To the women and girls who inspired us, and this book:
Ursula Vogel, Lynda Harris, Kitty Cooke and Maeve Lippmann,
thank you.

Contents

List of tables and figures

Tables

Figures

Acknowledgements

This book is the result of a project carried out by the Gender Research Network, an interdisciplinary network of researchers working in the School of Social Sciences at the University of Manchester with an interest in issues of gender. As New Labour prepared for election for what turned out to be a historic third term in 2005, we wanted to draw on research carried out in social sciences from discipline areas as diverse as political science, sociology, economics, international relations and social policy, to examine the question of what New Labour had achieved for women in politics and policy.

Research and writing for collections such as these can often be a lonely, competitive affair, and we quickly realised that we needed to put into practice some of the lessons we had learned from feminist scholars about the research process. As editors we therefore made a conscious effort to make it as collaborative a process as possible, without losing any intellectual rigour. We convened a series of workshops whereby authors were given the opportunity to develop their ideas with the help of constructive feedback from other authors and from invited discussants. We gave as many of our PhD students as possible the opportunity to contribute to the process, by taking part in the seminars and by co-authoring chapters with more experienced academics. Finally, as if to test everyone's commitment to feminising the research process, one of the editors decided to have a baby halfway through, resulting in some rescheduling and challenging editorial meetings – a useful case study in itself of policy being personal.

This book is therefore the result of a lot of hard work but also a lot of joy, and we hope that readers will agree with us that it was worth the effort. We would like to thank the authors who took part in the process: working in such a collaborative way was definitely challenging at times and it took a great deal of courage. This book would not have been possible without the involvement of the discussants, Sarah Childs, Janet Smithson, Bernard Walters and Georgina Waylen, and other participants at the seminars, including Wendy Olson, Natalie Bormann, Andrew Clifton, Chrissie Eason and Ursula Vogel. As editors we all owe personal and intellectual debts to a variety of mentors too numerous to mention here, but we would like to record a special debt to Ursula Vogel, who was a brave pioneer in the field of gender issues in political science when it was a very lonely field to be in, and who in many ways paved the way for us and helped to inspire this project.

The seminars themselves were made possible by funding from the School of Social Sciences at the University of Manchester, for which we thank Peter Halfpenny, outgoing Head of School and David Farrell, Head of Politics and now Head of School. Administrative support for the project was provided by Sharon Hammond, Charlotte Jackson and Gillian Whitworth. Particular thanks are due to Catherine Durose who played a central role in the final editing stage: any errors are our own responsibility and probably due to us ignoring her hard work.

Finally, projects of this kind inevitably take a toll on people's personal lives, and we would therefore like to record our deep gratitude to Rorden Wilkinson, Bill and Kitty Cooke, Pauline Rummery, and Simon, Euan, Rohan and Maeve Lippmann, without whose love and support none of this would have been possible.

Foreword

Women and New Labour: Engendering Politics and Policy? is the product of a collective inter-disciplinary research project conducted by the Social Science Gender Research Network at the University of Manchester. In September 2005 we were invited to act as discussants for one of the project workshops and we were pleased to be asked to write this foreword. In exploring various policy outcomes *Women and New Labour* facilitates gender and politics scholars in the analysis of key themes of the sub-discipline, particularly the relationship between the descriptive and substantive representation of women and the interaction between actors and institutions (increasingly becoming known as feminist institutionalism). Its focus on policies that have been relatively neglected by feminist scholars, such as economic policy, alongside analyses of welfare, care and sexuality and its acknowledgement of differences between women, is a strength of this book. Moreover, *Women and New Labour* constitutes a much-needed initial contribution to the task of gendering the mainstream literature on policy-making and governance in British politics.

Our aim in this foreword is to position the collection within the wider contemporary debates in the gender and politics literature. The issues raised here could be taken further in future research and analysis in the UK and elsewhere, and contribute to the development of a comparative politics of gender. On reading *Women and New Labour*, four key questions that have more general applicability stand out: (1) How is a particular political formation or government gendered, in terms of both its ideology and practice? (2) How is the policy-making process gendered? (3) What is the impact of the wider political opportunity structure, and (4) What are the gender outcomes?

How is New Labour gendered?

As this volume details, the incoming New Labour government in 1997 was, in terms of sex, the most descriptively representative ever. Party change in the 1980s and 1990s established internal party sex quotas that ensured a rough parity of representation at all levels of the party; all women shortlists guaranteed a better representation of women in the Parliamentary Labour Party in 1997. There were also record numbers of women in the Cabinet and government alongside the establishment of new forms of gender machinery – a Women's Minister and a Women's Unit – and the adoption of gender mainstreaming. As a result, female bodies and institutions devoted to women's concerns were more visible than ever before.

However, it is more difficult to determine the extent to which New Labour has acted for women and whether it has been committed to the principle of gender equality for its own sake rather than for instrumental reasons. For example, have New Labour strategies to maximise women's participation in the labour market been driven by a concern to increase economic productivity, reduce poverty or improve women's lives?

The 'business case for gender equality' is often employed by New Labour, but whether this can be called feminist, even given feminism's multiple definitions, is open to debate. In part, these difficulties also reflect the ongoing discussions about the ideological underpinnings of New Labour.

Addressing how New Labour is gendered raises what is perhaps the key question in contemporary gender and politics scholarship: What is the relationship between women's descriptive (the number of women present) and substantive representation (the representation of women's concerns and perspectives)? This relationship cannot be understood without an overarching and systematic analysis of both the policy-making processes and the wider political environment in which these processes occur.

How is the policy-making process gendered?

Analysing the gendered dimensions of policy-making has become a central concern of current gender and politics literature. It is becoming increasingly clear that in order to understand how gendered policy outcomes occur, both under New Labour and more widely, we need to understand how women's concerns and perspectives are initially articulated, how they can be put on the political agenda and then, sometimes, translated into policy. Contemporary research highlights the role of critical actors and strategic alliances (for example, between political actors inside and outside government and the state) in all these processes.

What is the impact of wider political opportunity structure?

Of course, policy-making occurs within wider political environments which may provide more or less favourable contexts for gendered political change. In the domestic context this includes socio-economic and cultural structures, institutional legacies and the organisation of government and the state. Yet, as gender and politics scholars are increasingly recognising, the international context also influences the national arena. The diffusion of international gender norms, which have been developing over the last 30 years, has been more widespread than has often been acknowledged in the British context. The adoption of quotas, gender mainstreaming and Women's Policy Agencies, embodied, for example, in the Platform for Action, adopted at the UN's Fourth World Conference on Women, in Beijing, 1995, is part of this global trend. Similarly, the role of the EU in promoting gender equality in member states must be recognised.

What are the gender outcomes?

Once these questions have been incorporated into an analytic framework it is possible to assess the nature of gendered outcomes. In evaluating the case of New Labour, gender and politics scholars can easily assess improvements in descriptive representation, whether at the party, parliamentary, governmental and bureaucratic level. It is much harder to reach an unambiguous conclusion with respect to the substantive representation of women, casting serious doubt on the concept of critical mass. Nonetheless, under New Labour, it is possible to identify feminist critical actors who often work as part of strategic alliances comprising sympathetic actors inside (such as the Women and Equality Unit, or individual Ministers) and outside the state (women's civil society groups).

Understanding the interaction between such actors and institutions and acknowledging the multiple sites of representation can better capture the processes by which gendered policy change can take place and enrich the study of gender and politics.

Sarah Childs and Georgina Waylen
September 2006

List of abbreviations

AEEU	Amalgamated Engineering and Electrical Union
AGM	Annual General Meeting
AMS	Additional Member System
APEX	Association of Professional, Executive, Clerical and Computer Staff
ASHE	Annual Survey of Hours and Earnings
AWS	All Women Shortlists
CAWP	Centre for Advancement of Women in Politics
CEDAW	Convention on the Elimination of All Forms of Discrimination against Women
CEHR	Commission for Equality and Human Rights
CEO	Chief Executive Officer
CIPD	Chartered Institute of Personnel and Development
CLP	Constituency Labour Party
CLPD	Campaign for Labour Party Democracy
COHSE	Confederation of Health Service Employees
CSA	Child Support Agency
DfEE	Department for Education and Employment
DfES	Department for Education and Skills
DfID	Department for International Development
DoH	Department of Health
DSS	Department for Social Security
DTI	Department for Trade and Industry
DNA	Norwegian Labour Party
DWP	Department for Work and Pensions
EOC	Equal Opportunities Commission
ESC	(Norwegian) Equal Status Council
ESRC	Economic and Social Research Council
EU	European Union
EWERC	European Work and Employment Research Centre
F!	(Norwegian) Feminist Initiative
FPTP	First Past the Post
GDP	Gross Domestic Product
GMB	Britain's General Union
GMWU	General and Municipal Workers' Union
IFS	Institute for Fiscal Studies
ILO	International Labour Organisation
IMF	International Monetary Fund
IPEG	Institute for Political and Economic Governance

IPU	Inter-Parliamentary Union
LCC	Labour Coordinating Committee
LGBT	Lesbian, Gay, Bisexual and Transgender
LO	(Norwegian) National Labour Organisation
LPC	Low Pay Commission
MSF	Manufacturing, Science, Finance
NAFTA	North American Free Trade Association
NEC	National Executive Committee
NFPI	National Family and Parenting Institute
NHO	Confederation of Norwegian Business and Industry
NHS	National Health Service
NMW	National Minimum Wage
NUPE	National Union of Public Employees
ODPM	Office of the Deputy Prime Minister
OECD	Organisation for Economic Co-operation and Development
OMOV	one member one vote
OSCE	Organisation for Security and Co-operation in Europe
OWOS	one-woman-on-the-shortlist
PAC	policy advocacy coalition
PFI	Private Finance Initiative
PLP	Parliamentary Labour Party
PSA	Public Sector Agreements
SDA	Social Development Adviser
SRE	Sex and Relationship Education
SSLP	Sure Start Local Programme
TGWU	Transport and General Workers' Union
TUC	Trades Union Congress
TUPE	1981 Transfer of Undertakings (Protection of Employment) Regulations
UN	United Nations
UNIFEM	United Nations Development Fund for Women
USDAW	Union of Shop, Distributive and Allied Workers
WAC	Women's Action Committee
WBG	Women's Budget Group
WEU	Women and Equality Unit
WFI	Work Focused Interviews
WFTC	Working Families' Tax Credit
WNC	Women's National Commission
WTC	Working Tax Credit
WU	Women's Unit

Notes on contributors

Claire Annesley is lecturer in European politics and convener of the Gender Research Network at the University of Manchester, UK. Her research interests focus on the transition of the welfare state in the direction of the Adult Worker Model in the UK, Germany and the European Union. Recent publications on these themes have appeared in *Journal of European Social Policy, Parliamentary Affairs, Comparative European Politics,* the *British Journal of Politics and International Relations* and *German Politics.* She is currently undertaking an Economic and Social Research Council-funded research project 'Engendering the Adult Worker Model Welfare State: The UK Case' (RES-000-22-1615).

Guro Buchanan is a PhD candidate in politics at the University of Manchester, UK, and has research interests in international relations, feminism, Norwegian foreign policy and Scandinavian social democracy. Her thesis 'Towards a Feminist Theory of the State' engages with feminist critiques of orthodox international relations theories and seeks to show how the personal is international.

Karen Clarke is a senior lecturer in social policy at the University of Manchester, UK. Her main research interests are in gender roles, policies in relation to children and state–family relations. Her current research examines the origins and development of New Labour's Sure Start. She is currently the co-editor of *Social Policy Review* (The Policy Press 2005, 2006, 2007).

David Coates currently holds the Worrell Chair in Anglo–American Studies at Wake Forest University in North Carolina, US. He previously taught at the universities of York, Leeds and Manchester in the UK, and for the Open University. Recent publications include the jointly authored *Blair's War* (Polity Press 2004) and *Prolonged Labour: The Slow Birth of New Labour Britain* (Palgrave 2005).

Catherine Durose is a doctoral student based at the Institute for Political and Economic Governance at the University of Manchester, UK. This research is concerned with how frontline public sector staff manage and negotiate the issues and tensions that face them, and how within changing governance structures the literature around policy implementation, and particularly the concept of street-level bureaucrats, can be reassessed. The empirical part of this work is being conducted within the neighbourhood management structure adopted by a North West authority. Additional research interests include interpretive policy analysis and methods, public sector reform and modernisation, the neighbourhood agenda, social capital and social entrepreneurs.

Juanita Elias is senior lecturer in international politics at the University of Adelaide, Australia. Her research interests include gender and the international political economy, the politics of corporate social responsibility and the political economy of Malaysia and Southeast Asia. She is author of *Fashioning Inequality: The Multinational Company and Gendered Employment in a Globalising World* (Ashgate 2004). Most recently she has published work in the journals *International Feminist Journal of Politics* and *New Political Economy*.

Lucy Ferguson is a PhD candidate at the University of Manchester, UK. Her doctoral research explores the gendered implications of tourism as a development policy in Latin American countries. Her key thematic interests include gendered political economy, gender and development and feminist approaches to international politics.

Francesca Gains is a senior lecturer in the School of Social Sciences and senior research fellow at the Institute for Political and Economic Governance at the University of Manchester, UK. She is currently the research coordinator for the Evaluating Local Governance research project (see www.elgnce.org.uk) for the Department of Communities and Local Government. Her previous research was in the introduction of new political management arrangements in central government through the establishment of executive agencies. Recent publications have been in *Public Administration*, *Journal of Public Policy* and *Public Policy and Administration*.

Damian Grimshaw is Professor of Employment Studies at the Manchester Business School at the University of Manchester, UK, and Director of the European Work and Employment Research Centre. His research interests include low-wage employment, women's employment, the employment effects of outsourcing and changes in national employment models within Europe. Recent books and reports include *Fragmenting Work: Blurring Organisational Boundaries and Disordering Hierarchies* (OUP 2005, with Marchington, Rubery and Willmott), *The Undervaluation of Women's Work* (Equal Opportunities Commission 2006, with Rubery) and *Knowledge Intensive Business*

Services: Organisational Forms and National Institutions (Edward Elgar 2006, with Miozzo).

Jill Lovecy is a lecturer in politics at the University of Manchester, UK. Her current research is focused on processes of Europeanisation in the field of human rights. She has other recent publications on gender and politics relating to France, on the parity legislation and the constitutionalisation of gender (in *Government and Opposition* 2000), and to mainstreaming at the European level (in *Feminist Legal Studies* 2000) and a longer standing specialist interest in French political institutions.

Sarah Oettinger graduated from Wake Forest University, US, in 2006 with a degree in political science. While at Wake Forest, she researched UK politics with David Coates. She is currently attending the University of North Carolina at Chapel Hill School of Law, from which she will graduate in 2009.

Kirstein Rummery is Professor of Social Policy at the University of Stirling, UK. Her research interests include disability, citizenship and access to services, and partnership working and governance in the welfare state. She is the author of *Disability, Citizenship and Community Care: A Case for Welfare Rights?* (Ashgate 2002) and co-editor (with Glendinning and Powell) of *Partnerships, New Labour and the Governance of Welfare* (The Policy Press 2002). She recently edited the themed section of *Social Policy and Society* on 'Partnerships, Governance and Citizenship' (2006, 5(2)).

Angelia R. Wilson has taught social policy feminist political theory at the University of Manchester, UK, for over 12 years. Her work explores the intersection between feminist political theory, queer theory and policies regulating sexuality. Her book *Below the Belt: Sexuality, Religion and the American South* (Cassell 2000) articulates the tensions of sexual politics in a hostile culture. More recent publications offer a theoretical analysis of UK, European Union and US 'family' policies in relation to families of choice. She is currently the president of the American Political Science Association Lesbian, Gay, Bisexual and Transgender Caucus.

Part One
Introduction

ONE

Feminising politics and policy: the impact of New Labour

Claire Annesley and Francesca Gains

Introduction: Women and New Labour

The iconic, but now rather clichéd, image of Tony Blair and the 101 female Labour MPs elected to the 1997 House of Commons sent a signal to the world that New Labour and women somehow go 'hand in hand'. Undeniably, the 1997 General Election was significant in gender terms because Labour returned a record number of female MPs thanks to its use of all women shortlists (AWS) in selecting candidates for that election. Moreover, the party's landslide victory that year was made possible by the massive swing in the female votes from the Conservatives to New Labour: remarkably, in 1997, 44% of women voted for Blair's government. And, in government, Labour has made bold claims about what it is doing for women. Indeed, in 2005 the then Minister for Women, Tessa Jowell, went so far as to claim that the Blair administration was the 'most feminist Government in our history' (*The Times* (2005) 'Gender pay gap "may never go"', 5 December).

At face value, New Labour in government appears to have done much to 'feminise politics'. That means, using Lovenduski's (2005) definition, to act for women, to take on women's concerns and to make a difference to women's lives. Of course, there is no consensus on what 'women's concerns' entails or on what the feminist movement demands (Bacchi 1999; Chappell 2004). Labour has implemented changes within the party itself, the UK system of governance and in key policy areas – from economic to welfare to international policy – all of which have had significant implications for women. Yet, the jury is still out on whether New Labour really is committed to feminising politics or whether these achievements are the unintended consequences of other policy initiatives.

Meg Russell (2005) argues that New Labour only became associated with progress for women because the party's election in 1997 coincided with the election of 101 women MPs. Yet that achievement in women's representation was really the consequence of a longer campaign by women and Left-wing activists in the party dating back to the early 1980s; it was not New Labour's doing. Anna Coote (1999) argues that women or gender issues has never been part of New Labour's 'Third Way' programme. Traditionally, the Labour Party has pursued egalitarian positions, but based on the category of class rather than gender (Lovenduski 2005, 60). As a party dominated by trade unions, it represented the interests of male unionised workers rather than women, who were present as subordinates: as wives and mothers (Perrigo 1999). At most, Coote (1999) argues, New Labour saw women as 'sub-categories' in need of policy attention (welfare claimants, lone parents, low earners), but they were not perceived of as a coherent whole. Other commentators still have argued that New Labour is still very much a 'boys' club' that excludes and alienates women (Bradberry 1998; Coote 1999; Bright 2005).

Despite the party's heritage, what we can perhaps observe is an awareness on the part of New Labour of the significance of women as political and social citizens who have agency. This attitude is shaped by a mixture of internal and external influences. Internally, that is, inside the party, a shift in politics and policy has been pushed by committed feminist, Left-wing and trade union activists. These groups can now claim success in promoting gender democracy in the party despite the fact that their campaigns have generally met with ambivalence from the party leadership from Kinnock to Blair (Russell 2005). In Chapter Four, Jill Lovecy sets out the feminist project to improve women's representation in politics and a focus on policy areas of concern to women.

Externally, a feminisation of politics and policy under New Labour has been triggered by electoral imperatives associated with socio-economic change. As a consequence of the shift towards a service sector economy which is dominated by women, and the fact that more women are now in paid employment, women are therefore more likely to vote for progressive parties rather than conservative ones. Indeed, the trades union became aware of this fact during the 1980s and allied themselves to campaigns in the party for women's representation (Russell 2005). But the party as a whole has been slower to respond to women's issues. As has been widely noted, Labour would have won the 1992 General Election had it gained the support of women voters and it learned a valuable lesson from this: that winning the female vote was central to its future electoral campaigns (Worcester 2005).

In *Feminizing Politics* Lovenduski claims that in European party democracies, such as the UK, the arguments for feminising politics 'must first be won in political parties, which then take the ideas into government' (2005, 91). It seems clear that a modernising, social democratic party such as New Labour has the potential to play a defining role in altering the perception and position of women in British politics similar to the way in which the Norwegian and Swedish social democratic parties have since the 1970s.

Women and New Labour: Engendering Politics and Policy? assesses the extent to which New Labour has feminised politics in the UK. Has it acted for women? Has it taken on women's concerns? Has it made a difference to women's lives? The book starts from an optimistic premise: that the Labour governments elected in 1997 and re-elected in 2001 and 2005 have been more inclined than any other UK party in government to forge politics and policy with a concern for women. It then looks critically at the achievements that the party has made in terms of improving the opportunities to increase women's inclusion in the decision-making process and to promote policies of concern or benefit to women. It examines the ways in which women have been politically empowered and the extent to which this has changed the content or focus of policy-making. Significantly, the book does not just look at what policies were developed but also assesses concrete policy outcomes in a range of areas. The book also considers not only arenas that are of traditional 'women's interests', for example childcare and women's health issues, but also more 'mainstream' policy domains such as economic and foreign policy.

This introductory chapter presents the framework developed in the book to help assess the process through which a feminisation of politics under New Labour might occur. In a first step, this framework, in contrast to approaches which focus predominantly on political representation, outlines the range of opportunities available to a political party to promote women's representation and interests. In a second step, by drawing on a public policy approach, the framework highlights the series of constraints which can hinder a successful exploitation of these opportunities.

Opportunities for feminisation

Most studies of the feminisation of politics have tended to have as their starting point the issue of women's political representation. Certainly, increasing the number of women in Parliament is a crucial way to improve the opportunity for a feminisation of politics and policy. But there is a broader repertoire of mechanisms through which a political party might contribute – directly or indirectly – to a feminisation of politics and policy. These might be: appointing women to the core executive; feminising the policy platform; strengthening women's policy agencies and implementing constitutional reform. There is evidence that Labour has seized the opportunity to feminise politics in all these ways. However, the extent to which any action has led to noticeable improvement for women is potentially limited by a range of constraints which are highlighted in the next section.

Representation of women

Increasing the number of female representatives in national, regional and local legislatures is a central pillar of a project to improve the opportunities to feminise politics. There are two cases for why women's representation should be increased, which Lovenduski (2005, 22) refers to as the 'justice arguments' and 'pragmatic arguments'. The former refers to the claim that it is unjust and undemocratic for men to dominate institutions of decision-making (Phillips 1995) while the latter case is made on the grounds that fielding women candidates will attract women's votes.

The Labour Party introduced a range of mechanisms to increase women's representation in the party and within the House of Commons. The most significant measure was the AWS used in the selection of parliamentary candidates for the 1997 and 2005 General Elections. As a consequence, in 1997 women made up 24.6% of Labour candidates and 24.1% of elected Labour MPs (Lovenduski 2005, 121).

The issue of whether women's presence makes a difference to parliamentary processes and outcomes is unclear. Feminist scholars argue that women being inserted into male institutions with male cultures and norms will find it hard to make a difference. Scholars such as Kanter (1977) have used the concept of 'critical mass' to argue that a certain number of women – say 30% – is required to make a difference or trigger change. Others such as Yoder (1991) argue that the success of a critical mass of women depends on the context and institutional framework. Dahlerup (1988) has argued that women might make a difference if they are successful at changing the culture of the party or legislature (Lovenduski 2005, 141-5).

Since the election of the 101 Labour women, research has sought to answer the question of whether this descriptive presence has led to a substantive representation of women. Or, in other words, does the increased numerical presence of women make a difference to the kinds of issues raised and legislated. Childs' research (2004), based on interviews with Labour MPs, has demonstrated that the women do perceive themselves to be acting for women, and that they have made a difference on a range of women's issues such as childcare, breast screening and cutting VAT on sanitary protection. Yet in interviews for other research projects, women MPs also report a range of constraints and sexist treatment in the House of Commons (Ashley 2004). The steps taken by New Labour in opposition to increase the representation of women in the party is dealt with further in Chapter Four by Jill Lovecy and the activities of the party in power and research assessing the impact of increased representation are summarised in Chapter Five by Catherine Durose and Francesca Gains.

Women in the core executive

Feminist scholars tend to focus largely on the opportunities for feminisation presented by increased numbers of female representatives. Yet as Chappell argues, although many feminists are reluctant to engage with the state, all bureaucracies offer openings and constraints for feminist actors (2004). In fact it is crucial to look at the opportunities for feminising politics via state bureaucracies. This is particularly the case in the UK since the contemporary policy analysis literature almost entirely bypasses Parliament and parliamentarians in understanding policy change and instead focuses attention on activity in the 'core executive' (Rhodes and Dunleavy 1995; Burch and Holliday 1996, 2004; Richards and Smith 1997; Smith 1999) The core executive is 'all those organisations and procedures which co-ordinate central government, and act as final arbiters of conflict between different parts of the government machine' (Rhodes 1997, 12). The argument that core executive studies make is that researchers need to understand how key political and administrative actors situated at the top of departments and in the central coordinating departments of Number 10, the Treasury and the Cabinet Office interact in networks, exchanging resources to achieve their goals.

It can be argued that parliamentarians have less chance of implementing change than government Ministers, but that the increase in women parliamentarians provides a greater pool of women who could be given ministerial portfolios. Indeed, five women were appointed to Blair's first Cabinet and between 1997 and 2001, a total of 35 women served on the front benches, 26 in the House of Commons and nine in the House of Lords (Lovenduski 2005, 161). Ministers included prominent party feminists such as Clare Short, Harriet Harman and Patricia Hewitt, but, until Margaret Beckett was appointed as Foreign Secretary in May 2006, none held one of the four key offices of government

(Prime Minister, Chancellor, Foreign Secretary and Home Secretary). Currently, there is a higher proportion of female Ministers (35%) than female MPs (19.5%) (Bryant 2007, 4).

However, there is no systematic research to assess the degree to which such female Ministers, especially those with overtly feminist perspectives, have managed to push women's interests into government policy. What research does suggest, however, is that female Ministers' success in part depends on the amount of support they get from women's policy machineries. A further assessment of the changing gender balance in the New Labour Cabinets is provided in Chapter Five by Catherine Durose and Francesca Gains.

Women's policy machineries

An important and growing body of research on 'state feminism' highlights the important role women's policy machineries play in translating women's or feminist goals into policy (McBride Stetson and Mazur 1995). In this research, state feminism refers to 'activities of government structures that are formally charged with furthering women's status and rights', for example, women's ministries or women's policy units (McBride Stetson and Mazur 1995, 1-2). The research demonstrates that countries develop a high degree of state feminism if they are (among other things) established by social democratic governments under pressure from feminists and a women's movements and if they are centralised organisations with widespread influence over a range of policy areas (McBride Stetson and Mazur 1995, 287-91).

One further way in which states can seek to change policies is through gender mainstreaming strategies. The concept of mainstreaming has achieved wide currency since its emergence as a strategy for effecting policy change at the UN Conference on Women in Beijing in 1995 and subsequent widespread adoption internationally. However, the meaning of mainstreaming is described as both vague (Squires 2005, 4) and contested (True 2003, 369). As Wilson discusses further in Chapter Two, mainstreaming issues can vary from more narrowly conceived policy instruments designed to ensure more gender equitable outcomes to a more broadly conceived and radical agenda to include into policy-making a recognition of gendered differences 'transforming it to take account of gender inequality' (Squires and Wickham-Jones 2002, 59).

In the UK, women's policy machinery has been traditionally organised as the Women's National Commission (WNC) and the Equal Opportunities Commission (EOC) (Lovenduski 1995). Following the election of Labour in 1997, a new Women's Unit (WU) was established and this later became the Women and Equality Unit (WEU) in 2001 (Squires and Wickham-Jones 2004). The WU was given the job of 'scrutinising legislation to promote sexual equality and with promoting female friendly policies' (Squires and Wickham-Jones 2004, 82-3). Its self-declared aim was to 'put women's interests into the mainstream of government policy' (WU 1998, cited in Squires and Wickham-Jones 2004, 83). This has included a focus on disseminating guidance to departments on Policy Appraisal for Equal Treatment and directly on issues such as reducing the pay gap, work–life balance, women in public life and public services.

The work of the WU was supported by a Women's Minister – the first was Harriet Harman – but the portfolio was secondary to a main ministerial portfolio; in Harman's case, she was also secretary for Social Security and the portfolio of Minister for Women has not always been remunerated. Moreover, the WU was located in four different government departments in the years 1997 to 2004 (Lovenduski 2005, 164). According to Squires and Wickham-Jones (2004, 96) the weakness of the WU and mainstreaming initiatives has been that there is confusion about its remit, and it does not have credibility with senior civil servants (see Durose and Gains, Chapter Five).

Constitutional reform

A significant opportunity for women to feminise politics in the UK came with the devolution project proposed and executed by the Labour Party following the 1997 General Election. Labour held referendums on devolution to Scotland and Wales and the first Scottish Parliament and Welsh Assembly were elected in 1999. This process presented a significant opportunity for women on a number of grounds. Feminists had been involved in campaigns for devolution since the 1970s. An integral part of the project of devolution was therefore the feminisation of politics in the devolved administrations. The political institutions were designed to avoid the confrontational nature of Westminster politics and an electoral system was selected (additional member system (AMS)) which is effective in maximising female representation.

In 1999, female representation was 37% in Scotland and 30% in Wales; this rose to 40% and 50% respectively in 2003. In the Welsh executive, over 50% of Ministers are currently women and a range of policies have been introduced which directly address women's interests. For example, the Scottish Parliament has passed a Bill to make it an offence to prevent a mother from breastfeeding in public (BBC 2004) while the Welsh executive cut the gender pay gap in the Welsh civil service (Meehan 2005). This impact of the constitutional reform on feminising politics is discussed in more detail in Chapter Five, but the differentiated policy outcomes that are the consequence of devolution are not addressed in this book – for this further research would be required. The policy case studies in this volume relate to the UK or England.

Feminising the policy platform

A final opportunity for feminising politics arises from a party's need to secure the female vote. Lovenduski argues that 'to court women voters, political parties try to feminise their image, their manifesto and their personnel' (2005, 150). Women in the UK have traditionally voted Conservative. However, women's participation in the labour market increased from the 1980s, and has been matched by a de-alignment of women's voting behaviour in favour of progressive parties (Inglehart and Norris 2003). This is discussed further by Jill Lovecy in Chapter Four. The Labour Party leadership certainly chose to develop policy to promote women's interests in order to attract the shifting women's votes following successive electoral defeats during the 1980s and early 1990s (Russell 2005).

In 1992, women were 8% less likely to vote Labour and party strategists were aware that this propensity cost Labour the election (Bradberry 1998). There is evidence that women – and young women in particular – moved their allegiance to the Labour Party and in 1997 the swing to Labour was larger among women than among men (Kellner 1997 cited in Lovenduski 2005, 151). In 1997, 44% of women voted Labour, although this fell to 42% in 2001 and again to 38% in 2005. Nevertheless, New Labour appears to have benefited from its appeal to women voters with the pollster Bob Worcester beginning his analysis of how the 2005 electorate voted by saying, 'It was women voters who … delivered a comfortable majority for Tony Blair' (Worcester 2005).

The decisive influence of the women's vote acted as an incentive for the Labour Party to develop policy that appeals to women. As one Labour insider put it, 'women have always been at the heart of the campaign … what is obvious is that women are an important part of the New Labour coalition – always have and always will be' (Bright 2005). However, Lovenduski argues that, 'once in power, Labour forgot the gender lesson of the 1997 victory' (2005, 151). During the 2005 General Election, campaign coordinator, Alan Milburn, was criticised for refusing to campaign specifically on women's issues to attract the disillusioned female vote (Lobel and Happold 2003) and for not using Labour women prominently in the front line of the campaign. The subsequent fall in female support for New Labour in the 2001 and 2005 General Elections has been put down to women's dissatisfaction with Tony Blair, with Labour's delivery in public services and the party's stance on the war in Iraq.

What must be borne in mind, however, is that a party might decide on a platform of feminising policy in order to achieve other goals. For example, a policy to increase female employment or improve the provision of childcare might be framed as part of a feminised policy agenda but in actual fact be concerned with economic growth and efficiency. Indeed, New Labour has been so concerned with establishing itself as a party with sound and stable economic management that many policies regarding gender equality are made against the backdrop of the economic case. Indeed, a dominant strand of New Labour's policies to act for women, take on women's concerns and make a difference to women's lives relates to the commitment to insert women into paid employment, an approach referred to as the 'adult worker model' (Lewis 2001). The case study chapters in Part Two of this book examine in detail New Labour's policy stance, activity and outcomes for women in a range of economic, social and foreign policy areas.

Constraints to the feminisation of politics

New Labour has had abundant opportunities to feminise politics and policy in the UK. Whether these opportunities actually translate into policy with concrete outcomes for women depends on the party's ability to overcome a series of constraints. At the most general level feminist scholars might argue that a feminisation of politics and policy is constrained by patriarchy: that states are patriarchal entities which seek to preserve male power (Chappell 2004). From a more public policy perspective, we argue that New Labour's capacity to feminise politics is constrained by features of the policy-making process generally and in particular by the norms and institutions of policy-making in the UK system.

It is common to hear British politicians talk of making policy change in the UK as like trying to 'turn a tanker mid ocean'. Despite the political and electoral authority which the British Prime Minister and her or his Cabinet colleagues have, and the huge state resources at their disposal, the business of trying to introduce, implement and deliver policy change is fraught with difficulty. Most recent contemporary policy analyses of the UK state focus upon the activities of the core executive rather than the legislature in seeking to understand how the party in government attempts to develop its policy proposals into policy programmes.

The way in which the New Labour government has sought to 'steer the ship of state' and push through its preferred policy proposals is the subject of many public policy analyses (for example, see Ludlam and Smith 2001 and 2004; Savage and Atkinson 2001). In general, this literature highlights the electoral drivers for particular policy platforms. The literature also points to the constraints which face New Labour in power operating in a 'hollowed out' system where decision-making power is tempered by globalisation, the European and regional settings and where delivery is undertaken by a range of arm's length bodies both elected and non-elected, network management is also key (Bevir and Rhodes 2006).

The New Labour government, like all executives, needs to be able to bring to bear the administrative resources at its disposal in order to deliver their aims. Actors in the core executive hold resources at their command but need to cooperate and exchange resources to achieve government goals. This creates a power dependency between actors in government. Ministers, their advisers and senior civil servants operate in networks requiring trust and good communication (Heclo and Wildavsky 1981; Smith 1999; Gains 2004).

There is considerable analytical interest in the public policy literature into how New Labour has organised and operates the core executive (Rhodes 2000; Flinders 2002; Burch and Holliday 2004; Richards and Smith 2004). The main findings are that New Labour has strengthened resources at the centre of government in the Prime Minister's Office, the Cabinet Office and the Treasury (Burch and Holliday 2004; Bevir and Rhodes 2006). In particular the Treasury under Gordon Brown has become more powerful and extends its reach into the work of departments through setting up a system of public service agreements (Stoker 2002; James 2003; Bevir and Rhodes, 2006). Policy advice comes from a wider range of sources including special advisers, task forces, policy think tanks, as well as civil servants (Foster 2001). However, analysts still find that the work of individual Ministers in their departments is key and is linked to particular policy outcomes (Flinders 2002; Richards and Smith 2004, 118; Bevir and Rhodes, 2006, 18).

One notable aspect of this whole genre is, with a couple of exceptions – the discussion of the Women's Policy Unit by Flinders (2002) and Squires and Wickham-Jones (2004) – the *lack* of attention paid to gender or gender issues. Conversely, although the public policy literature has been drawn on by feminist scholars (for example Chappell 2004 and Mazur 2002, 12 for summary) to examine the influence of feminist social movements and agenda setting and to examine the women's policy units, there is little overtly feminist empirical work looking at issues of policy implementation and policy outcomes in the UK. The next section of this chapter looks at the public policy literature theorising the policy process generally (and where relevant in the UK specifically) to outline the features of policy-making which could act to facilitate or constrain the feminist policy-making intentions of New Labour. While public policy theorists emphasise stability and continuity in policy-making, there is renewed interest in how constraints are overcome and 'important governmental programmes are sometimes altered dramatically even if most of the time they continue as they did the previous year' (True et al 1999, 97).

Is there a window of opportunity?

According to Kingdon (1984), the policy process is very messy involving an interplay of three different kinds of processes. First, is the existence of policy problems – which may or may not get described as such. Second, is the advocacy of policy proposals developed among specialists in a policy area who Kingdon refers to as 'policy entrepreneurs', the politicians, civil servants, and pressure group leaders waiting to offer policy solutions. Third, political events can provide an impetus to how policy problems and are defined and solutions examined. At key times these processes come together to create a 'window of opportunity' where an idea moves high on to a political agenda and it is possible for policy advocates to progress proposals. Windows can arise from both large systemic events such as elections and small events such as crises in policy delivery or media pressure (Cortell and Peterson 1999). As Baumgartner and Jones suggest 'issues considered high on the political agenda tend to be dealt with during periods of tremendous optimism or after waves of pessimism have swept through the political system' (1993, 236). Without a 'window of opportunity' pressing policy problems and likely policy proposals will continue to exist, but without impacting upon policy implementation awaiting a future opportunity to move up the political agenda.

A first constraint upon feminist policy-making would arise, therefore, if there is no window of opportunity, and if policy problems and possible solutions do not coincide with political events. The election of the first Labour government for 17 years represents a potentially sizeable electoral window of opportunity, however the policy streams may not all come together in a fortuitous way for that opportunity to be realised.

Is there a committed policy actor to drive change?

Cortell and Peterson highlight that even where a window of opportunity exists there needs to be a committed policy actor prepared to drive through change (1999). Governments and governmental actors are limited in the attention they can give to issues at any one time (Baumgartner and Jones 1993). For Sabatier and Jenkins–Smith it is elite policy entrepreneurs, the politicians, officials, pressure group and academic experts who form policy advocacy coalitions (PACs) in policy subsystems who drive change (1993). Actors in each PAC share core beliefs about the nature of policy problems and how they may be tackled. The coalition acts over long periods of time to seek change in policy goals following electoral or economic windows of opportunity (Sabatier and Jenkins–Smith 1993, 375). Gender policy entrepreneurs are said to be key in 'leveraging' policy change through the promotion of policy learning and coalition building (True 2003, 372 and 379) and how widely feminist PACs (of the sort within the Labour Party pre-1997 described by Lovecy in Chapter Four) have gone on to act as policy advocates in government is a key empirical and analytical question. The advocacy coalition framework was developed to explore policy-making in the federal US with its multiple points of access. In the more parliamentary and party dominated UK theorists have taken a more state centric approach focusing more on actors, networks and coalitions within the core executive even when acknowledging challenges to the idea of a 'Westminster model' (Richards and Smith 2002; Bevir and Rhodes 2006).

In the UK core executive, the Prime Minister has always been recognised as being able to support an initiative by indicating an interest in the policy area. This was seen under Blair's leadership by his association with social exclusion and the outbreak of foot and mouth, for example. However, despite the growing staff of Number 10, the British Prime Minister also faces weaknesses in that the extent to which a Prime Minister can attend to policy areas is limited and the Prime Minister has no delivery mechanisms under her or his control (Bevir and Rhodes 2006). One insider 'femocrat' account of the gender mainstreaming initiatives of the WEU noted that the patchy support from the Prime Minister's Office indicated the low political saliency of this agenda (Veitch 2005).

Despite the New Labour concern to advocate joined-up government and the proliferation of cross-cutting units like the WU, it is the departments of state where policy actors – departmental Ministers – have the hierarchical and infrastructural power (Smith 1993; Gains 1999; Smith et al 2000; Flinders 2002). If those key elites do not have intentions to feminise policy, then this will constrain the process despite the existence of women's policy machineries or cross-governmental initiatives, for example, gender mainstreaming. Conversely, having the support of non-feminist elites will facilitate the feminisation of policy-making (Mazur 2002). Policy chimneys, where policy-making is funnelled through hierarchies within departments, still exist in UK government and therefore the extent to which individual Cabinet Ministers sign up to change is a critical factor to facilitate or block change. This links to the third constraint highlighted in the public policy literature: the need for committed actors to have the institutional capacity to act.

Does the policy actor have capacity to act?

Here the literature highlights that even committed actors faced with windows of opportunity must be able to translate that possibility for change into action. This requires institutional capacity, for example, bureaucratic staff and infrastructural support, to prepare proposals and network within and beyond government to reach agreement on a plan of action. Arguably, this is one of the reasons why the WU was seen to be ineffectual in Labour's first term, the first Secretary of State for Women shared responsibility for that brief with her responsibilities for the giant Department of Social Security (DSS) and capacity to support the women's brief was not there (Flinders 2002; Squires and Wickham-Jones 2004). The second Minister for Women had no paid portfolio and effectively no institutional capacity. Even where a policy actor has capacity in the sense of sitting in control of a department, other factors relating to their authority and standing within government or with their parliamentary colleagues may limit the extent to which they are able to forge alliances and make the trade-offs to win support. For example, resource dependencies in the core executive arise where actors need to exchange resources to achieve policy goals (Gains 2003b). If policy actors do not have resources to exchange or do not recognise their dependency then achieving goals is unlikely (Smith 1999).

One structural feature which has also changed under New Labour and is critical to this question of institutional capacity is the extent to which departmental agendas are closely tied in with Treasury targets. The Treasury is more than ever before a fixed feature of policy development discussions, and Treasury approval for domestic policy initiatives is a necessity for a committed policy actor to utilise a window of opportunity and flex their institutional capacity to make a reality of feminist policy proposals (Deakin and Parry 2000). As Veitch notes in respect of mainstreaming initiatives 'ministerial interest produces resources and outcomes' (2005, 603). The core executive literature sees the operation of resource dependencies in government, such as that between Treasury and departmental officials and politicians, as key to understanding policy formulation (Burch and Holiday 2004).

The impact of policy networks

The fourth constraint on action moves the analysis to what happens when policy proposals are translated into legislative or administrative programmes of action. Here, attention needs to be given to the activities of wider policy networks. One of the puzzles of the Thatcher government is that their radical policy ideas did not translate into radical policy change on the ground in many substantive policy areas. Marsh and Rhodes argue this was primarily due to the protective and constraining effect of the functional policy networks surrounding many policy areas (1992b). Policy networks arise where actors within government need to exchange resources with each other and with outside organisations (Marsh and Rhodes 1992a; Smith 1993, Gains 2003b). The dependency this creates can lead to very close policy communities which are insulated from outside pressures, for example the alternative policy solutions offered from competing PACs in the policy sub-sector. The operation of these closed policy communities is extremely influential in controlling which issues reach the agenda and how policy problems are perceived and should be addressed (Cortell and Peterson 1999; Gains 1999). Even where there is an actor with capacity committed to feminising politics, if the professional pressure group networks needed to deliver the policy are not supportive, any policy activity may be diverted or diluted.

Path dependency in institutions

A final constraining feature of policy-making raised in the historical institutionalist literature is that even when policy change is set in motion either constitutionally, legislatively or administratively there is strong path dependency in how actors interpret and enact new policy aims reflecting pre-existing standard operating procedures and existing policy goals. For Pierson, this arises because of the costs of moving to new ways of organising, and because policy actors become locked into existing ways of operating (2000). In *substantive* policy areas where governments are only steering delivery networks, policy enforcement is therefore difficult (Richards and Smith 2002). This effect has also been noted in the adoption of *administrative* policies, for example, in how the machinery of government responded to the UK's changing relationship to the European Union (EU); in the impact of arm's length Next Steps agencies in central government; and in how local government authorities responded to the choice of reform options when the separation of powers was introduced in local government (Bulmer and Burch 1998; Gains 2003a; Gains et al 2005). Squires and Wickham-Jones in their analysis of the work of the WU note that 'many officials remain culturally entrenched within their departments and resentful of cross cutting bodies' (2004, 92).

In terms of New Labour's gender agenda, this line of argument suggests that even where a strong policy actor grasps a window of opportunity, has the policy capacity and is not blocked by policy networks, a resulting policy change (in substantive policies or in administrative policies like mainstreaming aimed at supporting substantive policy development) may be diluted in implementation.

Intended and unintended outcomes

Analysis of the 2005 General Election indicates that women overwhelmingly endorsed New Labour and that, had only women voted in the election, the government's 66-seat majority would have increased to 90 (Worcester 2005). However, this electoral endorsement is too blunt an instrument to answer the final question we set out at the beginning of this chapter, which is: Has New Labour made a difference to women's lives? Isolating and assessing cause and effect here is problematic. Governmental action is designed to address policy problems and achieve specified aims. However, the public policy literature highlights that it is very difficult to predict the outcomes of policy change (Select Committee on Public Administration 2000). For example, the Conservative government plans to revitalise the private rented sector in the late 1980s through lifting rental values had the consequent and, at the time, unforeseen effect of inflating the housing benefit bill. The impact of changes in the school meal system on childhood obesity is only just being assessed (Select Committee on Health 2004). A final twist in any assessment of whether New Labour utilised the opportunities, without stumbling over the constraints, is that the outcomes of policy proposals have both intended and unintended policy consequences.

Thus it is perfectly possible for policy proposals and actions directed at helping women to have the opposite effect. Likewise, it is possible for policy platforms and changes which are gender neutral or gender blind to provide positive gendered outcomes. One advantage of looking at policy sectors in general and not at specific policy proposals for feminist policies, is that we can take a broader view about the outcomes of policy both intended and unintended.

The structure and key arguments of this book

The chapters in *Women and New Labour* look for evidence of feminising politics and policy making in the UK. Part Two of the book focuses on whether and how New Labour has opened up opportunities for women. This part of the book begins with a theoretical chapter by Angelia Wilson (Chapter Two). In recognition of the fact that no consensus exists on what 'feminising politics' means to different women, the aim of this chapter is to set out and problematise the range of concepts appropriate to any discussion of women and New Labour. In particular, this chapter raises the contrasts, tensions and contradictions between feminisms that address women and those which are concerned with gender and engendering politics and policy.

To place the New Labour experience in a comparative context, Guro Buchanan and Claire Annesley (Chapter Three) look at the experiences and achievements of social democratic parties in Norway and Sweden in a project to feminise politics. They make clear that despite obvious progress, there are still clear limitations to the achievements in these women-friendly societies and argue that New Labour might learn from these constraints. Jill Lovecy (Chapter Four) then traces the stance of the Labour Party on women and feminising politics from so-called 'old' to New Labour, illustrating how feminist activists within the party were able to mobilise their demands. In the last chapter in Part Two, Catherine Durose and Francesca Gains (Chapter Five) review the opportunities taken by New Labour to engender the machinery of governance at national, regional and local levels.

Part Three is an empirical section: it is concerned with reform policy under New Labour via a series of case studies in the key policy areas of economic, social and international policies. These chapters will form a multiple case study (Yin 2004) of New Labour to explore the feminisation of policy-making. To do this we use the opportunities and constraints framework developed in the introductory sections to examine a number of thematic policy areas. The policy chapters describe the policy discourse and outcomes with regards to women and will consider how in this area the Labour Party has: (1) acted for women; (2) taken on women's concerns into policy; and/or (3) made a difference to women's lives. The chapters seek to explain how this change was able to come about through a discussion of opportunities, constraints and outcomes and the impact of gender assumptions and consequences.

The case studies represent a range of domains related to economic, social and foreign policy. Our selection of case studies is by no means exhaustive and there are some obvious omissions, such as health or education. However, they have in common the fact that they are mainstream policy areas and not ones conventionally regarded as women's issues. Moreover, they reflect the expertise of the members of the Gender Research Network at the University of Manchester. The policy case studies are as follows: David Coates and Sarah Oettinger (Chapter Six) examine the gender implications of New Labour's macro-economic policy and Damian Grimshaw (Chapter Seven) assesses the effects of New Labour's labour market policy on women's pay. Then Karen Clarke (Chapter Eight) examines New Labour's policies in relation to parenting responsibilities and their implications for gender roles in work and care. Kirstein Rummery (Chapter Nine) looks at the way New Labour's policies have offered opportunities and constraints for older and disabled women and Angelia Wilson's chapter on family values (Chapter Ten) looks behind the policies and practices that New Labour has introduced to support gay and lesbian families. Finally, Juanita Elias and Lucy Ferguson's chapter (Chapter Eleven) assesses the gender dimensions of New Labour's international development policy.

In the final chapter, the editors bring together the research findings. This conclusion emphasises the fact that New Labour has taken a number of opportunities to address women's issues and that as a consequence the policy framework in the UK has been significantly altered. For the first time, gender as well as class features firmly on New Labour's political agenda.

At the same time, the conclusion acknowledges the limitations of New Labour's approach and concrete policy outcomes. For example, the government's achievements, it is argued, are constrained by the fact that by insisting on a work-centred approach to policy, it fails to acknowledge the complexity of women's lives as workers, carers and the receivers of care. As a consequence, and as the conclusion sets out in some detail, New Labour's policies have a differentiated impact on different groups of women.

New Labour's achievements are also limited by the constraints specific to the British system of public administration and the difficulty of 'turning a tanker mid ocean'. There was clearly a window of opportunity to engender politics and policy and even committed policy actors and entrepreneurs pushing for change, but these did not always preside over the capacity to act or the resources required to implement significant policy change.

A final, but significant, constraint is that New Labour is focusing on feminising politics and policy, which means developing policy for women, rather than engendering politics and policy which seeks to address and alter existing gender structures and patterns. Equating gender with women, the conclusion argues, places distinct limits on what New Labour, however ambitious, can achieve. Hence, we call for New Labour – or its Conservative successor – to adopt a serious engendering politics and policy approach.

Women and New Labour builds on existing research into the performance of the Labour Party in government (Coates and Lawler 2000; Ludlam and Smith 2001, 2004) and on the relationship of the Labour Party to women (Perrigo 1999; Russell 2005). The book makes a contribution to the established literature on the impact of women representatives in shaping the outcomes of policy (Childs 2004) and on the feminisation of public policy (Coote 2000). What differentiates this work from other work on the capacity of a party to engender politics and policy is that first, we are looking beyond women's representation or women's policy agencies in order to examine the mechanisms for change. Second, we have drawn much more extensively on the public policy literature – which has hitherto been gender blind – to inform our research design especially on the constraints to policy change. Third, we are looking beyond classic women's issues of domestic violence, abortion or breast screening to include a wider range of policy areas such as macro-economic and foreign and security policy thus permitting some grounded theorising about feminist policy processes. Finally, we are examining outcomes to assess the linkage between deliberative action and the impact on women's lives. By looking at the way New Labour has acted in power we hope to learn something about the political and policy processes of feminising politics more generally and contribute to the range of empirical and methodological approaches to researching feminist politics.

References

Annesley, C. (2007) 'Women's political agency and welfare reform: engendering the "adult worker model" welfare state', *Parliamentary Affairs*, 60(4).

Ashley, J. (2004) 'Women MPs bullied and abused in Commons', *Guardian*, 7 December.

Bacchi, C. (1999) *Women, Policy and Politics: The Construction of Policy Problems*, London: Sage.

Baumgartner, F. and Jones, B. (1993) *Agendas and Instability in American Politics*, London: University of Chicago Press.

BBC (2004) 'Breastfeeders bill gains approval', 18 November, http://news.bbc.co.uk/1/hi/scotland/4021137.stm

Bevir, M. and Rhodes, R.A.W. (2006) 'Prime ministers, presidentialism and Westminster smokescreens', *Political Studies* 54(4), 671-90.

Bradberry, G. (1998) 'Blair's laddish New Labour', *The Times*, 24 November, 17.

Bright, M. (2005) 'Labour's trouble with women', *The Observer*, 20 February, http://observer.guardian.co.uk/focus/story/0,,1418531,00.html (accessed 16 June 2005).

Bryant, C. (2007) *Financial Times*, 5 January, 'Size of gender gap in top jobs "woeful"'.

Bulmer, S. and Burch, M. (1998) 'Organizing for Europe: Whitehall, the British State and European Union', *Public Administration* 76(4), 601-28.

Burch, M. and Holliday, I. (1996) *The British Cabinet System*, Hemel Hempstead: Prentice Hall.

Burch, M. and Holliday, I. (2004) 'The Blair government and the core executive', *Government and Opposition* 39(1), 1-22.

Chappell, L. (2004) *Gendering Government: Feminist Engagement with the State in Australia and Canada*, Vancouver: University of British Columbia Press.

Childs, S. (2004) *Women Representing Women: New Labour's Women MPs*, London: Routledge.

Coates, D. and Lawler, P. (eds) (2000) *New Labour in Power*, Manchester: Manchester University Press.

Coote, A (1999) 'It's lads on top at Number Ten: Feminism just doesn't fit into Blair's vision of a pain-free politics for middle England', *Guardian*, 11 May, 15.

Coote, A. (ed.) (2000) *New Gender Agenda*, London: IPPR.

Cortell, A. and Peterson, S. (1999) 'Altered states: explaining domestic institutional change', *British Journal of Political Science* 29(1), 177-203.

Dahlerup, D. (1988) 'From a small to a large minority: women in Scandinavian politics', *Scandinavian Political Studies* 11(4), 275-98.

Deakin, N. and Parry, R. (2000) *The Treasury and Social Policy*, London: Macmillan.

Flinders, M. (2002) 'Governance in Whitehall', *Public Administration* 8(1), 51-75.

Foster, C.D. (2001) 'The civil service under stress: the fall in civil service power and authority', *Public Administration* 79(3), 725-50.

Gains, F. (1999) 'Implementing privatisation policies in Next Steps agencies', *Public Administration* 77(4), 713-30.

Gains, F. (2003a) 'Adapting the agency concept: variations within the 'Next Steps', in C. Pollitt and C. Talbot (eds) *Unbundled Government: A Critical Analysis of the Global Trend to Agencies, Quangos and Contractualisation*, London: Routledge.

Gains, F. (2003b) 'Executive agencies in government: the impact of bureaucratic networks on policy outcomes', *Journal of Public Policy* 23(1), 55-79.

Gains, F. (2004) 'Hardware, software or network connection? Theorising crisis catalyst in UK Next Steps agencies', *Public Administration* 82(3), 547-66.

Gains, F., John, P. and Stoker, G. (2005) 'Path dependency and the reform of English local government', *Public Administration* 83(1), 25-45.

Heclo, H. and Wildavsky, A. (1981) *The Private Government of Public Money: Community and Policy Inside British Politics*, London: Macmillan.

Inglehart, R. and Norris, P. (2003) *Rising Tide: Gender Equality and Cultural Change Around the World*, Cambridge: Cambridge University Press.

James, O. (2003) *The Executive Agency Revolution in Whitehall: Public Interest versus Bureau-shaping Perspectives Basingstoke*, Basingstoke: Palgrave Macmillan.

Kanter, R.M. (1977) 'Some effects of proportion of group life: skewed sex rations and responses to token women', *American Journal of Sociology* 82(5), 965-90.

Kingdon, J. (1984) *Agendas, Alternatives and Public Policies*, Boston, MA: Little Brown.

Lewis, J. (2001) 'The decline of the male breadwinner model: implications for work and care', *Social Politics* 8, Summer, 152-70.

Lobel, M. and Happold, T. (2003) 'Profile: Alan Milburn', *Guardian*, 12 June.

Lovenduski, J. (2005) *Feminizing Politics*, Cambridge: Polity Press.

Ludlam, S. and Smith, M.J. (eds) (2001) *New Labour in Government,* Basingstoke: Macmillan.

Ludlam, S. and Smith, M.J. (eds) (2004) *Governing as New Labour: Policy and Politics under Blair,* Basingstoke: Palgrave.

Marsh, D. and Rhodes, R.A.W. (eds) (1992a) *Policy Networks in British Government,* Oxford: Clarendon Press.

Marsh, D. and Rhodes, R.A.W. (eds) (1992b) *Implementing Thatcherite Policies: Audit of an Era,* Buckingham: Open University Press.

Mazur, A.G. (2002) *Theorising Feminist Policy,* Oxford: Oxford University Press

McBride Stetson, D. and Mazur, A.G. (1995) *Comparative State Feminism,* London: Sage.

Meehan, E. (2005) 'Women and citizenship: constitutional reform in the UK as a new enlightenment for feminist politics?', Paper presented to MANCEPT conference *Feminism, Citizenship and the Enlightenment: Themes from Ursula Vogel,* University of Manchester, 11 March.

Perrigo, S. (1999) 'Women, gender and New Labour', in G. Taylor (ed) *Impact of New Labour,* Basingstoke: Palgrave.

Phillips, A. (1995) *The Politics of Presence,* Oxford: Oxford University Press.

Pierson, P. (2000) 'Increasing returns, path dependence, and the study of politics', *American Political Science Review* 94(2), 251-67.

Randall, V. and Lovenduski, J. (2004) 'Gender in contemporary British politics', *British Journal of Politics and International Relations* 6(1), 1-3.

Rhodes, R.A.W. (1997) *Understanding Governance,* Buckingham: Open University Press.

Rhodes, R.A.W. (2000) 'New Labour's civil service: summing up joining up', *Political Quarterly* 71(2), 151-71.

Rhodes, R.A.W. and Dunleavy, P. (1995) *Prime Minister, Cabinet and Core Executive,* London: Macmillan.

Richards, D. and Smith, M.J. (1997) 'How departments change: windows of opportunity and critical junctures in three departments', *Public Policy and Administration* 12(2), 62-79.

Richards, D. and Smith, M.J. (2002) *Governance and Public Policy in the UK,* Oxford: Oxford University Press.

Richards, D. and Smith, M.J. (2004) 'New Labour and the reform of the state', in S. Ludlam and M.J. Smith (eds) *Governing as New Labour: Policy and Politics under Blair,* Basingstoke: Palgrave.

Russell, M. (2005) 'Women in the party: the quiet revolution', in M. Russell *The Building of New Labour: The Politics of a Party Organisation,* Basingstoke: Palgrave.

Sabatier, P. and Jenkins-Smith, H. (eds) (1993) *Policy Change and Learning,* Boulder, CO: Westview.

Savage, S. and R. Atkinson (2001) *Public Policy under Blair,* London: Palgrave Macmillan.

Select Committee on Health (2004) *HC 23 Obesity,* 3rd Report, 2003/2004 Session, London: The Stationery Office.

Select Committee on Public Administration (2000) *HC238 v Making Government Work, Evidence from Professor Christopher Pollitt and Professor R.A.W Rhodes,* 2000/2001 Session, London: The Stationery Office.

Smith, M.J. (1993) *Pressure, Power and Policy,* London: Harvester Wheatsheaf.

Smith, M.J. (1999) *The Core Executive in Britain,* London: Macmillan.

Smith, M.J., Marsh, D. and Richards, D. (2000) 'Re-assessing the role of ministers', *Public Administration* 78(2), 305-26.

Squires, J. (2005) 'Evaluating gender mainstreaming in the context of EU diversity strategies', Paper given at the Political Studies Association Conference, 5 April, University of Leeds.

Squires, J. and Wickham-Jones, M. (2002) 'Mainstreaming in Westminster and Whitehall: from Labour's Ministry for Women to the Women and Equality Unit', *Parliamentary Affairs* 55(1), 57-70.

Squires, J. and Wickham-Jones, M. (2004) 'New Labour, gender mainstreaming and the Women and Equality Unit', *British Journal of Politics and International Relations* 6(1), 81-98.

Stoker, G. (2002) 'Life is a lottery: New Labour's strategy for the reform of developed governance', *Public Administration* 80(3), 417-34.

True, J. (2003) 'Mainstreaming gender in global public policy', *International Feminist Journal of Politics* 5(3), 368-96.

True, J., Jones, B. and Baumgartner, F. (1999) 'Punctuated-equilibrium theory: explaining stability and change in American policymaking', in P. Sabatier (ed) *Theories of Policy Process,* Boulder, CO: Westview.

Veitch, J. (2005) 'Looking at gender mainstreaming in the UK government', *International Feminist Journal of Politics* 7(4), 600-6.

Worcester, B. (2005) 'Women's support gave Blair the edge', *The Observer,* 8 May, 6.

Yin, R. (1994) *Case Study Research: Design and Methods,* London: Sage.

Yoder, J. (1991) 'Rethinking tokenism: looking beyond numbers', *Gender and Society* 5(2), 178-92.

Part Two
Engendering politics?

TWO

Theoretical underpinnings: women, gender, feminising and politics

Angelia R. Wilson

Introduction

This volume is primarily concerned with the assessment of New Labour as it purposefully sought to promote the interests of women and reduce inequalities between the sexes. In Parts Two and Three each author teases out the implications of the politics and policies underpinning New Labour's celebrated attraction to, and for, 'women' and 'women's issues'. Along their journey in interpreting 'the needs of women', authors traverse a conceptual terrain which, while crucial to reaching their final destination, might take more time to detail sufficiently than possible within the confines of one chapter. Moreover, given that most of the authors share a general perspective on this conceptual terrain it seems suitable that one chapter could offer a brief picture of the theoretical underpinning through an examination of key concepts found in the political and policy discourse in relation to gender specificity. Such is the task of this chapter.

To begin, it is worth articulating the boundaries of this chapter as it is an overview of a few fundamental concepts employed within this text and conceptually motivated readers may wish to consult references for further elaboration. Moreover, any 'bird's eye view' necessarily involves the eye of a particular 'bird', or author. My own account of the terrain shares in a set of values which I believe informs this collection. Undoubtedly, each individual author may find their particular understanding more informative to their own analytical journey and we have worked together to avoid overlap while encouraging lively conversation of ideas and perspectives. Nevertheless, the articulated aims of 'reducing inequalities' and 'promoting the interests of women' rests upon familiar, but contested, ground within feminist discourse. For example, 'the interests of women' reflects the desire to articulate a common experience of patriarchy that permeates much of second-wave feminism. Even a call to 'reduce inequalities between the sexes' raises questions about the kinds of (in)equality between the sexes; the desirability to reduce 'inequalities'; and the binary distinction between male/female and how this may map on to gender construction.

Potential perils of essentialism, assumptions of 'feminism', and agendas of liberalism can be traced through key 'policy and politics' textbooks. Social policy literature over the last 50 years has employed a similar 'women and x' formula for policy analysis. For example, Elizabeth Wilson's *Women and the Welfare State* (1977); Ungerson's *Women and Social Policy* (1985); and even Jen Dale and Peggy Foster's *Feminist and State Welfare* (1986); Pascall's *Social Policy: A feminist analysis* (1986). While some include a brief discussion of 'feminism' or an overview of 'feminisms', their primary concern has been the relationship between the state and women via welfare issues of caring, need, dependency, etc. Likewise, those in political studies have asked questions about 'women and x' albeit often using 'gender' as synonymous with 'women', such as Anne Phillip's *Engendering Democracy* (1991); Susan Moller Okin's *Justice, Gender and the Family* (1989). Some of the discussions of politics and policy found in this volume flow in a similar vein of questioning; as do the gendered intentions and outcomes of New Labour. However, this volume sits apart from others in its awareness that policies designed with 'women' in mind, as well as those that are not, touch upon deeply embedded notions of gender within our society perpetuating some even in the process of disrupting others.

Recently, in the new journal *Politics and Gender*, Karen Beckwith highlights the need to 'disaggregate the meaning of "women"... "women" are no longer treated as a monolithic undifferentiated constituency of identified, shared implicitly homogeneous preferences' (Beckwith 2005, 128). Beckwith acknowledges the shift within policy and politics discourse from 'woman/women' to 'gender', particularly where the concept of gender has benefited from both social constructionist and postmodernist exploration of the relationship between 'gender' and 'body'. Continuing, she clarifies how gender has come to be understood as a 'category' and as a 'process':

> Gender as a category: 'multidimensional mapping of socially constructed fluid, politically relevant identities, values conventions, and practices conceived of as masculine and/or feminine, with the recognition that masculinity and femininity correspond only fleetingly and roughly to male and female'.

> Gender as a process: 'behaviours, conventions, practices
> and dynamics engaged in by individuals, organizations,
> movements, institutions and nations … manifestations in
> recent gender and political research: 1) as the differential
> effects of [gender-neutral] structures and policies upon
> women and men and 2) as the means by which masculine
> and feminine actors … actively work to produce favourable
> gendered outcomes'. (2005, 130)

The path from essentialised assumptions about 'women' to more
recent analysis of gender and its construction is worthy of mapping as
a collection such as this, which questions the relationship between a
government and women, must remain mindful of the historical context
of feminist theory and gender theory. Judging whether a governmental
action is in the 'interest of women' critically depends upon contested
interpretations of 'gender', 'women' and 'women's interest'. To that end,
the next section offers a brief consideration of the equality/difference
debate and subsequent questioning of gender construction. Following
from that, the second section interrogates the language of 'feminisation'
as employed Lovenduski, as well as that of 'gender mainstreaming'
appearing in policy contexts. The conclusion situates New Labour and
its 'women'-friendly policy focus within this complex and changing
conceptual terrain.

Feminism and gender construction

The cornerstone of modern political theory is the public/private
distinction. The public, where citizens deliberate on issues of governance,
is constructed, by liberals for example, as a place of rationality. Historically,
men were seen as capable of such rationality while women, different
in body, were not. Thus mind/body distinction motivated arguments
about citizenship, rationality and appropriate limits of 'public' policy.
Mary Wollstonecraft challenged this construction claiming that the
mind has no sex. Women should not be confined to the private sphere
but, like men, could be rational public actors and citizens. Moreover,
she added, if men participated in the caring roles within the home
they would be better husbands and citizens themselves:

> Make them [women] free, and they will quickly become
> wise and virtuous, as men become more so; for the
> improvement must be mutual, or the injustice which one
> half of the human race are obliged to submit to, retorting

on their oppressors, the virtue of men will be worm-eaten
by the insect whom he keeps under his feet. (1983, 175
– first published in 1792)

Wollstonecraft maintained that women should be educated and full
participants in public life and that men should be better husbands and
carers. However, much to the discomfort of current liberal feminists,
she also recognised some, biological and socially constructed, differences
between men and women. Each of these strands to her position is
relevant to contemporary debates about women in politics, welfare
and economic policy and gender construction.

Highlighting the 'Wollstonecraft dilemma' in *The Sexual Contract*,
Carole Pateman locates the conceptual division of male/female in the
mind/body dualism of male subjectivity and female sexuality:

> It is the implicit assumption of modern political theory
> that men are able to dissociate themselves from sexuality,
> reproduction and natural passions. Male subjectivity and
> male sexuality are divorceable conceptually and spatially in
> a way that female subjectivity and female sexuality are not.
> As Rousseau puts it, 'man is only man now and again, but
> the female is always a female' ... She tends to his natural,
> corporeal needs while he is transforming himself into
> rational 'social man'. (1988, 123)

The 'differences' between men and women then have served to
underpin the public/private divide where men are public actors and
women private servants. Where Wollstonecraft had argued that the
mind was not sexed, Pateman demonstrates that this answer does not
go far enough:

> While feminists continue to accept the liberal emphasis on
> the essential neutrality of the mind, sexual discrimination
> will continue to be 'justified' by natural bodily difference ...
> the female body will appear as the natural site of women's
> oppression, turning attention from the socio-political
> organization that can then present itself as an effect, rather
> than a cause. (1988, 123)

While it is important to claim the mind as unsexed, it does not fully
challenge the 'embodied' oppression of socio-political norms of

'masculine' and 'feminine' which are constructed directly from bodily difference.

Liberal feminists and socialist feminists, lumped together as 'equality feminists', interpreted social and material outcomes of gender as reasons why the state should perceive and treat citizens in a gender neutral manner. Judith Squires comments that equality feminists saw it as vital to argue that, irrespective of their sex, women were 'equally capable of the rational, individualistic and competitive characteristics commonly deemed to be masculine' (1999, 55). Equality feminists, such as Okin, would prefer to emphasise the similarities between men and women as 'human persons' and minimise differences arising from sexed bodies (1989; see also Cott 1988; Scott 1997). In particular, liberal feminists utilised the language of equality of rights and opportunities endorsing 'gender blind' legislation that would emancipate both sexes from gender expectations.

Set against this approach were feminists who maintained that biological differences were significant and that women naturally brought a 'different voice' to the public political arena (Rich 1980, 1986; Gilligan 1982; Daly 1987). This approach was employed by feminists with divergent political ideals, for example, libertarian/conservative, mothering feminist, radical lesbians. While each envisioned contrasting policy outcomes, they shared in the motivation to construct a society that valued differences, particularly emphasising a woman's identity as 'woman' (see Segal 1999). For example, Carol Gilligan's research offered empirical 'evidence' to 'the different voice of women' through which she believes they articulate an ethic of care (1982). Her work launched the delineation of a political ethics that resonates with themes that dominate policy debates concerning welfare, employment, family life and political representation.

Gilligan's claim that women have a different moral voice contrasted an 'ethic of justice' concerned with 'rights and rules' with an alternative 'ethic of care' concerned with 'relationships and responsibilities' (1982; see also Squires 1999, 140-65). An ethic of justice, it is claimed by Gilligan and others, conceptualised the individual moral actor as an autonomous individual capable of abstract rationality, particularly in relation to rights and universality. Contrastingly, an ethic of care, articulated by women reflects a situational reasoning, empathy, connectedness and an understanding of relationships and needs of others. This binary understanding of moral reasoning can map onto the historical debates within feminist theory regarding public/private; mind/body distinction, male/female nature; equality/difference. As such, it is has impacted upon feminist political theory, particularly regarding the appropriate ethical mode of reasoning underpinning the relationship between the state and citizens. Various scholars have raised methodological questions about Gilligan's research. One of the most compelling, from Joan Tronto, maintains that while these may be distinctive ethical perspectives, they do not necessarily arise from either biological differences, or be exclusively a phenomenon of gender (1993). Instead, Tronto argues that moral reasoning is more likely a function of socio-political subordination. While in Gilligan's work this may appear in relation to 'women', shifting the methodological focus would offer a clearer picture regarding power, oppression and capacity for caring.

Tronto's intervention reflects yet other friction that haunts feminist essentialism. The equality versus difference construct masks biological, relational, and socially constructed differences among women. The cacophony of different voices challenging essentialism within feminist theory was most eloquently heard in Audre Lorde's 'An Open Letter to Mary Daly' in which she accuses Daly of racism for assuming all women's experience of oppression to be the same (1983). The 1980s was marked by a plethora of writing from women of colour – Gloria Anzaldua, Angela Davis, bell hooks, Amina Mama and Pratibha Parmar to name but a few – well rehearsed in the dangers of biological essentialism and the need to understand socially constructed oppression and the possibility to 'overcome' it. In Britain, socialist feminists such as Michèle Barrett, Mary McIntosh, Juliet Mitchell, Anne Phillips and Elizabeth Wilson presented another challenge to American liberal essentialist 'feminism' (see Lovenduski and Randall 1993). Thirty years on, it remains surprisingly easy to find references to 'women's issues' and 'feminism' which do not account for differences of experience, reasoning and subjectivity. Questions of difference – initially raised by 'black' feminists, lesbians, and others of mixed/fluid/multiple identities – led to a proliferation of difference in which identity politics based on the category 'women' continues to struggle (Fraser and Nicholson 1990).

Alongside these challenges, others began to endorse a more robust theoretical deconstruction of 'gender' categories. For example, in the late 1980s, Connell argued for the deconstruction of masculinities by breaking the connection between being male and 'doing masculinities' (1987, 83). His later work aligns generally with those who question the power of patriarchy or 'hegemonic masculinity' – 'current practices and ways of thinking which authorise make valid and legitimise the dominant position of men and the subordination of women' through institutions such as 'the family, corporate business, government and the military' (Cranny-Francis et al 2002, 16). The 'patriarchal dividend' benefits all men whether or not they individually oppress women and as such, involves complicity with the hegemonic project. So, while women of difference picked away at the (dis)comfort-blanket of feminism, men were also questioning the construction of 'masculinity' and 'patriarchy' setting the scene for the implosion of an identity politics based upon fixed subjectivities.

Deconstructionist Rosie Braidotti, for example, observes that 'the signifier "woman" is no longer sufficient as the foundational stone of the feminist project' (1994, 4). The (in)famous Judith Butler's *Gender Trouble* posits gender as a verb – the enactment or performance of gender appears as natural, stable and therefore unchangeable (1999). On this particular point, many would agree. However, she continues by claiming that binary oppositions are produced in relation to each other and as such sex and identity are determined discursively through repetition or resistance. The subject is not an autonomous chooser as found in modern political theory, liberal feminism, or a wilful agent of emancipation. Only parody and performance discursively disrupts the heterosexual matrix (Butler 1999, 1993). It is with this disabling of the subject as agent that many feminists take issue. Martha Nussbaum, for example, rails against Butler as the 'Professor of Parody' and the enemy of feminism, and more importantly, of women whose lived experience of oppression, abuse, poverty appear to be dismissed by Butler's elitist theorising (1999).

While some question Butler's feminist credentials, what is clear from the given overview is that it is now conceptually dubious to claim 'woman' as an essentialised category of socio-political analysis. The journey from the women/men binary; to recognition of the differences between 'women'; and continuing on to perceptions of the complexity of relational fluid subjectivities constituted, at least in part, by discursive connections between signifiers, has led us to the contested political terrain of contemporary feminism. Postmodernism poses infinite challenges to gender identity as a permanent political fixture. 'Gender sensitivity' or 'gender awareness' is no longer the linguistic equivalent of policy or politics reflective of 'women' or 'women's needs'. Instead, any claims of sensitivity or awareness involve not only the material and social construction of gender, but also a fundamental understanding of gender fluidity and linguistic construction. Gender becomes a linguistic power tool in both deconstructing and reconstructing social discourses on women and men, difference and sameness, apparitions of truth and metanarratives.

Rosemary Pringle and Sophie Watson comment on the implications of this 'discursive turn' for feminism:

> If 'women's interests' are constructed rather than pre-given, then so are men's. If we have to let go of the authentic female subject, then we can let go too of the male subject. Patriarchal discourse need not be seen as homogeneous and uniformly repressive, and women do not need to be portrayed as victims. This opens up possibilities of exposing differences between men and where appropriate, creating alliances ... women's interests will be articulated in a variety of competing ways ... our subjectivity will have been formed within a multiplicity of discourses, many of them conflicting and contradictory ... rather than seeking a politics based on 'unity', we can move towards one based on respect for the differences of others, and on alliances with them. (1992, 68-70)

The variety of analysis offered in this volume on New Labour and women attests to the complexity of determining whether New Labour has promoted 'the interests of women and reduce inequalities between the sexes.' 'No policy will be a gain for all women ...' (see Chapter One). Each and every instance of policy-making reflects a different configuration of power relations and networks. Policy and its implementation will 'depend not only on how strongly these different interests are articulated, but on how they mesh with the demands of other groups' (Pringle and Watson 1992, 69). With this in mind, the following section considers a couple of attempts to negotiate the complexity of gender while maintaining a political agenda resonant with motivations of feminism.

Feminising politics and gender mainstreaming

In her recent text, *Feminizing Politics*, Joni Lovenduski notes the difficulty in utilising essentialised notions of 'women' but nevertheless claims to demonstrate the importance of women's representation to changing politics and political institutions (2005). She considers the growing number of women MPs and whether or not increased representation has led New Labour to act for women; take on women's concerns in policy; and make a difference to women's lives. To this end, New Labour, or women MPs can be seen to be 'feminising' politics. In light of the previous discussion, this particular selection and ordering of words deserves more consideration as it seems to impose a static 'feminine' gender onto a, discursively constructed, masculine 'politics'.

The binary construction of masculine/feminine within modern political theory establishes the latter as weak, unable to handle power, domestic, caring and cheap labour. To feminise politics could refer then to making politics less 'masculine' for example, a less confrontational, rational, autonomous state policing and/or providing for citizens; and the desire for it to be more 'feminine', for example, a more communal, empathetic, connected/'in touch' state which protects and cares for all citizens. A few examples might demonstrate this: the debate over whether women MPs could breastfeed in the public spaces of the Houses of Parliament or, more negatively, references to the state provision of welfare as the 'nanny state'. Over the years, New Labour has given voice to the need to have a less confrontational style in debate; the need for local/community based services; the need to understand structural and situational context producing inequalities; and a more organic 'joined up' style of governing. This approach has risked New Labour politics being perceived as a 'politics light': not as powerful, strong, focused or lacking coherent trajectory. Critics of the Third Way typically made such accusations suggesting that it was incoherent, reactive rather than leading, not ideologically sound and therefore without a rational plan of action and ideals (Hall 1998; Lukes 1999; Ryan 1999; Giddens 2000).

To feminise politics could refer to the projected image of a more 'feminine' politics through the increasing representation of women. Cynically, this could be seen as a capitalist marketing strategy where one presents a 'more appealing' image in order to soften the tough exterior of a political 'hard man' and/or as a marketing strategy tailored to constituents in order to invoke an imagined identification with the product because it now 'looks' slightly more like 50% of the voting population. Perhaps less cynically, it could be construed as a nod towards an ideology of just democracy where at least some of those in power should share an identity (and presumably a political agenda) with those governed (Phillips 1991).

The language of 'feminisation' could be seen to rest upon essentialised understandings of 'women', of 'women representatives', 'women's issues', and, of course, 'feminine'. Traces of such essentialism can be found in Lovenduski's work (2005), as well as that of Childs (2004), with their research exploring the impact of increased representation of women and discussions of 'women's agenda' or 'feminist agenda' among those representatives. To this end, to 'feminise' maintains an affinity to a historical construct/artefact labelled the 'feminist agenda' which appeared to highlight policies affecting 'women's lives'. The Center for American Women and Politics (1995) study *Voices, Views, Votes* considered the unprecedented increase of women elected in 1992, their subsequent voting records and policy influence. Their findings support the assumption of women's collective agenda across party lines and that women representatives do feel a 'special responsibility' to represent 'the life experiences of women'. However, what is defined as a collective 'women's' agenda tended to include health care, abortion and crime, particularly violence against women. Moreover, in a relation to economic policy, specifically debates over North American Free Trade Association (NAFTA), there was little intervention by women. So, considering the impact of representation should highlight the spaces in which women can collectively work together, but it must also acknowledge the lack of opportunities to do so and, importantly, the deep political divisions between women which thwart attempts to locate a shared 'feminist' agenda. Even among the women of New Labour, one might imagine a less than 'sisterly' scramble for individual power.

To 'feminise', then, may linguistically conjure an essentialised unity of purpose, experience and an understanding of 'self' (as woman) and of 'other' (the political). To feminise the 'other' (the political) likewise locates the other, including the power of the other, as a coherent 'body' in need of alteration. To feminise 'politics' may call attention to a divide between 'politics' and 'feminine' that may leave little linguistic space for 'feminine politics' or 'non-gendered politics' or 'variously gendered politics'. One must not confuse feminising politics with a feminist politics. Where once feminists argued that the 'personal is political', some women's lives are not constructed as 'politically viable', do-able or cost-effective. It is the intention of this collection to examine the impact of New Labour on the lives of women. And while New Labour may be, comparatively speaking, the 'most feminist Government in our history' (*The Times*, 'Gender pay gap "may never go"', 5 December 2005), that does not make it 'a feminist government' or a 'government with a clear feminist agenda'. 'Feminising politics' – politics light; feminine politics; unmasculine politics – may be a good description of politics under New Labour. But surely the preference would be for a politics that negotiates the complexities of gender seriously and confidently.

One example of this may be found in the concept of gender mainstreaming. The 1995 Beijing United Nations Fourth World Conference on women endorsed a strategy of gender mainstreaming in which 'governments and other actors should promote an active and visible policy of mainstreaming a gender perspective in all policies and programmes, so that before decisions are taken, an analysis is made of the effects on women and men, respectively' (UN 1995). The Council of Europe Directorate of Human Rights Specialist Group on Mainstreaming responded to this mandate with the publication of *Gender Mainstreaming: Conceptual Framework, Methodology and Presentation of Good Practices* in 2004 (UN 2004). In that document, gender mainstreaming is defined as: 'the (re)organisation, improvement, development and evaluation of policy processes, so that a gender equality perspective is incorporated in all policies at all levels and at all stages, by the actors normally involved in policy-making' (UN 1995, 8). Setting aside the effectiveness of this document in the ensuing years, what is pertinent here is the section which established the conceptual foundation for such policies. First, gender mainstreaming is seen as a strategy to achieve gender equality: 'For a long time – and it is often still the case – gender equality in Europe was defined as giving girls and boys, women and men, *de jure* equal rights, equal opportunities, equal conditions and equal treatment in all fields of life and in all spheres of society. Nowadays, it is recognised that equality *de jure* does not automatically lead to equality *de facto* ... Gender equality is not synonymous with sameness, with establishing men, their lifestyle and conditions as the norm' (UN 1995, 7). Clearly, the ideal of equality between women and men motivates the need to give attention to gender within the policy process and, particularly, policy outcomes. However, the document does not make the conceptual mistake of assuming biological essentialism or fixity of categories of gender. Consider the definition of gender detailed in the very next paragraph.

> Gender is a socially constructed definition of women and men. It is the social design of a biological sex, determined by the conception of tasks, functions and roles attributed to women and men in society and in public and private life. It is a culture-specific definition of femininity and masculinity and therefore varies in time and space. The construction and reproduction of gender takes place at the individual as well as the societal level. Both are equally important. Individual human beings shape gender roles and norms through their activities and reproduce them by conforming to expectations. (UN 1995, 7)

Here one finds notions of gender fluidity over 'time and space' and gender 'constructed' by individuals, society and policies producing and reproducing structural and discursive relations between men and women. The document continues noting, what can only be identified as a foundational principle of feminism, that 'society is characterised by this male bias: the male norm is taken as the norm of society as a whole, which is reflected in policies and structures' (UN 1995, 8). In addition, the document recognises the demands of difference: 'Gender equality includes the right to be different. This means taking into account the existing differences among women and men, which are related to class, political opinion, religion, ethnicity, race or sexual orientation' (UN 1995, 8). At the very least, it is interesting that theories of gender are not conversations exclusive to the academy and, perhaps more so, that relational, discursive and fluid understandings of gender and difference have been so readily accepted by policy makers. Moreover, this document shows how policy makers can cling to a meta-narrative concept such as 'equality' while accepting the conceptual complexity of gender construction.

Judith Squires notes that gender mainstreaming is widely perceived as 'the new equality strategy' and as such is conceptualised in three distinct ways: as a means of pursuing equal opportunities policies via bureaucratic policy tools; as a means of pursuing women's perspectives via consultations with women's organisations; or as a means of pursuing complex equality via inclusive deliberation. This third conceptualisation in conjunction with mechanisms of deliberative democracy may offer an excellent strategy for transformation (2005). It is beyond the scope here to consider in detail how 'gender mainstreaming' may be embodied as a policy. However, seen in contrast to 'feminising politics' the breadth and depth of conceptual complexity at the heart of the EU articulation of gender mainstreaming appears capable of moving beyond equality/difference, masculine/feminine, public/private dichotomies. Taking Squires' suggestion, deliberative democracy opens space for conversations between those with multiple and fluid identities as well as engaging with the multiple faces of the state in a variety of domains. This conceptual terrain opens up discursive space for, in Chantal Mouffe's phrase, the *Return of the Political* – intentional communication in which we can negotiate respect of differences as well as norms for socio-political interaction (1993).

Conclusion

This chapter has offered an overview of conceptual concerns that motivate the chapters which follow. Without a doubt New Labour offered more of an opportunity to be more feminist than any previous government. There remain a number of questions, however. For example, worries persist over who precisely has been involved in determining what are 'women's issues'; which 'issues' were prioritised within policy; and, more telling perhaps, whose 'issues' were left unheard, and unaddressed. There are more women working, but does this indicate that women are more financially independent or that women are more pressured to be economically active as well as fulfilling the social/family expectations of caring? I am reminded of an advert in the early 1980s celebrating the post-sexual revolution woman who could 'bring home the bacon, fry it up in the pan, and never let you forget you're a man'. 'Women having it all' very quickly, for individual women, translates into 'women doing it all'. The outcomes of addressing some concerns of some women may not be as desirable as outcomes which fundamentally challenge the construction of gender in all its diverse manifestations.

Finally, it is worth noting a few constraints in motivating more fundamental challenges of gender within the political agenda. Interestingly, the rise of New Labour and its 'agenda for women' bizarrely coincided with a crisis within what has been labelled historically 'the women's movement'. This crisis of feminism became the topic of at least three books published at the dawn of the millennium by women associated with, or previously associated with, feminism: Germaine Greer's *The Whole Woman* (1999), Lynne Segal's *Why Feminism?* (1999) and Roz Coward's *Sacred Cows: Is Feminism Relevant to the New Millennium?* (1999) (see Wilson, 2006). In *The Whole Woman*, Germaine Greer writes 'it's time to get angry again' and encourages women to take up the mantle of radical feminism. Roz Coward asks 'Is feminism relevant to the new millennium?' and her answer is only if feminists sacrifice a few *Sacred Cows*. For Coward, the 20 years post-1970s feminism saw the feminisation of the economy and the breakdown of traditional family norms. The result of which was not a 'gender trouble' to be celebrated but bemoaned. Lynne Segal asks *Why Feminism?* and her account offers a clear guide to the varied terrain of feminist and gender theory. What is significant about these is that each one recognises the lethargy of feminism as a social movement. Moreover, although each was published post-1997 elections, not one of them celebrates the potential arrival of a feminist utopia under New Labour, not one of them hints at the possibility of New Labour actively pursuing a feminist agenda. Coward's lament of the feminist hangover aside, neither Greer nor Segal seems excited about the potential of New Labour. Both articulate continued worries about the realities of women's lives within a patriarchal capitalist society. While Greer's book rallies the feminist troops, Segal's details why feminism must engage with issues of gender construction. Undoubtedly, one constraint in recent political discourse has been the lack of a clear feminist voice. Of these three, Segal's intervention stood alone at the millennium challenging New Labour: 'Why feminism? Because its most radical goal, both personal and collective, has yet to be realised: a world which is a better place not just for some women, but for all women. In what I still call a socialist feminist vision, that would be a far better world for boys and men, as well' (1999, 232). Some would argue that such a 'socialist feminist' agenda was 'so last season'; perhaps similarly, given the conceptual discussion in this chapter, is New Labour's worry about 'women' rather than 'gender'.

References

Beckwith, K. (2005) *Politics and Gender* 1(1), 128-36.

Braidotti, R. (1994) *Nomadic Subjects – Embodiment and Sexual Difference in Contemporary Feminist Theory*, New York, NY: Columbia University Press.

Butler, J. (1993) *Bodies That Matter: On the Discursive Limits of 'Sex'*, New York, NY: Routledge.

Butler, J. (1999) *Gender Trouble*, London: Routledge.

Center for American Women and Politics (1995) *Voices, Views, Votes: The Impact of Women in the 103rd Congress*, New Brunswick, NJ: Rutgers.

Childs, S. (2004) *New Labour's Women MPs: women representing women*, London: Routledge.

Connell, R.W. (1987) *Gender and Power*, Cambridge: Polity.

Cott, N. (1988) *The Grounding of Modern Feminism*, New Haven, CT: Yale University Press.

Coward, R. (1999) *Sacred Cows: Is Feminism Relevant to the New Millennium?*, London: HarperCollins.

Cranny-Francis A., Waring, W., Stavropoulos, P., and Kirkby J. (2002) *Gender Studies: Terms and Debates*, London: Palgrave.

Dale, J. and Foster, P. (1986) *Feminists and State Welfare*, London: Routledge.

Daly, M. (1987) *Gyn/Ecology*, London: The Women's Press.

Fraser, N. and Nicholson, L. (1990) 'Social criticism without philosophy', in L. Nicholson (ed) *Feminism/Postmodernism*, London: Routledge.

Giddens, A. (2000) *The Third Way and Its Critic*, Cambridge: Polity Press.

Gilligan, C. (1982) *In a Different Voice*, London: Harvard University Press.

Greer, G. (1999) *The Whole Woman*, London: Doubleday.

Hall, S. (1998) 'The great moving nowhere show', *Marxism Today* Nov/Dec, 9-14.

Lorde, A. (1983) 'An open letter to Mary Daly', in C. Moraga and G. Anzaldua (eds) *This Bridge Called my Back: Radical Writings by Women of Color*, Latham, NY: Kitchen table, Women of Color Press.

Lovenduski, J. (2005) *Feminizing Politics*, Cambridge: Polity Press.

Lovenduski, J. and Randall, M. (1993) *Contemporary Feminist Politics: Women and Power in Britain*, Oxford: Oxford University Press.

Lukes, S. (1999) 'More than words?', in Social Market Foundation (ed) *The Third Way*, London: Social Market Foundation, 17-20

Mouffe, C. (1993) *The Return of The Political*, London: Verso.

Nussbaum, M. (1999) 'The professor of parody', *New Republic*, available at www.qwik.ch/the_professor_of_parody (accessed 22 February).

Okin, S.M. (1989) *Justice, Gender and the Family*, New York, NY: Basic Books.

Pascall, G. (1986) *Social Policy: A Feminist Analysis*, London: Routledge.

Pateman, C. (1988) *The Sexual Contract*, Cambridge: Polity Press.

Phillips, A. (1991) *Engendering Democracy*, Cambridge: Polity Press.

Pringle, R. and Watson, S. (1992) 'Women's interests' and the post-structuralist state', in M. Barrett and A. Phillips (eds) *Destabilizing Theory: Contemporary Feminist Debates*, Cambridge: Polity Press.

Rich, A. (1980) 'Compulsory heterosexuality and lesbian existence', *Signs* 5(4), 631-90.

Rich, A. (1986) *Of Woman Born*, London: Virago.

Ryan, A. (1999) 'Britain: recycling the third way', *Dissent* 46(2), 77 80.

Scott, J. (1997) 'Deconstructing equality-versus-difference', in D. Meyers (ed) *Feminist Social Thought*, London: Routledge.

Segal, L. (1999) *Why Feminism?*, Cambridge: Polity Press.

Squires, J. (1999) *Gender in Political Theory*, Cambridge: Polity Press.

Squires, J. (2005) 'Evaluating gender mainstreaming in the context of EU diversity strategies', presented at the Political Studies Association Annual Conference, 5 April, University of Leeds.

Tronto, J. (1993) *Moral Boundaries: A Political Argument for an Ethic of Care*, London: Routledge.

UN (United Nations) (1995) *Beijing Platform for Action*, Beijing Fourth World Conference on Women, UN.

UN (2004) *Gender Mainstreaming: Conceptual Framework, Methodology and Presentation of Good Practices*, available at www.coe.int/equality (accessed 22 May 2006).

Ungerson, C. (ed) (1985) *Women and Social Policy*, London: Macmillan.

Wilson, A. (2006) 'Practically between postmenopause and postmodern', in D. Richardson et al (eds) *Intersections between Feminism and Queer Theory*, London: Palgrave.

Wilson, E. (1977) *Women and the Welfare State*, London: Tavistock.

Wollstonecraft, M. (1983) *Vindication of the Rights of Woman*, Harmondsworth: Penguin Classics, first published 1792.

THREE

Women and Nordic labour parties

Guro Buchanan and Claire Annesley

Introduction

Many accounts of the politics and policy of New Labour have tended to emphasise the strong influence of New Right or American thinking on the party's reform agenda. Yet key figures in Labour Party policy circles have highlighted that much policy learning has in fact been done by looking towards the social democratic Nordic states. Geoff Mulgan, former director of the Prime Minister's Strategy Unit, said that Labour's welfare to work policies are 'actually borrowed more from Scandinavia than from America' (2003). In much of the comparative literature on democracy, welfare states and state feminism, the Nordic states are held up as role models for gender equality policies. This chapter therefore looks at the strategies used by social democratic parties in Norway and Sweden to feminise politics and seeks to assess the extent to which New Labour can learn from these states.

At the same time, it is necessary to take a critical look at the achievements of the Nordic states in terms of gender policies and therefore question the value of Nordic states as a role model for New Labour. Scholars such as Hernes (1987a, 1987b) have, for example, questioned the degree of influence that Nordic women have in policy making. While they tend to be well represented in Parliament, they are under-represented in the corporatist decision-making bodies where economic and social policies are drafted. Hakim (2004) highlights the economic inequality that exists in Nordic states: that the labour market is segregated in occupational terms, with women over-represented in the public sector; and that there is a lower proportion of women in managerial positions than in the US or the UK. Other scholars have highlighted that while welfare policies are women-friendly, policies on issues like domestic violence are not.

This chapter seeks to offer an evaluation of the position of women in two Nordic states – Norway and Sweden. These countries have been selected as they have both developed women-friendly politics and policies since the 1970s, although the opportunities for this were different and the outcomes vary. The chapter will offer a review of the opportunities for a feminisation of politics in these countries since the 1970s under the headings of women's substantive representation, women in the core executive, state feminism and women's policy platform to gain female votes. It will then evaluate the respective degrees of 'women-friendliness' in the economy, welfare state and foreign policy – the main focus of the policy sections of this book. In doing so, the chapter will offer some pointers to New Labour regarding how a party can make a difference to women's lives and the pitfalls that it might encounter along the way.

The gender record in Norway and Sweden

Gender relations in Sweden and Norway are perceived to be among the most progressive in the world and this achievement is closely related to the long-standing presence of social democratic governments. The Nordic social democratic movements emerged in the early twentieth century and some important measures were taken. Norwegian and Swedish women were given the right to vote in 1913 and 1921 respectively. The first female Minister in Norway was appointed in 1945. In Sweden, a 1939 Act made it unlawful to dismiss a woman in the event of marriage, pregnancy or childbirth (Gustafsson 1994). But the 1950s was the 'decade of the housewife' in Sweden on account of joint taxation of incomes and a poor provision of childcare (Gustafsson 1994, 50). As late as 1970, only 23% of Norwegian women held waged work (Raaum 1997). The housewife ideal also held a comparatively strong position in the Norwegian society well into the 1970s. Indeed, the Nordic gender revolution did not take place until the 1970s.

The transformation in Nordic states in the 1970s was two-fold. First, women entered the labour market on an unprecedented scale. In Sweden from the 1960s, economic policy reorganised around stimulating the labour supply of married women. Given the labour shortage, the preference was to bring women into the labour market rather than the more costly strategy of inviting over foreign workers (Gustafsson 1994). The social democratic ideal of the 'semi-professionalised housewife' became replaced by a series of state reforms to support working women, notably childcare for all (Curtin and Higgins 1998). Other women-friendly policies in Sweden included parental insurance (1974), the abortion law (1975) and the 1980 Equal Opportunities Act (Eduards 1991).

It can be questioned whether women or family-friendly welfare policies were introduced in order to facilitate the commodification of women in the labour market. Women's economic activity was encouraged to increase the labour supply as an alternative to immigration. Alternatively, such policies can be read as strategies to win the votes of female voters.

Second, and at the same time, women gained access to political power in national and local assemblies. In 1973 women achieved 10% of the seats in the Norwegian Parliament and then reached 20% in 1977 which was late compared to the other Nordic countries. Raaum (1997) argues this could be explained by the traditional character of the Norwegian society, as exemplified by the late and slow influx of women into the labour market. In 1970, the Swedish Parliament consisted of 14% women; by 1979 this had increased to 28% (Freidenvall 2005).

In these years, social democracy was reoriented around a new gender contract. In Swedish social democracy, gender equality was subsumed under the broader goal of class equality. Policies to promote gender equality were gender neutral, that is, they ignored the power dynamics assigned to the genders in Swedish society. Progress, it was assumed, would follow from greater class equality and would emerge through cooperation between the sexes. One should not underestimate the impact the Labour Party has had on women's political participation and representation in Norway. As we will see, the party was instrumental in institutionalising and securing gender equality as well as championing a gender dimension to politics. Much progress was achieved through opportunities presented to and taken by women in the political system.

Opportunities taken by women in promoting gender equality

The path towards gender equality in the Nordic countries of Sweden and Norway was developed through a number of opportunities for women in the political system. These include the increase of women's representation in Parliament and the part that women have played in government, the role of women's policy agencies and the inclusion of women in the trade union movement.

Women in Parliament

Nordic women have among the highest levels of representation in national parliaments. In Sweden, female representation in Parliament currently stands at 45.3% (IPU 2006). In Norway, the current Parliament has 37.9% women representatives. Of the seven parties represented in the Norwegian Parliament, the Labour Party has the highest proportion of women with 52.6% but is followed closely by the Socialistic Left Party on 49.3%, with the Centre Party and the Christian People's Party both on 45.5%. The Conservative Party and the Progress Party are doing worst with 21.7% and 15.8% female representation respectively (Stortinget 2006).

These two states took different routes to boost the presence of women in their national Parliaments. According to Borchorst, Norway is the Nordic country with most far-reaching legislation on gender quotas and the most developed and specialised policy implementation and enforcement apparatus (1997). In 1988, the Labour government introduced the requirement of minimum 40% representation of either gender in public boards and committees. Although this does not apply to wholly elected bodies, the requirement is expected to be adhered to in selection processes for election candidates wherever possible. The Labour party has also been pushing for the 40% requirement to be applicable when electing political parties' central committees and nominating candidates for both general and local elections. It is now only the Progressive Party that has not adopted gender quotas (Christiansen 1997). In general elections there is little difference between the percentage of women candidates and women elected, and the level of female representation has been rather stable over the last 20 years, independent of whether there has been a conservative or a socialist majority. There is still among elite politicians as well as the general public, strong support for the use of gender quotas. Gender quotas are perceived as securing democratic ideals of political representation (for women) that would otherwise not be achieved and that would possibly regress were quotas abolished. In fact, rather than limiting its use, it has been suggested that gender quotas could also be introduced to private businesses and boards.

In contrast, no use of quotas has been made in Sweden. Rather, women demanding higher representation have relied on voluntary strategies based on cooperation between the sexes. The demands for quotas from women's sections of political parties have been made periodically as concerns about the slow pace of change have been raised. Following the drop in the representation of women in the 1991 election – the first since 1928 – the extra-parliamentary feminist network Stödstrumporna (The Support Stockings) threatened political parties that they would set up a women's party if the parties did not increase the number of women on their ballots (Freidenvall 2005). The women's section subsequently pushed for parties to introduce special measures to increase female representation. In response to this, the Swedish Social Democratic Party introduced a new rule – Varannan Damernas – whereby men and women were placed alternately on all social democratic party lists (Freidenvall 2005). The 1994 election produced a then world record of 43% female representation.

Women Ministers

The high proportion of women in Nordic Parliaments has translated into a high number of female Ministers, many of international reputation. In Norway, Gro Harlem Brundtland received her first Cabinet post as Minister of Environmental Affairs in 1974 and became the elected leader of the Norwegian Labour Party in 1981. In her address to the Labour Party Annual General Meeting (AGM) that year Brundtland pointed to the inclusion of right to abortion in the 1969 programme as the start of the party's emphasis on women and gender equality. But, as discussed below, her addresses to the party AGMs in the 1980s gave far more attention to employment issues and the protection of the welfare state, than to issues of gender equality and/or women's politics.

Gro Harlem Brundtland became the first and, to date, only female Scandinavian Prime Minister in 1981, and in 1986 she installed her world record-breaking Cabinet with eight women among 18 Ministers. The percentage of female representation in the Cabinet has since then never fallen below 40% (Statistisk Sentral Byrå 2006a) and has always been higher than in Parliament. Sweden, in 1999, became the first country to have more female Ministers than men. This included Anna Lindh, the Foreign Minister who was murdered in 2003. In 2004 there were 11 male Ministers and 11 female Ministers in the government. In Sweden 10 of 26 state secretaries, the rank immediately below Cabinet Minister, are women.

The current coalition government in Norway, consisting of the Labour Party, the Socialistic Left Party and the Centre Party, has 47.4% women in its Cabinet compared to 40.9% in the last Conservative/ Centre coalition. During the 1990s, however, the Conservative/centre coalitions did better than their socialist counterpart in representing women in Cabinet posts. In Norwegian ministry administration women are not doing as well as in the political offices with more women at the lower levels and few in managerial positions. The numbers for personal secretaries, political advisers and political secretaries are, however, similar for both conservative/centre coalitions and Labour governments since the 1970s (Informasjon fra regjerigen og departementene 2006).

Women's policy agencies

Women's policy agencies are formal state structures given the role by political leaders to improve the status of women by pursuing overtly feminist policy goals (Stetson and Mazur 1995). In Nordic states such bodies have gained a comparatively high degree of policy access and policy influence. The Swedish Equality Ombudsman – JämO – was established by the Equal Opportunities Act in 1979 to enforce new equal employment policy. It has played an important role in promoting gender equality in the workplace and highlighting the issue of sexual harassment. However, it has done little to give a voice to feminist activists or organisations, resisting, for example, the call from autonomous feminists to broaden its remit to include gender issues outside the labour market. Rather, it has collaborated with feminists in political parties and trades union thus embracing a 'state inspired definition of what would advance women's status by focusing on gender-neutral notions of equality' (Mazur and Stetson 1995, 281).

The Norwegian Equal Status Council (ESC) (located within the Ministry for Children and Family Affairs) was set up by the Labour Government in 1972 and replaced the Unit for Equal Pay, which had existed since 1959. The ESC was both proactive and reactionary. In 2004 it assessed 517 new cases of which 50% came from women, 30% from men and 15% were initiated by the ESC itself (Likestillings Ombudet 2006). Under the conservative/centre coalition government in office until October 2005, a new structure for the ESC was agreed. The new Ombud for Equality and Anti-Discrimination combines the responsibilities for protection from racial, sexual, gender and religious discrimination within one unit. The Ombud was established in January 2006, and replaced the ESC.

According to Mazur and Stetson (1995, 279) the ESC 'contributed to the emergence of an equality policy network, an "equal status segment" throughout Norway that has gone far in pushing the state to improve women's position in society'. It has 'empowered women's interests through coordinating and supporting equal status committees in counties and municipalities, which, with the support of the ESC in the 1980s served as important avenues of women's recruitment into elected office and corporate bodies' (Mazur and Stetson 1995, 279).

The corporatist channel – women in trades union

In the Nordic context, the corporatist channel is an important consideration in the process of exercising political power to promote women's interests. As Hernes (1987a and 1987b) has argued, it is in the tripartite decision-making bodies rather than Parliament where political deals are struck and key policy decisions made. Hernes argues that while the political representation of women has developed since the 1970s, their presence in the corporatist channel is low.

According to Hernes, the welfare state has been developed via the corporate channel, where women as a group have lacked political power and women's interests have lacked legitimacy. The corporate channel grew out of the need for mainstreaming interest representation. Generally, the corporatist channel has been perceived as an extension of democracy and representation. But we should remember that its participants are there by virtue of representing institutional and group interests. For a group to be considered 'in', aspects of education, professional status and links with institutions are all held to be relevant criteria. However, gender is not. As discussed above, gender has been accepted as 'political' in the numerical-democratic channel, but this has not been mirrored in the corporate-pluralist channel, and realisation of women's representation in it has therefore been difficult.

Norway has been characterised by a close relationship between the state and the organisations in the public and private sector and this is considered one of the contributing factors to its state-friendly society. Kuhnle and Selle describe this as a 'culture of cooperation' wherein the state, on the one hand, guarantees and supports attained rights and, on the other, is very open to pressure from below (1992). Raaum (1997) argues that this special relationship has meant that political participation has just as often been channelled through the political parties in the parliamentary system as through organisations within the market and civil society. In Norway, there are strong links between the trades union and the political parties, as seen with the Labour Party and the Arbeidernes Landsorganisasjon (LO – National Labour Organisation) and the Conservative Party and the Næringslivets Hoved Organisasjon (NHO – the Confederation of Norwegian Business and Industry) respectively.

Although women's representation has been less successful in the corporate sector, the closeness between the two channels does increase women's access points and makes overspill possible. The new quota requirements – discussed in the section on the economy – in private business alongside the developments within the NHO could serve to increase the representation of women within the corporate channel.

In Sweden, women are highly organised in the peak blue collar trade union LO yet under-represented in the organisation. Women make up nearly half of LO's membership of over two million and yet, as

Curtin and Higgins (1998) note, at the end of the 1980s 'only 65 of LO's 525 representatives on tripartite policy-making bodies and 26 of its delegates on bipartite labour market bodies were women'. Curtin and Higgins (1998) attribute this to the nature of the Swedish gender contract in which women still perform the bulk of unpaid domestic duties meaning that 'would-be women activists thus tend to remain too pinned down in an exploitative division of labour in the home to fight through their unions for justice in their paid work'.

A 'women-friendly' society? Policy outcomes under Nordic social democracy

Social democratic Nordic states are characterised by a high presence of women in both the formal labour market and formal political sphere, most notably in national assemblies. The task now is to assess the extent to which this presence has translated into 'women-friendly' policies. While Nordic states conventionally have strong reputations in this regard, more recent critiques have highlighted the shortcomings of the gender neutral approach to equality that Nordic social democracy has promoted. Such critiques have emerged in particular during the shift to the Right that occurred in the 1990s. This section reviews the records of Norway and Sweden in three policy fields: the economy, the welfare state and foreign policy.

Economy

In Norway and Sweden women's participation in the labour force is almost equal to that of men. In Norway, in 2004, women made up 47% of the workforce. In Sweden in 2004, 72.1% of women were employed. However, recent studies have highlighted the gendered characteristics of this 'equal' status in the labour market.

First, Nordic labour markets are strongly segregated along gender lines. As Hakim (2004) observes, Sweden has a stark occupational segregation, with women working predominantly in the public sector and men in the private. In Norway the government is seeking to incorporate more men into caring roles – both professionally and at home. In 2003, men made up only 7.9% of nursery employees, but the number is rising and has been for the last few years. The goal is to achieve 20% male employees by the end of 2007 and to get more men into nursery management.

Moreover, research in 1979 on the nature of women's work in Sweden highlighted that it is characterised by 'low pay, insecurity, part-time status, monotony, lack of job satisfaction and career path, inconvenient hours, and poor occupational health and safety' (cited in Curtin and Higgins 1998). More recent research indicates that little has changed, and that the liberalisation of the labour market in the 1990s has had a greater impact on women than on men.

Second, women are under-represented in management positions in Nordic economies, particularly in the private sector (Hakim 2004). In 2004, women accounted for just 23% of top management in Norway. In Sweden, women are better represented in the management of public companies than private ones: the proportion of female board members in companies listed on the Stock Exchange was 15% compared with 42% in state owned companies. There are just three female organisational Chief Executive Officers (CEOs) in 300 Swedish companies listed on the Stock Exchange. The number of female directors in other firms was 19% in the private sector and 56% in the public sector. In Norway, the commonly held view that women do better in the public sector than in private business is not the case. Two out of three employees in the public sector are women but only 3% of these have managerial positions, contrasted to the 6% for the private sector (Statistisk Sentral Byrå 2006b).

The gender gap in management has been addressed in Norway through the introduction of quotas. As from June 2003, public boards must now have had a minimum 40% of each gender represented. There is also a political majority for introducing quotas at management levels in the private businesses. Currently, voluntary measures within the sector have brought about some changes but the government has threatened that quotas will be introduced if significant improvements are not made. The reasoning behind this is that the particular competence women represent to the economy is not realised thus creating a 'national resource deficit' (Næringslivets Hoved Organisasjon 2005). This view is reflected in NHO's pilot project 'Female Future', which works with their member organisations to improve career opportunities for women and increase the number of female managers as well as setting up networks between women in management. The organisation also appointed a gender equality manager in 2002. Both LO and NHO had representatives on the government's board of the Equality Status Council.

Third, some writers argue that policies aimed at securing women's participation in the labour market have been so institutionalised that there is a shift in the conceptualisation of the worker whereby the demands of social reproduction may take priority over those of production. However, this is opposed by Skjeie (1992) who claims that there was an evident over-emphasis on women as workers in the new labour market policies and that this led to women's roles and needs as carers being ignored. Her argument is characteristic of recent criticism of the Norwegian welfare system as too closely linked to participation in the labour market and to the social democratic ideal of full employment. Hernes (1982) also criticised the strong link between welfare provisions and paid work. She claimed that any notion of women's particular needs as salary-earners was non-existent in the evolution of the welfare state.

Welfare

Indeed the social democratic vision of the welfare state is premised on the norm of full employment for men and women. To facilitate this, Nordic welfare states have developed large-scale provisions for parents to balance work and caring responsibilities. In the following we outline the welfare provisions available to parents with young children. In research carried out by Skjeie (1992), respondents mentioned this as the policy area where women's political integration has had the most impact and where women's presence has had most influence on policy formation.

The provisions for parental leave related to childbirth in Norway are among the world's best. In cases where both parents or only the mother have had paid work for at least six months out of the last 10 prior to childbirth, one of them will receive full pay for 10 months, or receive 80% for 12 months. If only the father fulfils the requirements they receive 39 weeks with 80% or 29 weeks with 100% wage compensation. An upper limit for maximum salary compensation is set by the government; in 2004 this was 352.668 NOK or roughly £30,000. However, because of the wage difference between men and women and the upper limit to salary compensation it is often not economically feasible for families to have the father at home. In 2002 the average parental salary compensation received by women was 233.662 NOK or roughly £20,300 compared to £25,100 for men.

As long as the system of childcare provision takes mothers as their point of reference the economic level of the benefits will reflect women's salaries and work situations. Hence it preserves a gendered structure of childcare within the home. Of the parental leave entitlements the last three weeks prior to and the first six weeks after childbirth are reserved for the mother. In 1993 the Labour government introduced a four-week quota reserved for the father. He can only take the four weeks, however, if the mother fulfils the requirements of prior paid work mentioned above. In 2003, 89% of eligible fathers decided to take parental leave; but 85% chose to only take their quota or even less. The government is now arguing that in order to increase this number, fathers need help to put more pressure on employers to achieve recognition for their paternal role (Brandt and Kvande 2003).

The Norwegian cash benefit scheme was introduced by the conservative/centre coalition government in 1998 as a support to children aged one to three who do not benefit from state-sponsored childcare. The scheme aims to let parents spend more time with their children. However, a public evaluation report from 2001 showed that mothers would, on average, reduce their paid work by 1.5 hours weekly whereas fathers would maintain their prior patterns or indeed increase hours spent on paid work. Hence the cash benefit arrangement seems to have contributed to consolidate the gendered division of labour in families with children (Danielsen 2000).

The increase in parental leave during the 1990s and the introduction of paternity leave in 1999 both received high levels of political consensus. The cash benefit scheme, on the other hand, was the issue of the most heated debate since the Norwegian referendum on EU membership. In the election programme for 2005, the Labour Party promised to withdraw the cash benefit scheme and redirect the money into publicly funded childcare. Today, Norway is doing far worse than the other Nordic countries in providing funded childcare (Danielsen 2000).

In Sweden, there is a high provision of childcare which is provided by municipalities and funded by local and national government as well as parental contributions, which are calculated according to income levels. This provision is available to working parents, students and the unemployed. Around 43% of one-year-olds, 77% of two-year-olds and 82% of three-year-olds attend full-time childcare. Only 2% of Swedish women are 'homemakers' (SWEDEN.SE 2006).

In addition, parental insurance is offered to all working parents. Entitlement is linked to employment and benefits are related to pay. Parents are entitled to 13 months' benefit worth 80% of the previous salary plus a further three months' benefit at a fixed daily rate. Parents are entitled to between one and two months' parental leave. In an attempt to increase the number of men taking parental leave, since 1995 one month of parental leave entitlement is reserved exclusively for the father. A second 'Daddy Month' was added on 1 January 2002 (Bergman and Hobson 2002). However, take-up is still low; Kolbe (2001) argues that such policies need to be combined with campaigns to encourage active fathering and take-up.

Critics of the Nordic model of welfare highlight that the state plays a strong role in the caring of children and that caring responsibilities undertaken at home are undervalued. The system of social benefits in Norway has for all of the 20th century been linked to the duty and will to participate in wage work. The link has, however, been particularly strong since the 1990s, and has always been central to the Norwegian Labour Party's welfare policies. Danielsen (2000) highlights the link between paid work and care work benefits by looking at the situation for home-working mothers. Whereas paid working mothers will, in the majority of cases, receive full pay while on parental leave, women who have worked in the home will only receive the one-off payment, while they are, in fact, doing the same work. The care work that the paid work mother carries out is thus valued higher than the essentially identical care work a home-working mother does. It therefore seems to be the case that we are not here dealing with the appreciation of childcare as such, but rather a bonus-based system where incentives are being paid for previous paid work carried out (Danielsen 2000).

Moreover, while sophisticated welfare policies have been developed with regards to the state provision of childcare and support for working parents, recent scholarship has highlighted the neglect of welfare issues in the private domain such as violence against women by present or former partners. While violence in intimate relationships has, in Nordic countries, traditionally been viewed as a private issue, increasingly it is being perceived as a public matter (Lindstrom 2005). In 1998 Sweden introduced a new offence into the penal code called 'gross violation of a women's integrity', which regards 'less serious but repeated violent acts committed by a man against a present or former female partner … as one serious offence' (Lindstrom 2005).

Foreign policy

Whereas in the domestic context gender equality has been largely subsumed under the broader goal of class equality, in international affairs Nordic states have consciously promoted women's rights. As Linder (2001) argues, Scandinavian women made impressive contributions to efforts at the UN on behalf of women's equality. Not only were Scandinavian women well represented in international organisations, they tended to be feminists and worked in collaboration with other Nordic women to achieve their aims (Linder 2001).

Today, within the UN system, Norway is the fourth biggest voluntary contributor to the International Labour Organisation (ILO). Norway is also the fourth biggest contributor to United Nations Development

Fund for Women (UNIFEM) and makes up 12% of its budgets (Barne og Familie Departementet 2005). Norway supports UN projects that incorporate women into peace processes and reconstruction programmes as according to Resolution 1325. This is also a central issue for those peace processes that Norway supports outside the UN such as Sri Lanka and in the conflict between Haiti and the Dominican Republic. Since 1987, Norway has also supported work within the World Bank to study and develop operational directions that incorporate and institutionalise gender awareness. This support has been channelled into the creation of the Bank's Gender Sector Board.

In development terms, Norway is doing very well for women and all Ministers of Aid and Development, except one, have been women. But the Minister does not hold a separate portfolio, instead it is a sub-department of the Ministry of Foreign Affairs. All Ministers of Foreign Affairs have been men. The field of diplomacy and the home departments of foreign affairs similarly fall short of the regulations for gender quotas. Only one in 10 ambassadors is a woman and 97% of the consuls are men. Only two out of 10 section leaders in the Ministry of Foreign Affairs are women (Viken 2001). Within Europe, Norway has supported the work on gender equality awareness among member seeking countries. Through the Organisation for Security and Co-operation in Europe (OSCE), Norway channels money to women refugees in the Caucasus and central Asia.

Domestically, the Norwegian Ministry for Foreign Affairs has mainstreamed gender equality into all its multilateral and bilateral partnerships as well as supporting specific projects achieving rights for women all over the world. In bilateral aid, more than 30% of the resources are allocated to women-specific projects. This level has stabilised over the last few years and reflects the strong integration of gender equality aims into foreign aid policy. The incorporation of women-specific considerations and gender equality aims are central factors in judging the sustainability of potential aid receiving projects (Barne og Familie Departementet 2005).

Conclusion

There is no denying that major achievements have been made towards a feminisation of politics in Norway and Sweden. Both states have, under social democratic governments since the 1970s, led the world with regard to the representation of women in the labour market, national Parliaments and women's policy agencies. This presence has led to women-friendly policies which, among other things, support women in combining their working and caring responsibilities.

Progress towards women-friendly policies since the 1970s has, we would argue, been instrumental rather than ideological. The aim has been, on the one hand, to secure high participation of women in the labour market in order to meet the demand for labour and promote economic growth and, on the other hand, to secure votes and support among the newly politicised women. It certainly seems the Norwegian Labour Party capitalised on the electoral advantages innovative women-friendly politics presented in the 1970s and 1980s – not least by electing a female party leader – and used their leverage to introduce issues of gender equality. However, as the other major parties also adopted women-friendly policies and caught up with the Labour Party in terms of female representation, the party's advantage decreased. Hence in the 1990s the party had to adapt to the new electoral reality and their focus changed from 'woman' to 'individual'. This can be exemplified by looking at the party leaders' speeches to the Labour Party AGMs. Whereas full employment and the protection of the welfare state always received some attention, increasingly since the mid-1980s the individual and the need for social critique and reforms are mentioned. Nilsen and Østerberg (1998) argue that the Norwegian Labour Party under Brundtland ceased to be a programme manifested socialist party and became more clearly a social liberal party, while the Norwegian state went through a transition from social democracy to elitist social liberalism. In her 1990 speech to the Labour Party's AGM Brundtland described the Norwegian social democratic state as a compromise between labour and capital, governance and market and the individual and civil society, claiming the Labour Party had always perceived public governance as a necessary tool rather than an aim in itself (Det Norske Arbeiderparti 2005).

Frustration has been mounting among feminists in the Nordic states who are especially critical of the development of the welfare state under the women-friendly banner. The under-representation of women in corporatist institutions of economic power, which are arguably as significant as positions of political power in the Nordic context, is strongly criticised. In Norway, some women have been critical of the undervaluing of unpaid caring roles in the state-dominated welfare state, especially regarding the unfair link to paid work and caring benefit. In Sweden the focus has been on how in the process of economic liberalisation and 'flexibilisation' of the labour market the brunt of the burden has fallen on women.

Recent evaluations of Swedish gender relations since the 1990s have been more critical of the achievements of social democratic governments. Most prominent in such assessments is the gender neutral stance taken by social democratic governments in their pursuit of gender equality. This took citizens to be genderless workers in the social democratic state. With gender subsumed under the broader goals of class equality, the assumption was that equality between the sexes would follow automatically from a reduction in the gap between the rich and the poor. However, this gender neutral stance underestimated the gendered power dynamics that still exist in the private and public spheres. As a consequence, gender inequality is still apparent in the form of occupational segregation, the under-representation of women in management positions and in the corporatist channel, and the unequal division of labour in unpaid work.

The development of the welfare state combined with the representational strength of the Norwegian Labour Party can be said to have achieved a certain level of political representation and economical participation for women in Norway. Gender blind policies are very much 'yesterday' and gender mainstreaming combined with positive discrimination is the order of the day. After the success of the Labour Party and the welfare state in working for equality for women, it is significant that both the women's movement within the Labour Party and the government's Centre for Gender Equality have now been closed down. Whereas the feminisation of politics from above has, on the one hand, made the Norwegian state more women-friendly, on the other hand, feminism has to some extent been coopted by the state and has, as a result, lost some of its force and intensity. Hence, although the need for protection of gender equality measures is widely accepted, there is little debate about the norms and meanings that made them necessary in the first place.

In Sweden, the frustration at the slow pace of change in gender politics under the traditional social democratic regime which promotes cooperation between men and women has led to the setting up of a women's political party, Feministiskt initiativ (F! – Feminist Initiative). The third-wave feminist movement, founded in April 2005, established itself as a political party in September 2005 and at one point even threatened to stand in the 17 September 2006 general election.

F! states that it is no longer prepared to wait for established parties to pursue feminist political issues; until now, it argues, they have failed to challenge the prevailing gender order. The party holds that in Sweden, women are systematically subordinated to men in a range of spheres and is committed to freeing women from gender based inequality and injustice. It departs from the traditional stance that gender equality can be improved without affecting men and argues that men must relinquish some of their privileges to achieve gender equality (F! för en feministiskt politik 2006).

The emergence of the F! potentially marks a new era for gender politics in the Nordic context and challenges the prevailing view that Sweden and Norway are gender paradises that states aspiring to promote gender equality should emulate.

Certain characteristics of the Nordic context, for example, their so-called state-friendly societies and the well developed corporate-numerical channel, have presented Norway and Sweden with particular opportunities to feminise their politics. Some policy learning should, however, be possible. As our study of Sweden shows, gender quotas are not the only way to achieve women's representation. However, there seems to be evidence to argue that little change can be realised through gender neutral policies alone and that there needs to be a certain inclusion of gender specificity when addressing issues of gender inequality, both in the political and the economic sphere. Given the critique of the over-emphasised link between paid work and welfare benefits, we have also shown that gender equality is not always best served through a capitalist welfare state.

This chapter does show, however, that little can be achieved without well developed parental leave and cash support system. Here the issue is not merely to provide a longer time available for paid leave, but also to include the fathers in the caring of young children. Measures such as these combined with an awareness of, and focus on, women's absence at management level in the economic sector can go a certain distance in achieving a less gender segregated state and society. In order for any of these suggestions to materialise into women-friendly policies for the 21st century, however, it is paramount to be gender-wise in setting policy agendas and to be proactive in seeking out opportunities to feminise politics. And these are important lessons for New Labour to bear in mind.

References

Barne og Familie Departmentet (Norwegian Ministry of Children and Family Affairs) (2005) *Kjønnsperspektiv i budsjettarbeidet 2004-2005*, www.odin.dep.no/filarkiv/222719/Kjonnsperspektivet_i_budsjettet.pdf (accessed 3 March 2006).

Bergman, H. and Hobson, B. (2002) 'Compulsory fatherhood: the coding of fatherhood in the Swedish welfare state', in B. Hobson (ed) *Making Men into Fathers: Men, Masculinities and the Social Policies of Fatherhood*, Cambridge: Cambridge University Press.

Borchorst, C. (1997) 'Likestillingsinstitutionerne', in C. Berqvist et al (eds) *Likestilte Demokratier? Kjønn og Politikk i Norden*, Oslo: Universitetsforlaget, 158.

Brandt, B. and Kvande, E. (2003) *Fleksible Fedre*, Oslo: Universitetesforlaget.

Christiansen, A.D. (1997) 'Kvinder i de politiske partier', in C. Berqvist et al (eds) *Likestilte Demokratier? Kjønn og Politikk i Norden*, Oslo: Universitetsforlaget.

Curtin, J. and Higgins, W. (1998) 'Feminist and Unionism in Sweden', *Politics and Society* 26(1), 69-94.

Danielsen, C. (2000) 'Den kjønnskonservative velferdsstaten', in C. Holst (ed) *Kjønnsretferdighet. Utfordringer for feministisk politikk*, Oslo: Gyldendal Akademisk.

Det Norske Arbeiderparti (The Norwegian Labour Party) (2005) *Landsmøte Protokoller 1981-1998*, Oslo: Arbeidernes Hus.

Economist (2005) 'A spoil the men's party. A new women's party threatens the ruling Social Democrats', 14 April.

Eduards, M. (1991) 'Towards a Third Way: Women's politics and welfare policies in Sweden', *Social Research* 58(3), 677-706.

F! för en feministiskt politik (2006) www.feministisktinitiativ.se (accessed 12 May 2006).

Freidenvall, L. (2005) 'A discursive struggle – the Swedish National Federation of Social Democratic Women and gender quotas', *Nordic Journal of Women's Studies* 13(3), 175-86.

Gustafsson, S. (1994) 'Childcare and types of welfare state', in D. Sainsbury (ed) *Gendering Welfare States*, London: Sage, 45-61.

Hakim, C. (2004) *Key Issues in Women's Work: Female Diversity and the Polarisation of Women's Employment*, London: The Glasshouse Press.

Hernes, H.M. (ed) (1982) *Staten –Kvinner Ingen Adgang*, Oslo: Bergen Tromsø: Universitetesforlaget.

Hernes, H.M. (1987a) *Welfare State and Women Power: Essays in State Feminism*, Oslo: Norwegian University Press.

Hernes, H.M. (1987b) 'Women and the Welfare State: the transition from private to public dependence', in A.S. Sassoon *Women and the State: The Shifting Boundaries of Public and Private*, London: Routledge, 71-91.

Informasjon fra regjerigen og departementene (Information from the Government and from the Ministries) (2006) www.odin.no (accessed 9 May).

Inter-Parliamentary Union (IPU) (2006) www.ipu.org/wmn-e/classif.htm

Kolbe, W. (2001) 'Vaterschaftskonstruktionen im Wohlfahrtsstaat: Schweden und die Bundesrepublik in historischer Perspektive', in P. Doge and M. Meuser (eds) *Männlichkeit und soziale Ordnung*, Opladen: Leske + Budrich.

Kuhnle, S. and Selle, P. (eds) (1992) *Government and Voluntary Organisations: A Relational Perspective*, Avebury: Aldershot.

Likestillings Ombudet (The (Norwegian) Equality and Anti-Discrimination Ombud) (2006) www.likestillingsombudet.no/om/nokkeltall.html (accessed 3 March 2006).

Linder, D. (2001) 'Equality for women: the contribution of Scandinavian women at the United Nations 1946-66', *Scandinavian Studies* 73(2), 65.

Lindstrom, P. (2005) 'Violence against women in Scandinavia: a description and evaluation of two laws aiming to protect women', *Journal of Scandinavian Studies in Criminology and Crime Prevention* 5(2), 220-36.

Mazur, A. and Stetson, D.M. (1995) 'Conclusion', in D.M Stetson and A. Mazur *Comparative State Feminism*, Thousand Oaks, CA: Sage, 272-91.

Mulgan, G. (2003) 'The future of the welfare state. a contribution to the dialogue on progressive government', Friedrich-Ebert-Stiftung Conference, 17 March, available at www.fesonline.dial.pipex.com/sems02/MULGAN.HTM (accessed 9 September 2005).

Nilsen, H. and Østerberg, D. (1998) *Statskvinnen. Gro Harlem Brundtland og Nyliberalismen*, Oslo: Forum Aschehoug.

Næringslivets Hoved Organisasjon (Confederation of Norwegian Business and Industry) (2005) www.nho.no/ff/article13277.html (accessed 11 March).

Raaum, N.R. (1997) 'Kvinner i Offisiell Politikk: Historiske Utviklingslinjer', in C. Berqvist et al (eds) *Likestilte Demokratier? Kjønn og Politikk i Norden*, Oslo: Universitetsforlaget, 35.

Skjeie, H. (1992) *Den Politiske Betydning av Kjønn. En studie av norsk topp-politikk*, Oslo: Institutt for Samfunnsforskning.

Statistisk Sentral Byrå (Norwegian Central Bureau of Statistics) (2006a) www.ssb.no/vis/samfunnsspeilet/utg/200406/03/art-2004-12-09-01.html (accessed 9 May 2006).

Statistisk Sentral Byrå (Norwegian Central Bureau of Statistics) (2006b) www.ssb.no/ola_kari/makt (accessed 8 August 2006).

Stetson, D.M. and Mazur, A. (1995) 'Introduction', in D.M. Stetson and A. Mazur *Comparative State Feminism*, Thousand Oaks, CA: Sage, 1-21.

Stortinget (The Norwegian Parliament) (2006) www.stortinget.no/ representantene/navn_tall/statistikk.html (accessed 9 May).

SWEDEN.SE (The official gateway to Sweden) (2006) www.sweden. se/templates/cs/CommonPage____12528.aspx (accessed 13 July).

Viken, S.T. (2001) 'Diplomatiet, ein manssbastion', *Statistisk Sentralbyra*, www.ssb.no/magasinet/norge_verden/art-2001-03-15-01.html (accessed 3 March 2006).

FOUR

Framing claims for women: from 'old' to 'new' Labour

Jill Lovecy

Introduction

As noted in Chapter One, it was the adoption of AWS that secured New Labour's dramatic gender breakthrough in the June 1997 elections, when it virtually trebled the number of women MPs in the Parliamentary Labour Party (PLP) from 37 to 101. The party's resort to this strong measure of positive discrimination was sealed under John Smith's leadership at the party's 1993 Annual Conference, in the immediate aftermath of the party's fourth successive electoral defeat in 1992 (Short 1996, 19-21; Russell 2005, 111-5). Crucially, what AWS offered was a means of operationalising gender quotas within the framework of the UK's single-member constituency, first-past-the-post (FPTP) electoral system. In adopting AWS, the 1993 Conference committed the party to achieving a 50% quota in two categories of winnable seats: vacant safe seats, where a Labour MP was retiring at the next election; and the party's target marginals that it needed to win if it was to secure a working majority.

In the event, an industrial tribunal ruling (discussed further later) in January 1996 forced the party to abandon this procedure before it had completed its countrywide selection process. Nevertheless, as Table 4.1 shows, the bulk (35) of the party's 54 women MPs elected in these two categories of seats owed their selection to AWS; while a further seven were beneficiaries of 'informal' AWS procedures concluded after the tribunal ruling. The result was that whereas women comprised just 15% of the incumbent Labour MPs re-elected in June 1997 and 17% of the MPs elected in the 'surprise-gain' category, where AWS had not been implemented, in its non-incumbent safe and target seats the party was able to achieve women candidacy levels of 34% and 51% respectively and went on to win all of these seats.

AWS was devised and adopted as the post-1992 sequel to a much larger 'package' of gender reforms within the party's internal organisation that

Table 4.1: Labour's new women MPs in June 1997 (by type of seat and selection process)

Type of seat	All women shortlist	Open shortlist	By-election panel	Number of women selected	Number of men elected	Total number of seats	Women as % of candidates
Safe	2	4 (*2)	5 (*2)	11	21	32	34.4
Target	33	10 (*3)	0	43	42	85	50.6
Surprise gain	n/a	11	0	11	55	66	16.7
Total	35	25	5	65	118	183	37.5

Note: * informal AWS: completed after January 1996
Source: adapted from Eagle and Lovenduski (1998, 9-10)

had been put together in the latter years of Neil Kinnock's leadership, following the party's previous defeat in 1987. Adopted at the Party's Annual Conferences between 1989 and 1992, these reforms introduced an extensive, rolling programme of mandatory gender quotas (of between 40% and 50%) for positions of responsibility at all levels of the party: from local wards through to constituency parties up to delegates to the Annual Conference, members of National Executive Committee (NEC) and the new National Policy Forum (Perrigo 1995, 413-5; Russell 2005, 102-9). The PLP also introduced a modest gender quota (three out of 18 seats) for elections to the Shadow Cabinet from 1989 and in that year the Annual Conference had set the party the target of achieving gender balance in the PLP within 10 years or after three elections (Short 1996, 18-19).

How can we best explain the Labour Party's development of these policies and its commitment to securing, and sustaining over the longer term, a much more substantial representation of women within the party's own policy-making processes and a gender rebalancing of its parliamentary representation? As Russell emphasises, a simple leadership-driven account is clearly inadequate: '[W]omen's quotas were never part of the project of either of its famously modernising leaders. Indeed both Kinnock and Blair were resistant to moves towards positive action' (Russell 2005, 125).

Instead, studies of this period all demonstrate the key role of women's agency within the party in getting policies of positive action and positive discrimination onto the party's agenda (Perrigo 1995, 1996,

1999; Lovenduski 2005, 109–21; Russell 2005, 96–128). But how did women's agency operate within the Labour Party in this period? What kind of demands were put forward within the party – in respect of women's representation and of other substantive policy commitments relating to women and gender issues, when and why? How did these demands evolve over time in the two decades prior to 1997? In order to address these questions in this chapter I will employ an institutionalist analytic framework similar to that set out in Chapter One for analysing public policy, but adapted here to capture the dynamics of policy framing within a quite differently constituted political space, that of a political party.

The British Labour Party in comparative context

Before outlining this analytic framework, some preliminary points should be made setting developments within the Labour Party in their wider comparative context. A first point here is that both in adopting these reforms and in the sequence in which it adopted them – establishing internal gender quotas within the party before moving on to parliamentary candidacy selection quotas – the Labour Party aligned itself on broader international trends of this period. Research undertaken in the early 1990s showed that, worldwide, gender quotas were more extensively used internally, within parties' own structures, than for their parliamentary representation (IPU 1994). Nevertheless, by the mid-1990s, 84 parties in 36 different states are recorded as having established formal quotas in their parliamentary candidate selection processes (IPU 1997).

More specifically, the British Labour Party was participating in a rising trend among its sister social democratic parties, particularly in Europe. It is true that from the 1960s, the Swedish Social Democratic Party had built up its impressive record of women's representation in its parliamentary party and in government (discussed in Chapter Three) employing only *informal* means of positive discrimination (Sainsbury 1993, 279–82). But in 1983, the Norwegian Labour Party (DNA) opted in contrast for a formal parliamentary gender quota and another five parties – the Austrian Socialist Party (1985), Dutch Labour Party (1987), German Social Democratic Party (1988), Italian Democratic Left (1989) and Irish Labour Party (1991)[1] – had followed suit before the British Labour Party did so in 1993 (Caul 2001, 1220–1).

Moreover, at the regional level, interplaying with these developments, a broader process of European norm construction can also be observed. This got underway from 1986 as the Council of Europe focused on the need for positive action to achieve much enhanced levels of presence and participation by women in public life at the national level in Europe as 'a *sine qua non* of democracy and an imperative of social justice'; these normative claims were also subsequently taken up within the European Union (Lovecy 2002, 280–3). However, from the mid–1990s, in the aftermath of the UN's Fourth World Conference on Women, in Beijing, 1995, this 'politics of women's presence' agenda (Philips 1995) was to be increasingly displaced at the regional level in Europe by the rather different strategy of 'gender mainstreaming' (Pollack and Hafner–Burton 2000; Lovecy 2002, 279–81), developments which the concluding section of this chapter will return to and which are examined further in Chapter Five.

Comparative research on parliamentary candidacy quotas and internal party quotas also sheds light on where the British Labour Party's experience has been more mainstream, and where it has been most distinctive. Quantitative cross–national research has, for example, found the timing of the adoption of parliamentary quotas to be most positively correlated, first, with a greater number of women sitting on a party's highest decision-making body and, second, with a party having leftist values (Caul 2001, 1226–7). However, in the case of AWS, the NEC's decision to recommend this to the 1993 Annual Conference was taken when the new internal party quota rules had produced only a modest increase, from five to eight women out of 29 NEC members (Russell 2005, 107). Nevertheless, the bulk of the larger package of internal gender quotas was adopted in 1989/90 when, for the first time, the Labour NEC had a woman chair, Jo Richardson. More intriguingly, this quantitative research does not support the hypothesis that a shift from old to new Left is of itself a favourable factor, the correlation with leftist values being as strong for parties with 'old' as for those with 'new' Left values (Caul 1999, 87–8; Caul 2001, 1225). A third finding relates to a 'contagion effect' deriving from the prior adoption of parliamentary candidacy quotas by a competitor party. There is some limited evidence for such party-system competitive dynamics having influenced the British Labour Party in the mid- to late 1980s.[2] However, a different form of contagion effect can be identified, through lesson-drawing from the successful implementation of internal party gender quotas in other member-parties of the Socialist International. Such lesson-drawing was facilitated by representatives from these parties being invited in 1988 to address the Women's Conference and also an Annual Conference fringe meeting (Russell 2005, 104), through publications (Brooks et al 1990) and via the involvement in the NEC's Women's Committee from 1990 of Clare Short, who was active in the women's section of the Socialist International (serving as its vice-president from 1992) and had been elected as an MP in 1983. She was to chair that committee in 1992, when it was tasked by John Smith with preparing proposals for implementing the 1989 Conference's 50-50 gender target for the PLP (Short 1996, 18; Russell 2005, 103-4).

The very real difficulties that FPTP posed for implementing parliamentary quotas in the UK is underlined by other research findings, positively correlating higher levels of women's parliamentary representation with proportional representation systems using larger multi-member districts (Norris 1993, 312-15; Matland and Studlar 1996). And whereas the cross-national data identifies more localised control over candidate nomination as being conducive to higher levels of women's parliamentary representation (Caul 1999, 80-1, 85), in contrast, the UK's electoral system meant that the party would need instead to shift control over the candidate selection process upwards from the constituency level, in order to implement a gender quota (as discussed further later in the chapter).

Another body of qualitative research has been more directly concerned with addressing the issue of women's agency, employing process-tracing in single-party and single-country case studies.[3] Its methodologies and main findings are broadly consistent with the studies of women and gender in the British Labour Party in this period (Perrigo 1995, 1996, 1999; Lovenduski 2005, 109-21; Russell 2005, 96-128). This research points to the arrival within the mainstream parties, and most especially those of the Left, of newer generations of women bringing with them the mobilising ideas of second-wave feminism of the late 1960s and 1970s. It also underlines the more or less prolonged periods of activist mobilisation that were required to open up a space on party agendas for a varied range of positive action and positive discrimination policies (notably Lovenduski and Norris 1993). Characteristically, these feminist activists are shown to have developed pragmatic practices drawing on the two competing principles of equality and difference, outlined in Chapter Two. Sainsbury terms this a 'dual strategy' of working both through separate women's sections – where these existed within parties – and also through their male-dominated mainstream structures (Sainsbury 1993, 279). But what these studies bring out, above all, is the complexity of the processes of adjustment and accommodation operating between the nature of women's claims and the strategies used to press them, on the one hand, and party responses, in terms of programmatic and organisational change, on the other (Lovenduski 1993, 4-15).

Strategic framing and the political opportunity structures of the Labour Party

In order to 'unpack' these complex processes as they operated within the Labour Party during its long period of 18 years in opposition, this chapter takes as its central organising focus a concept drawn from the comparative social movements literature, that of *strategic framing*. This will enable the author to establish an overall argument about the pattern of gendered policy commitments developed by the Labour Party in the context of its renewal and modernisation in the 1980s and 1990s that marries in with the central concerns of the book and sets the scene for the chapters that follow, examining how New Labour has acted in government.

Strategic framing has been developed in the comparative social movements literature as one of a set of three key concepts, along with *political opportunity structures* and *mobilising structures*, in order to model how social movement actors pursue normative change, and with what success, within a variety of institutional contexts (McAdam et al 1996; Smith et al 1997). This literature reflects the institutional turn in comparative politics in positing that the extent of social movement mobilisations and the forms of their collective claims are shaped by the broader set of political opportunities and constraints unique to the specific institutional context in which a given movement is embedded (McAdam et al 1996, 2–3). It therefore offers a theoretical perspective cognate to that outlined in Chapter One, which can be applied here to analyse the role of actors influenced by the mobilising ideas of second-wave feminism, but who sought to engage with the wider public policy domain by engaging in the internal policy processes of a mainstream UK political party and re-shaping its public policy commitments. After mapping out how this approach can be applied to the Labour Party, the following two sections of the chapter will employ it in respect of representational and substantive policy claims for women, to account for the evolving ways in which these two types of claim came to be framed in the Labour Party from the late 1970s.

The concept of strategic framing itself focuses on the institutional incentives for (relatively resource-poor) 'outsider' actors to shape their claims in ways that 'resonate' and are congruent with the established policy concerns and preferences of (resource-richer) 'insider', and especially elite, actors; such framing enables them to engage in alliance-building and, as part of a wider *policy advocacy coalition*, to gain access to, and weight within, key decisional *venues*. In the case of feminists who brought to the Labour Party a gendered understanding of power and policy, this theoretical perspective means that the representational and substantive policy claims they have constructed over time, and also the *mobilising structures* in which they have sought to organise themselves, are to be treated as dependent variables of the analysis, to be explained by reference to the particular constraints and opportunities provided by shifting organisational and ideational features of the Labour Party, and its wider political environment, at successive points in time. This approach therefore posits that the extent to which the different competing feminist principles surveyed in Chapter Two got taken up within the Labour Party, and when they did so, depended largely on how feminist actors responded to shifting opportunities for alliance-building in the party.

Applying the comparative social movements literature to the Labour Party, we can identify four key dimensions (McAdam et al 1996, 10 and 23-4) of its political opportunity structures, and changes within them over time, that served to shape the behaviour of feminist actors within the party in this period:

A. The relative openness or closure of its institutional processes (that is, the formal and informal rules governing its internal organisation and access to its main decisional venues).
B. The relative stability or instability of the elite alignments under-girding these institutional processes.
C. The presence or absence of elite or 'insider' allies.
D. Highly charged 'symbolic' events affording specific 'windows of opportunity', including notably the cycle of parliamentary elections and their outcomes.

A number of studies have documented how, in the period up to the early 1970s, the Labour Party's organisational arrangements impacted on its women members and were linked in to a wider dynamic of gender relations in the party (McDonald 1977; Hills 1981; Graves 1994; Perrigo 1996, 118-9; Black and Brooke 1997, 430-3; Francis 2000, 195-9). Conceptualised here as 'political opportunity structures', what is most notable is the party organisation's high degree of closure in respect of women (dimension A), largely because of the entrenched weight of the trade union movement in the party's organisation and the broader party culture this had given rise to. As Perrigo emphasises, 'male-domination was ... embedded in Labour's rule-bound, bureaucratic ways of working. Heavily influenced by trade unions, the rules fostered fraternal feelings and a system of shared meanings about what the party "stands for", which tended to exclude women and make it difficult for them to participate on equal terms' (1995, 408). However, Francis notes that 'sexual difference in the discourses (both hegemonic and subordinate) of the Labour Party was rarely disentangled from a larger matrix of identities, derived from religion, region, age, and (most critically) social class' (2000, 199). From the 1970s the younger generation of women joining the party included large numbers of university-educated professional women and white-collar workers.

The result of this pattern of closure was that, until the mid-1970s, no woman had ever been elected to the trade union section of the party's leading body, the NEC, and, although women constituted some 40% of the Labour Party's individual membership, around 30% of its local general management committees and 11% of delegates to the Annual Conference, only two women had ever been elected to the NEC's constituency section: Barbara Castle serving from 1951 to 75 and Joan Lestor from 1966 to 75 (Middleton 1977, 204-5; Hills 1981, 17-19, 23). There were of course five reserved seats for women on the NEC but since these were elected by the party Annual Conference their allocation was effectively subject to the trades union, whose block votes controlled over 90% of the votes at conference (Hills 1981, 19). Equally, trade union delegates dominated the 'selectorates' of constituency parties in most safe seats, controlling access to parliamentary nominations.[4] Thus the October 1974 General Election saw just 18 women returned as Labour MPs, 5.6% of the PLP (Russell 2005, 110), even though Labour continued, as it had in the inter-war and post-war periods, to have a significantly better record in this respect than the Conservatives, and in this year almost 15% of its local councillors were women (Brooks et al 1990, 3).

Alongside the party's mainstream organs, separate structures had existed for women party members since the amalgamation of the independent Women's Labour League into the Labour Party in 1918 when the suffrage was first extended to some women in the UK. There were structures such as women's sections at branch (ward) level; women's councils at constituency or district level; conferences at the regional level, and at the national level the annual Women's Conference; the (nominated) National Labour Women's Advisory Committee and Chief Woman Officer, both reporting to the NEC and the latter also to the party agent; but none of these bodies enjoyed any formal powers within the party's local and national policy processes (Francis 2000, 196). These separate structures had come under threat when the 1968 Committee of Enquiry into the Party Organisation advocated their abolition, but survived thanks to a spirited campaign of defence by the National Labour Women's Advisory Committee, although the latter's publication, *Labour Women*, ceased in 1971 (McDonald 1977, 152-3).

The Advisory Committee produced its own counter-report, *Woman and the Labour Party*, advocating the retention of separate structures and the NEC reserved seats until something like parity of presence between men and women had been achieved, recording that already by the early 1970s the number of women's sections was expanding (Labour Women's Advisory Committee, 1971). This was to continue through the seventies, thanks in part to the arrival in the party of a younger generation of women familiar with the practice of separate organisation within the broader second-wave feminist movement (Rowbotham et al 1979; Byrne 1996).

However, in the course of the following two decades the party's political opportunity structures underwent a number of changes of critical importance for the argument developed here about the strategic framing of claims on behalf of women. We will focus here on four such changes. First, from the early 1970s what had been a relatively stable elite alignment (dimension B) between the moderate leaderships of the PLP and the trade union movement broke down, ushering in a protracted period of intense intra-party struggles with a successful alliance of the party's Left drawn from the PLP, the unions and the constituency parties in the ascendancy in the NEC and annual conference by the mid-1970s, but bitterly at odds with the moderate majority in the PLP. This Left–Right polarisation in the party (with each of these wings in any case internally divided) was increasingly displaced by the rise to prominence of a new breed of party modernisers, who succeeded in constructing a coalition drawing from both wings of the party under the leaderships of Kinnock 1983-92, Smith 1992-94, and Blair from 1994 (Russell 2005, 10-33). Kinnock had been on the Left of the party prior to his election as leader, while Smith had been a leading figure in the moderate majority of the PLP. It is this context which provided institutional incentives for different groupings and networks of feminist activists to engage in a number of distinct episodes of strategic framing as they sought to use and gain access to the key decisional venues within the party by establishing a succession of differently configured elite alliances (dimension C). But from the late 1980s the formal arrangements of the party (dimension A) were increasingly supplemented by informally networked decisional venues through which the new modernising elite alignment consolidated its control over the party.

Second, for all that the intra-party struggles of this period centred at heart on conflicting visions of what the party should stand for and how these could be linked to building a winning electoral coalition, for each of the competing factions the key to success lay in securing, or resisting, changes to the formal rules governing the party's institutions and policy process (dimension A). It is this dominance of the debate over party rules that helps to explain why the energies of those who mobilised to pursue a feminist agenda within the party in the two decades up to 1997 were so largely directed to achieving an appropriate voice and presence for women within the party, rather than to further developing specific substantive policy issues. Prioritising party representational claims was, of course, logical, for without women achieving more effective representation, how could the party develop properly thought-through substantive policies for women? This chapter reflects this balance, dealing more fully with the strategic framing of representational claims in the next section and considering the strategic framing of substantive policy issues more briefly in the following section.

A third set of critical developments in this period concerns alterations in the availability of potential elite allies for feminist activists (dimension C) as a result of far-reaching changes underway in the trade union movement, changes which complicated the unions' role as actors within the party in a period when the party's modernisers were increasingly concerned to reduce the most publicly visible forms of their voting power within the party. In effect, the economic policies of the Thatcher governments combined with longer-term patterns of change within the UK labour market, and notably the rising participation rates of women in the active workforce, to alter the balance of power within the trade union movement in two important ways. First, power shifted from the predominantly male skilled and general workers unions to those based in varying categories of the white-collar public and private sector workforce. Second, leaders of these latter unions in particular, and also some general unions, faced new incentives to reposition themselves in relation to their current female membership and to potential women members by developing substantive policies for women and new representational procedures for them within their own decisional structures (Cockburn 1987, 6–14). The Trades Union Congress (TUC) had published its 10-point charter, *Equality for Women Within Trade Unions* in 1979 (Cockburn 1987, 12) and by the mid-1980s an EOC survey of the 11 largest unions showed that women made up 40% of their members, 16% of their executive bodies, 6% of their full-time officials and 20% of their delegates to TUC conferences (EOC 1985). These developments therefore transformed some leading trade unionists into potential allies for feminists, and facilitated alliance-building with them through the presence in the Labour Party of new networks of trade union women's and equality officers and researchers pursuing their own trade unions' gender agendas (Wainwright 1987, 185–8;

Short 1996, 18). However, in this same period other elements on the Right in the unions, who organised with their allies in the PLP in the 'St Ermins Group' to defeat the Left in the party, targeted the women's sections seats in particular to build a moderate majority on the NEC (Hayter 2005, 117-23, 188, 193).

Finally, there are the ways in which electoral outcomes provide particular 'windows of opportunity' for strategic framing and alliance-building (dimension D). The four successive defeats of this period, which served to fuel competitive struggles over the party's identity and organisation, certainly also provided opportunities for developing persuasive narratives linking representational as well as substantive policy claims on behalf of women to the party's interest in offsetting its electoral 'gender-gap', as significantly fewer women than men from some key class and generational groups voted Labour (Norris 1993). While these cycles of electoral defeat have been employed as the organising framework for a number of analyses of gender representation within the Labour Party in this period (Perrigo 1995, 1996; Lovenduski 2005, 109-30), in the following two sections the analytic focus will, instead, be on successive cycles of strategic framing structured around, and stimulated by, shifting alliance-building opportunities within the party.

Strategic framing and representational claims for women

In examining representational claims, we can separate out four distinct episodes, in which claims concerning the representation of women were successively framed in terms of:

- the collective empowerment of women within the party;
- empowering executive representation through a Ministry for Women;
- empowering individual women party members through gender quotas;
- extending parliamentary representation through AWS.

As will be seen, each of these episodes centred on its own distinctive logic of strategic framing, with important differences in terms of: the *mobilising structures* involved, and which feminist activists they organised; the alliance-building and *policy advocacy coalitions* in which they engaged; and the decisional *venues* in the party they could mobilise in and to which they sought to gain access. For each case, it will be argued here, the specific configurations of such factors are best understood as responses to key shifts over time in the party's political opportunity structures discussed above.

The collective empowerment of women within the party

This first episode of strategic framing in the 1980s centres on the development of claims for women's representation that fitted with the overall strategy of the party's organised Left. It involves the only formally organised mobilising structure to emerge within the Labour Party specifically concerned with promoting women's rights and gendered policies: the Women's Action Committee (WAC), set up in 1980. WAC brought together primarily London-based activists influenced by second-wave feminism, but it was as much a product of the party's Left–Right polarisation as of the wider feminist movement, initially being an off-shoot of the Campaign for Labour Party Democracy (CLPD), formed in 1973 with Kinnock as one of its founding members. Although some WAC activists were closer to the 'softer' Left Labour Coordinating Committee (LCC) established in 1978 (Wainwright 1987, 181-3; Russell 2005, 97). From the outset, when its key demands were formulated, WAC was therefore firmly embedded in a wider policy advocacy coalition pursuing a strategy of party renewal and democratisation aimed at securing the accountability of the party's parliamentary and extra-parliamentary leadership to its activist membership.[5] For the CLPD this was to be achieved through the introduction of a wider electoral college to replace the PLP for election of the party leader; the mandatory re-selection of sitting MPs before each election; and by asserting the Right of the NEC – and not the Labour Cabinet (when the party was in government) or the Shadow Cabinet (when it was not) – to control the party's election manifesto. In line with this, WAC's founding platform focused primarily on representational concerns linking these into a broader Left-wing agenda: 'To campaign for action, including positive discrimination, to ensure that women are fully represented at every level of party life, and thereby to strengthen the fight for a fundamental shift in the balance of power and wealth in favour of women as well as working men' (cited in Wainwright 1987, 181).

From the early 1980s, WAC pursued two main sets of demands (Russell 2005, 97-100). The first of these sought to empower the collective (and separate) representation of women in the party, by giving the Women's Conference a formal role within the party's decisional processes via two new rights: to put two resolutions onto the agenda of the party's Annual Conference; and to elect the five NEC places reserved for women. The second, taken up from 1982, sought to establish a minimum of one-woman-on-the-shortlist (OWOS) for every parliamentary selection. The first of these claims, to enhance the status of the Women's Conference, was not new (Graves 1994, 110), but as formulated in the early 1980s it both took up the principles of difference and autonomous organisation from the second-wave feminist movement but also, quite crucially, fitted with the wider campaign of the CLPD and could be expected to increase the weight of the Left in shaping the agenda for the Annual Conference and, in particular more crucially, its weight within the party's leading body by bringing a slate of Left-wing women onto the NEC in place of a slate backed by the (moderate) unions (Hayter 2005, 102, 117-23, 188; Russell 2005, 98-9). The second claim, which was quite new, both grew from, and helped to further legitimise, the CLPD's wider case for mandatory reselection of all sitting MPs (Russell 2005, 99-100).

These two sets of representational claims were the subject of extensive, concerted campaigning, with circulated model resolutions taken in parallel by women's sections for debate at the Women's Conference and via adoption by sympathetic constituency parties to successive party Annual Conferences (Wainwright 1987, 181-3; Perrigo 1995, 412; Russell 2005, 98). WAC was thus very successful in initiating a wider debate within the party about strengthening women's representation within the party. In the event, however, it had only partial success with the more limited of its demands, for OWOS. This was finally adopted at the 1988 Annual Conference, against the NEC's opposition, with trade union backing. The fact that only three years earlier a similar WAC-initiated resolution on OWOS had secured NEC support but then been voted down by the unions' block votes (Russell 2005, 100) is itself testimony to the emergence of new gender commitments in a number of major unions. But this pattern of developments also reflects the ambiguity of Kinnock's position on these issues, given the tactical juggling he needed to engage in to construct a coalition around his party modernisation project in the aftermath of the Thatcher government's crushing defeat of the miners' strike in 1985; of his own excoriating attack on the Militant Tendency at the 1985 conference (Shaw 1996, 174-6); and given WAC's growing identification with the party's 'harder Left' in this period (Perrigo 1995, 412-13; Russell 2005, 95-7). In any case, the composite OWOS resolution as adopted with union support included a proviso ('where a woman has been nominated') which could potentially, and indeed did subsequently, allow sitting MPs to be reselected via a shortlist of one candidate (Russell 2005, 101).[6]

The attempt to enhance the powers of the Women's Conference, which both challenged and divided the trade union movement, proved altogether more problematic. WAC's success in securing majority-support for its resolutions at the women's conference in this period triggered a process of counter-framing in 1986 (Wainwright 1987, 183-7), in the form of a trade union-led reform strategy for the women's conference and a GMB–APEX (Britain's General Union and the Association of Professional, Executive, Clerical and Computer Staff) resolution to the party conference (Wainwright 1987, 183–7). This gave the Women's Conference a new voting structure rather than new rights, with the leading share going to the trades union (50%), constituencies having 45% and other affiliates 5% (Russell 2005, 102), but in the longer term it involved re-articulating the constituent parts of the party to a new, elected NEC Women's Committee, replacing the nominated National Labour Women's Advisory Committee (see later). Accounts of how this reform strategy was put together point to the emergence of new informal sites of party policy-making – foreshadowing developments that we will return to with the third episode of strategic framing – with key actors from the party's head office staff (including the party's new general secretary, Larry Whitty, himself an ex-official of the then General and Municipal Workers' Union, GMWU) networking together with trade union research and women's officers and some members of the NEC and its Women's (sub-) Committee (Wainwright 1987, 186; Russell 2005, 102).

Empowering executive representation: A Ministry for Women

If WAC's campaign for rule changes met with very limited success during the 1980s, it did firmly log the issue of women's representation within the party onto the party's agenda. In response, a very different exercise in counter-framing got underway as early as 1983; following the disastrous election defeat of 1983 (when Labour's share of the vote went down to its lowest level since 1918, with only 27.6% of the vote, and the loss of a crucial layer of its core support among trade unionists and skilled manual workers) and the election of Kinnock as party leader. This episode of strategic framing was undertaken by an altogether different kind of 'mobilising structure'. Although the party's archival record is not entirely clear on this, the key role here seems in effect to have been played by a solo feminist policy entrepreneur, Jo Richardson. A Left-winger and feminist active in the party from the late 1940s, she was elected to Parliament after a long stint of service to the PLP Left as secretary to the Tribune Group of MPs (1948–78), and then successfully took forward as a private member's bill the 1976 Domestic Violence and Matrimonial Proceedings Act (Roth 1992, 1246-8).[7] Elected to the Constituency Labour Party (CLP) section of the NEC from 1980, she would later be the first woman chair of the NEC (in 1989-1990).

Already in the party's 1983 General Election manifesto – arising from the very full package of gendered policy commitments developed in *Labour's Programme, 1982* discussed in the following section – reference had been made to appointing a Cabinet Minister (of unspecified gender) to promote equality been the sexes (Labour Party 1983, 16). With the Left of the party still controlling the NEC, what Richardson now proposed was to address the issue of women's representation within the party at the level of the party's elected leadership, with the nomination by the NEC of one of its members to act as Women's Rights Spokeswoman. The proposal was endorsed by the NEC, with Richardson duly appointed to the post in November 1983 (Roth 1992, 1247). At the same time, the NEC published a document, prepared by the National Labour Women's Advisory Committee, a 'Charter for Equality for Women in the Party' recording the party's rhetorical commitment to progress in women achieving positions of responsibility in, and on behalf of, the party but without specifying any new measures to achieve this (Perrigo 1996, 122; Lovenduski 2005, 112).

The wider electoral salience of the issue of women's representation in the party was to be underlined in 1985 with the publication of a new analysis of Labour's electoral defeats in 1979 and 1983 that identified a critical 'gender gap' in Labour's voting support in key sections of the electorate (Radice 1985). Growing concern in the upper echelons of the party about attracting women voters combined with continuing impasse over the wider rule changes designed to secure women's collective representation in the party, as advocated by WAC, set the context for Richardson to produce a more elaborate proposal in 1986, again using her base in the party's key policy venue, the NEC. In this she was aided by the presence of a number of more or less sympathetic women who had achieved positions of prominence and responsibility in the upper echelons of the party's formal organisation, including three other women NEC members drawn from different strands of the Left of the party – Audrey Wise, CLP section; and from 1985, Margaret Beckett and Joan Maynard, women's section (Hayter 2005, 159-60) – and also of the party's, re-titled, National Women's Officer, Joyce Gould

The proposal that the NEC now adopted was for Labour to commit itself to the *executive representation* of women in the party with the appointment of a Shadow Minister for Women's Rights and a party pledge to establish a Minister with Cabinet status when returned to government, in each case the appointee having a watching brief over, and coordination of, the party's gendered policy commitments across the full range of policy sectors (Labour Party 1987a; Perrigo 1995, 413; Perrigo 1996, 124–5; Squires and Wickham-Jones 2002, 60). This had the effect of aligning the question of women's representation in the party onto a quite different policy advocacy coalition, embracing the party leadership. Before being placed before the Annual Conference, the proposal was the subject of a broad, if in practice uneven, consultation exercise, with regional women's councils and constituency parties being asked to discuss and offer responses on the proposal (Perrigo 1986, cited in Wainwright 1987, 180). But the initiative itself was developed very much 'from above' and seems to have been strongly influenced by the example of the Mitterrand presidency, the Left in France having finally been returned to government in 1981, against a wider European electoral trend to the Right, but with a prominent commitment to creating a Ministry for Women's Rights of Cabinet status. This French experiment attracted widespread interest and commentary outside France in the early and mid-1980s, when Mme Yvette Roudy used her post at the national level to push forward a range of often controversial policies in France (Mazur 1995, 76-93), and at the European level to initiate a first round of meetings within the Council of Europe of national Ministers with responsibility for policies for women (Lovecy 2002, 277-8).

The strategic framing underlying this proposal was designed to ensure its congruence with the interests of the party leader, since the new Shadow Cabinet post would fall within the leader's political patronage powers. Along with the prominence given to the party's array of policies for women (discussed in the following section), this new post may have contributed to a sizeable swing to Labour among both younger women and among women manual workers at the 1987 General Election, a swing that only partially offset, however, its larger loss of male trade unionist and manual workers' votes (Cockburn 1987, 1-4). But as had been the experience in other countries, creating such a ministry raised as many problems as it sought to solve, in terms of its standing in relation to policies falling within the remit of other ministries (Short 1996, 23). Richardson held the position until 1992 when it briefly passed to Mo Mowlam before John Smith chose to appoint to the post Clare Short, a well-known feminist who was not (unlike her two predecessors) an elected member of the Shadow Cabinet, with a brief to review the party's commitment to what was now referred to as a Minister for Women (Short 1996, 22-3). However, the document that was finally published in 1995, following wider consultations in the party and with its women's organisations, *Governing for Equality*, while affirming a commitment to the appointment of a Minister for Women, did not commit the party to establishing a ministry for women but to 'a women's machinery with clear goals and access to information to be located in the Cabinet Office' (Squires and Wickham-Jones 2002, 61). How these commitments to a WEU (in the Cabinet Office), an enhanced Women's National Commission, 'conducting an annual consultation on priorities for advancement to women's equality' (Short 1996, 23), and a Minister for Women of Cabinet rank fared subsequently after 1997 are examined in Chapter Five.

Empowering individual women party members: gender quotas

The outcome of these first two episodes of strategic framing of women's representation in the party resulted in the creation of what was a new kind of 'insider' feminist mobilising structure within the party on this issue. The wider, informal policy network on women's representation embracing a mix of trade union women's/equality officers and Labour Party head office staff (Whitty and the party's Women's Officer: Vicky Phillips, until 1988 and then Deborah Lincoln, along with Joyce Gould, promoted to Director of Organisation) that had been at the core of the reform strategy developed for the Women's Conference in 1986/87 was now integrated into the new NEC's Women's Committee, and the newly created Shadow Minister for Women's Rights (Short 1996, 19; Russell 2005, 105). The latter comprised all the women members of the NEC, plus six elected women trade unionists, and 11 representatives elected by the party's regional organisations (Labour Party 1993, 12). Russell notes that six of the women trade union officers, drawn from: the Amalgamated Engineering and Electrical Union (AEEU), Confederation of Health Service Employees (COHSE), Manufacturing, Science, Finance (MSF), National Union of Public Employees (NUPE), Transport and General Workers' Union (TGWU) and Union of Shop, Distributive and Allied Workers (USDAW) – who had 'started to meet regularly behind the scenes with the party's women's officer ... to build support in the unions for change' subsequently gained seats on the NEC's women's committee in 1989, elected by the trade union section of the Women's Conference (Russell 2005, 104, 127).

A third episode of strategic framing thus got underway, as participants of this 'insider' mobilising structure sought to fit the issue of women's representation within the framework of the broad, modernising strategy that Kinnock and his closest supporters were developing for the party. This they did by learning from the experience of other sister-parties of the Socialist International (Short 1996, 18; Russell 2005, 104), as noted in the introduction to this chapter, taking up the idea of internal party gender quotas. It was the 1989 Women's Conference that first adopted a resolution on a 40% internal quota in the party. This was then taken forward by six resolutions submitted to the 1989 party conference, resulting in the adoption, on a show of hands, of Composite 54 moved by a CLP and seconded by the GMB (Russell 2005, 105, 107), committing the party to introducing internal party quotas for the constituency and trade union sections of the NEC, for a minimum of 40% of women on all party committees and local party delegations (for example, to party conference) and a minimum quota for the Shadow Cabinet (Labour Party 1990, 2). This new policy *after* it had been adopted was, like Richardson's previous NEC proposal for a Ministry for Women, the subject of a wide consultation exercise in the party, organised by the new NEC Women's Committee (Labour Party 1990, 1), and more detailed proposals were tested at the 1990 Women's Conference, where the unions voted in support (Russell 2005, 106). Three members of the reformed NEC Women's Committee, two trade union officers, Rachel Brooks of GMB (but who sat on the Women's Committee as a London party representative) and Angela Eagle of COHSE (a trade union section representative) and Clare Short, by then the Committee's chair, co-authored *Quotas Now: Women in the Labour Party* (1990), which set out the case for fully implementing the 1989 conference decision across the whole party. After 17 further resolutions were submitted to the 1990 annual conference, a more detailed composite was successfully moved by the GMB and the NEC finally in 1991, which recommended to party conference a rolling programme of quotas at all levels of the party to be implemented over several years, winning 98% support on a card vote. The NEC proposals left the contentious issue of parliamentary representation to one side in the run-up to the 1992 General Election, but included the requirement that trade union delegations to the party Annual Conference include women pro rata to their representation in each union's membership (Russell 2005, 107–8).

Undoubtedly, the case for some clear movement on the issue of women's representation within the party was aided by the persuasive analysis that could be developed for the party leadership around the decisive importance of winning women voters to Labour, after Labour's third successive General Election defeat. The election focus group research undertaken by the party's Shadow Communications Agency in late 1988 clearly demonstrated the popularity of Labour's policies and core values with women voters, but that such support was not being translated into votes because of the party's unattractively 'male' public identity among different social class and age groups of women (Hewitt and Mattinson 1989; Labour Party 1990, 1; Short 1996, 17-18). Reframing the issue of women's representation in the party in terms not of their collective representation, but of an enhanced presence of women as individuals in positions of responsibility at all levels that could be secured by internal party quotas offered, for the leadership, the advantage of making the party more 'electable' by being more women-friendly in its public image, not least at the party's conference.

If the internal quotas proposals were thus strategically framed to appeal to the party leadership, and the case for them often presented as part of an electoral-driven strategy, it is nevertheless true that the issue was not developed nor initially taken forward by Kinnock or the NEC, but rather, as Russell argues, the NEC, trade union leaders and Kinnock were effectively left in a reactive role, 'bounced' into supporting change by an active, feminist network in the unions supported by key party head-office staff (Russell 2005, 106-7). The longer-term outcome would be a radically changed gender composition for local executive bodies, for the Annual Conference and for the NEC where the number of women expanded from five out of 29 in 1991 to 18 out of 32 in 1998 (once the reserve section had been abolished in 1997, replaced by an increased quota in all other sections). This resulted in Clare Short's assessment, in 'an important and unremarked change in the ethos and balance of power of the party' (Short 1996, 19). In the longer term, enhancing the individual representation of women through internal party quotas (Perrigo 1999, 175), however, served to undermine the rationale of the separate women's sections and conference that had lain at the heart of WAC's strategy for the collective representation of women: within four years from 1994 the number of women's sections had fallen from 550 to 200 (most having less than 10 active members), and an NEC consultation exercise in 1998 recommended that the national Women's Conference should be redesigned as a training event for women members, while the new Policy Forums around which the party's policy process was now being re-built (Labour Party 1997a) should have equal numbers of men and women members attending (Labour Party 1998, 6-12; Perrigo 1999, 171-2)

Extending parliamentary representation: all women shortlists

With this final episode of strategic framing, we move on to a case of renewed activist mobilisation (of the kind that was central to our first episode) now centred on winning increased parliamentary representation but linked into the insider feminist network (that had been critical to the third episode) organised around the Women's Committee. The latter, following John Smith's election as party leader in 1992, was now integrated into the revamped party modernisation coalition which he, coming from the 'moderate' wing of the party, sought to build with a crucial emphasis on parliamentary selection rule changes that would remove the trades union local 'block vote'. The strategic framing of women's representation thus gravitated upwards, beyond the Women's Committee and the NEC, to which it reported, to the office of party leader. Having committed himself in his acceptance speech as leader of the party in July 1992 to introducing a one-member-one-vote (OMOV) system for parliamentary candidate selection (Hayter 2005, 41), Smith's decision to himself attend the key meeting of the Women's Committee that debated the options (Short 1996, 20-1) testified to his understanding of the strategic importance of tying in the development of a mechanism to implement the party's targets for women in its parliamentary party to the achievement of OMOV.

Any incoming leader in this period would have prioritised making the party's public image more women-friendly, in view of the focus-group research noted above and the gender gap that reopened in the 1992 General Election, the party's fourth successive General Election defeat. At these elections Labour had made only quite limited progress towards its PLP target of 50% women by 2000, with 37 incoming women MPs (13.7% of the PLP), in place of 21 (9.2%) elected in 1987 and just 10 women MPs (4.8%) in 1983 (Russell 2005, 110). From 1988, a number of prominent women had run Labour Women's Network to provide training for aspirant parliamentary candidates. But in the run-up to 1992 with 20 incumbent MPs retiring, only two were replaced by women candidates; the increased number of Labour women MPs therefore owed their success to the party's rising support in a range of more marginal constituencies (Short 1996, 20). For Smith, however, finding a viable mechanism for securing women candidates in safe and target seats and linking this to OMOV was of strategic importance to winning the wider battle over the latter.

It is in this context that AWS came to the fore. The Women's Committee could not draw on other countries' experiences, since most operated with list systems of proportional representation. AWS had been discussed within WAC in the mid-1980s (Russell 2005: 109-10), but WAC had not pursued it in a focused way, preferring OWOS as a broad policy feeding into the Left's wider campaign for subjecting incumbent MPs to regular reselection. LCC, however, had taken it up in its commission on party democracy in 1989 and in that year the party's General Secretary wrote to all CLPs encouraging them to use AWS (Russell 2005, 110-11). In 1990, the Fabian pamphlet, *Quotas Now*, argued for AWS to be adopted through a system of variable quotas for safe, marginal and no-hope seats organised within a regional framework (Brooks et al 1990, 20-2). From 1990, WAC and CLPD backed model resolutions on AWS for all seats with a retiring MP and all by-elections, but a composite resolution along these lines was heavily defeated at the 1992 party conference (Russell, 2005, 111). What was now proposed in the Women's Committee, with the support of the chair of the party's Organisation Committee, Gordon Colling, was a compromise: a commitment to AWS in half the safe seats with retiring MPs and half the party's target seats (Short 1996, 20), and a new regional framework to achieve consensus on which constituencies would operate with AWS (Eagle and Lovenduski 1998, 4-5; Russell 2005, 113).

Once adopted by the Women's Committee, these proposals were endorsed by the NEC in June 1993. The decision to link AWS to OMOV in a single parliamentary selection rule change proved critical. OMOV itself was opposed by many trade unions attached to retaining their block votes in local parliamentary electoral colleges, while Smith as leader argued that ending the block vote was vital to the party's credibility as a party of government. It was only because the USDAW union broke its members' conference mandate on OMOV in order to support AWS, while MSF abstained on this key vote (because its members' votes had formally committed it to support AWS and to oppose OMOV) that the rule change was passed (Short 1996, 21; Russell 2005, 49-56, 113).

The outcome in terms of the numbers of Labour women MPs elected in 1997 was examined at the beginning of this chapter. As noted there, AWS was, however, challenged as a breach of the 1975 Sex Discrimination Act in an industrial employment tribunal case in Leeds, *Jepson and Dyas-Elliot v. Labour Party 1996*.[8] Two Labour Party male members successfully argued that section 13 of the Act covered parties' selection processes because these governed access to gainful employment. The Labour Party decided not to appeal and subsequently it became clear that, as party leader and then Prime Minister, Tony Blair regarded AWS in 1997 as a one-off boost to women's representation rather than providing a continuing framework of positive discrimination (Eagle and Lovenduski 1998, 12–13; Lovecy 2002, 282–3; Russell 2005, 114–15). In the absence of new legislation permitting AWS, for the 2001 elections the NEC successfully proposed that all shortlists should be gender balanced (with 50% men and 50% women), but the numbers of women elected fell from 101 to 95. After the elections an amendment tabled at a National Policy Forum was accepted by the government and, once new amending legislation had been put onto the statute book with the 2002 Sex Discrimination (Election Candidates) Act, the NEC and Annual Conference in 2002 adopted a new system that would applying AWS to a percentage of all seats with incumbent MPs retiring at the next General Election (Childs 2003; Russell 2005, 120–1). This left gender-balanced selection processes in place for all other seats, and left full discretion to the NEC to designate the vacant safe seats where AWS would apply, in order to achieve the overall percentage of women candidates required in this category.

Strategic framing and substantive policy claims for women

In terms of substantive policies, we find a considerably greater degree of continuity in the patterns of framing policies for women that developed over the two decades to 1997. This continuity is to be explained in part because the new generations of women coming into the party with the distinctive values of second-wave feminism were able to build on a number of policies already underway or in place. More especially, as noted in the previous section, they succeeded in winning a framing of women's equal rights requiring positive discrimination during the Left's ascendancy, in the party programme adopted at the 1982 Annual Conference on which the 1983 manifesto was then based (Labour Party 1982), and they did so in terms that were fairly congruent with the Left's wider vision for the party. Once this had been achieved successive party leaders, concerned with extending Labour's support among different categories of women voters, as previously argued, accepted they should afford some prominence to policies, which opinion polling and focus group research showed to be attractive to many women voters. As a result, while there certainly was a Left–Right polarisation in the party over policies for women, and the way some of these were taken up and implemented by local Labour-run councils was targeted in key parts of the media as exemplifying 'the loony Left', it was not until the mid-1990s that a significant element of re-framing got underway under Blair's leadership. In any case, in the 1980s a key policy like abortion law, with attempted reforms to restrict its provision, proved divisive on both wings of the party.

In terms of gendered policies, Labour governments had been responsible for important legislation that responded to the concerns of feminists who joined the party from the 1970s on (even if such legislation was usually felt to 'not go far enough'). This included Barbara Castle's 1970 Equal Pay Act, enacted in response to the Dagenham women Ford workers' strike; the 1974 State-Earnings Related Pension scheme, whose biggest winners were women; the 1975 Sex Discrimination Act and Wilson's creation in 1975 of the National Women's Commission as a consultative body within the governmental policy process (Perkins 2003, 328-33, 378-9). The Labour government had also enabled a series of key private members' bills to come onto the statute book through free votes in the 1960s, legalising abortion, facilitating divorce for women and decriminalising male homosexuality in the 1960s (Francis 2000, 211). A decade later Richardson, working closely with the National Council of Civil Liberties, succeeded in winning new statutory protections for women subject to domestic violence, with the support of the Lord Chancellor's Office (Coote and Gill 1977). From the late 1960s the National Labour Women's Advisory Committee had identified discrimination against women operating in a broad range of policy areas, starting with its 1969 *Towards Equality* report on social security, and this work led to a formal party commitment in 1974 to end all forms of discrimination against women, set out in the manifesto's *Charter for Women*, and to the Committee's report, calling for gender balance in all nominated public bodies, *Obstacles to Women in Public Life*, that would be published by the party in 1974 (McDonald 1977, 149-51, 159).

Perrigo argues that the ascendancy of the Left in the NEC by the late 1970s then enabled feminists to win a fuller analysis of the problems facing women in contemporary Britain in *Labour's Programme 1982* (1996, 121-2). As a result, commitments to positive action policies – to remove discriminatory practices in the workplace, expand training opportunities for women, extend the 1970 Equal Pay Act and extend employment rights to part-time and home-workers, provide a major expansion of childcare and strengthen the 1975 Sex Discrimination Act – were taken forward; along with further improvements in maternity rights and grants, the ending of VAT on sanitary protection, improved support for carers and for victims of rape and domestic violence, and the expansion of NHS provision for family planning and abortion in the 1983 manifesto, *The New Hope for Britain* (Labour Party 1983, 14, 16-7), where they sat alongside the party's ambitious economic programme of public sector-led reflation, re-nationalisations and import controls to create full employment (Shaw 1996, 166-8).

Whereas economic policy, defence commitments and the party's stance on Europe were all to undergo a sea-change in the following period, for the most part these policy commitments for women were retained in the party's subsequent election manifestoes through to 1997 (Labour Party 1987b, 1992, 1997), or in some cases spelt out further so that, for example, Labour's *Charter for Women's Health*, referred to in the 1987 manifesto, included commitments to a full network of Well Women's Clinics, to better breast cancer screening and to the Right for women to choose to see a woman doctor (Labour Party 1987b, 8). The 1987 manifesto also set out the case for a Ministry for Women's Rights headed by a Cabinet Minister in terms of the need to tackle the many essential rights that women in Britain were still denied (Labour Party 1987b, 14-5, 39-43) and Jo Richardson was able to develop her own role, as a Shadow Minister, in this campaign, drawing on the 'insider' network of feminists that we saw developing with the framing of gender quotas. Cockburn records that 'the Labour Party for the first time had an all-woman team of organisers working more or less autonomously to put across a women's policy programme to the electorate' (Cockburn 1987, 23). In the Policy Review established following that electoral defeat, other women's organisations within the party were not formally represented but its report sustained the party's main range of policy commitments for women and Perrigo notes that 'criticism that women had not been formally involved led to a women's monitoring committee being set up, chaired by Jo Richardson' (1996, 125), while the party's subsequent publication on the ministry spelt out the party's policy commitments under a wider set of issue areas – women at work; safety and women; women as consumers; women and public life; and so on (Labour Party 1991).

Nevertheless, by the early 1990s the party's overarching policy frame was shifting from the 1983 objective of creating 'a fairer Britain' to what became 'Building a strong economy' in 1992 (Labour Party 1992, 11-14). In the process, some of the party's gendered policies began to be re-articulated to what would become a much clearer 'welfare-to-work' framework in the 1997 manifesto, *New Labour Because Britain Deserves Better* (Labour Party 1997b). Already by 1992 there was beginning to be a clearer focus on the family rather than more specifically on women, with policies set out in terms not just of achieving new rights for women but rather of creating a new framework for more prosperous and successful families and for achieving 'work–life balance' for both men and women (Labour Party 1992, 13-15). This latter was a perspective that Patricia Hewitt, who was by this time working in the party leader's personal office, was to develop further (Hewitt 1993). And this shift was to be taken considerably further in the 1997 manifesto, where there would be no sub-section on women and their rights as such. Instead, policy commitments relating to women were 'mainstreamed' and integrated under Blair's 10 key pledges ('mainstreaming' in terms of policy process is discussed further in Chapter Five), especially those on education, personal prosperity and 'build[ing] strong families and communities' (Labour Party 1997, 6-31).

Conclusion

This chapter has identified and charted the evolution of two very different trajectories of strategic framing in the cases of representational and substantive policies for women in the Labour Party in the two decades to 1997.

In the case of representational policies, differently constituted groups of feminist activists have been shown organising themselves over time in different kinds of mobilising structures, each linked to what were quite different wider policy advocacy coalitions and giving them access to differing decisional venues within the party. Changing opportunity structures in the Labour Party in the course of this period were shaped by changing elite alignments in the party's NEC and PLP and in the relations of these bodies to the trade union movement. Led, under successive party leaders, to the framing of representational issues, as we have seen, around four successive demands: for the collective empowerment of women in the party: for empowering their executive representation; for empowering individual women through gender quotas; and for expanding women's presence within the PLP.

In contrast, in the case of substantive policies, this chapter has shown that changes in the party's evolving opportunity structures had less of a direct impact on how feminist activists sought to extend the party's policy commitments to women from the late 1970s through until the early 1990s, indeed until as late as July 1994 when Clare Short, as Shadow Minister of Women, published *Labour's Strategy for Women – A Summary* (Labour Party 1994). Here processes of strategic framing by feminists were more clearly underpinned by the demonstrable electoral interests of the party and as a result there was a greater degree of continuity in how substantive policies were framed. However, Blair's leadership from 1994 and the development of Gordon Brown's economic strategy for the party brought with them a significant change in the political opportunity structures for the strategic framing of substantive policies for women as these were 'mainstreamed' into the party's main sectoral policies. At the same time, the advent of gender quotas 'mainstreamed' women into the party's organisations and decisional venues at all levels and by the time Labour won the 1997 General Election, this had led to the demise of the annual Women's Conference. This meant that in the elaboration and implementation of the policies that are the subject of the chapters that follow, there no longer was a distinctive arena in the party for its women members to publicly debate the relationship of the Labour Party, as a party of government, to the politics of gender.

Notes

[1] In addition, a full decade earlier than the DNA, the new French Socialist Party incorporated into its party statutes an initially modest gender quota of 10% (increased to 20% in 1979 and 30% in 1991) that was to apply both to the party's internal structures and also to candidacy selection for elections using proportional representation (Allwood and Wadia 2000, 59), thus excluding the party's parliamentary representation, where a variant on the UK's FPTP system (with two ballots) is employed. More recently, the Socialist Party in government has led the way in Europe by introducing statutory gender quotas for candidate selection in all elections (Lovecy 2000).

[2] For example, the breakaway Social Democrat Party in 1981 devised a shortlisting quota system (Perrigo 1996: 123).

[3] For single country studies see, notably, the set of country studies covering Australia, Canada, France, Germany, Ireland, Italy, the Netherlands, Norway, Sweden and the US as well as Britain brought together in Lovenduski and Norris 1993.

[4] Barbara Castle's selection in Blackburn in 1944 provides an interesting exception to this general rule, with the local agent mobilising local members to outflank the 'group of trade unionists who would prefer a trade union activist to a London-based journalist' (Perkins 2003, 77).

[5] Russell notes that from 1983 WAC constituted itself as a formally independent body but remained affiliated to the CLPD before 'becoming associated with the "hard" Left in the later 1980s' (Russell 2005, 97-8).

[6] Its effect was thus limited, as the Left's earlier 1979 mandatory selection victory had been (resulting in only eight de-selections by 1983, with only one woman, Clare Short, selected as a replacement) (Perrigo 1995, 410).

[7] Her feminist convictions were equally clear from the foreword she wrote the National Organisation of Labour Students' 1977 publication, *Women, Sexism and Socialism.*

8 *Jepson and Dyas-Elliot v. Labour Party* [1996] IRLR 116.

References

Allwood, G. and Wadia, K. (2000) *Women and Politics in France,* London: Routledge.

Black, A. and Brooke, S. (1997) 'The Labour Party, women, and the problem of gender, 1951-1966', *Journal of British Studies* 36(4), 419-452.

Brooks, R., Eagle, A. and Short, C. (1990) *Quotas Now: Women and the Labour Party,* London: The Fabian Society.

Byrne, P. (1996) 'The politics of the Women's Movement', *Parliamentary Affairs* 49(1), 55-70.

Caul, M. (1999) 'Women's representation in Parliament – the role of political parties', *Political Parties* 5(1), 79-98.

Caul, M. (2001) 'Political parties and the adoption of candidate gender quotas', *Journal of Politics* 63(4) 1214-29.

Childs, S. (2003) 'The Sex Discrimination (Election Candidates) Act', *Representation* 39(2), 83-92.

Cockburn, C. (1987) *Women, Trade Unions and Political Parties,* London: The Fabian Society

Coote, A. and Gill, T (1977) *Battered Women and the New Law,* London: National Council for Civil Liberties.

Eagle, M. and Lovenduski, J. (1998) *High Time or High Tide for Labour Women,* London: The Fabian Society.

Equal Opportunities Commission (1985) *Women and Trade Unions: A Survey,* Manchester: Equal Opportunities Commission.

Francis, M. (2000) 'Labour and gender', in D. Tanner, P. Thane and N. Tiratsoo (eds) *Labour's First Century,* Cambridge: Cambridge University Press, pp 191-220.

Graves, P.M. (1994) *Labour Women: Women in Working Class Politics 1918-1939,* Cambridge: Cambridge University Press.

Hayter, D. (2005) *Fightback! Labour's traditional right in the 1970s and 1980s,* Manchester: Manchester University Press.

Hewitt, P. (1993) *About Time: The Revolution in Work and Family Life,* London: IPPR/Rivers Oram Press.

Hewitt, P. and Mattinson, D. (1987) *Women's Votes: The Key to Winning,* London: The Fabian Society

Hills, J. (1981) 'Britain', in Lovenduski, J. and Hills, J. (eds) *The Politics of the Second Electorate*, London: Routledge and Kegan Paul, pp 8-32.

IPU (Inter-Parliamentary Union) (1994) *Plan of Action to Correct Present Imbalances in the Participation of Men and Women in Political Life*, Geneva: IPU.

IPU (1997) *Men and Women in Politics: Democracy in the Making*, Geneva: IPU.

Labour Party (1982) *Labour's Programme*, London: Labour Party.

Labour Party (1983) *The New Hope for Britain: Labour's Manifesto 1983. Think Positive Think Labour*, London: Labour Party.

Labour Party (1987a) *Labour's Ministry for Women*, London: Labour Party.

Labour Party (1987b) *Britain Will Win With Labour*, London: Labour Party.

Labour Party (1990) *Representation of Women in the Labour Party: Statement by the NEC*, Annual Conference 1990, London: Labour Party.

Labour Party (1991) *A New Ministry for Women*, London: Labour Party.

Labour Party (1992) *It's Time to Get Britain Working Again: Labour's Election Manifesto*, London: Labour Party.

Labour Party (1993) *Women in the Labour Party*, London: Labour Party

Labour Party (1994) *Labour's Strategy for Women – A Summary*, London: Labour Party.

Labour Party (1997a) *Partnership in Power*, NEC Consultation Document, January, London: Labour Party.

Labour Party (1997b) *New Labour Because Britain Deserves Better*, London: Labour Party.

Labour Party (1998) *Building a Healthy Women's Organisation*, NEC paper to Annual Conference, London: Labour Party.

Labour Women's Advisory Committee (1971) *Women and the Labour Party*, Report submitted to the December National Executive Committee, London: Labour Party.

Lovecy, J. (2000) 'Citoyennes à part entière? Gendered citizenship in France', *Government and Opposition*, 35(4), 439-62.

Lovecy, J. (2002) 'Gender mainstreaming and the framing of women's rights in Europe: the contribution of the Council of Europe', *Feminist Legal Studies*, 10(3), 271-83.

Lovenduski, J. (1993) 'Introduction: the dynamics of gender and party', in J. Lovenduski and P. Norris (eds), *Gender and Party Politics*, London: Sage, pp 1-15.

Lovenduski, J. (2005) *Feminizing Politics,* Cambridge: Polity.

Lovenduski, J. and Norris, P. (eds) (1993) *Gender and Party Politics,* London: Sage.

Matland, R.E. and D.T. Studlar (1996) 'The contagion of women candidates in single-member district and proportional representation electoral systems: Canada and Norway', *Journal of Politics* 58(3), 707–34.

Mazur, A.G. (1995) 'Strong state and symbolic reform: the Ministère des Droits de la Femme in France', in D.M. Stetson and A.G. Mazur (eds), *Comparative State Feminism,* Thousand Oaks, CA: Sage, pp 76–94.

McAdam, D., McCarthy, J.D. and Zald, M.N. (1996) 'Introduction: opportunities, mobilising structures and framing processes – towards a synthetic, comparative perspective on social movements', in D. McAdam, J.D. McCarthy and M.N. Zald (eds) *Comparative Perspectives on Social Movements: Political Opportunities, Mobilising Structures and Cultural Framing,* New York, NY: Cambridge University Press, pp 1–22.

McDonald, O. (1977) 'Women in the Labour Party', in L. Middleton (ed) *Women in the Labour Movement: The British Experience,* London: Croom Helm, pp 144–60.

Middleton, L. (ed) (1977) *Women in the Labour Movement: The British Experience,* London: Croom Helm.

National Organisation of Labour Students (1977) *Women, Sexism and Socialism,* London (Transport House): National Organisation of Labour Students.

Norris, P. (1993) 'The gender-generation gap in British elections', in D. Denver et al (eds) *British Elections and Parties Handbook,* London: Harvester Wheatsheaf, pp 129–42.

Perkins, A. (2003) *Red Queen: The Authorized Biography of Barbara Castle,* Basingstoke: Macmillan.

Perrigo, S. (1986) 'Socialism, feminism and the Labour Party: some experiences in Leeds', *Feminist Review,* no 23, 101–8.

Perrigo, S. (1995) 'Gender struggles in the British Labour Party from 1979 to 1995', *Party Politics* 1(3), 407–37.

Perrigo, S. (1996) 'Women and change in the Labour Party', *Parliamentary Affairs* 49(1), 17–25.

Perrigo, S. (1999) 'Women, gender and New Labour', in G. Taylor (ed) *The Impact of New Labour,* Basingstoke: Palgrave, pp 162–76.

Phillips, A. (1995) *The Politics of Presence,* Oxford: Clarendon Press.

Pollack, M and Hafner-Burton, E. (2000) 'Mainstreaming gender in the European Union', *Journal of Public Policy* 7(3), 432–56.

Radice, L. (ed) (1985) *Winning Women's Votes*, London: The Fabian Society.

Roth, A. (1998) *Parliamentary Profiles*, London: Parliamentary Profiles.

Rowbotham, S., Segal, L. and Wainwright, H. (1979), *Beyond the Fragments: Feminism in the Making of Socialism*, London: Islington Community Press.

Russell, M. (2005) *Building New Labour: The Politics of Party Organisation*, Basingstoke: Palgrave.

Sainsbury, D. (1993) 'The politics of increased women's representation: the Swedish Case', in J. Lovenduski, and P. Norris (eds), *Gender and Party Politics*, London: Sage, pp 263-90.

Shaw E. (1996) *The Labour Party since 1945*, Oxford: Blackwell.

Short, C. (1996) 'Women and the Labour Party', *Parliamentary Affairs* 49(1), 17-26.

Smith, J., Chatfield, C. and Pugnucco, R. (1997) 'Social movements and World politics: a theoretical framework' in J.Smith, C.Chatfield and R. Pugnucco (eds) *Transnational Social Movements and Global Politics*, New York, NY: Syracuse University Press, pp 59-77.

Squires, J. and Wickham-Jones, M. (2002) 'Mainstreaming in Westminster and Whitehall', *Parliamentary Affairs* 55(1), 57-70.

Wainwright, H. (1987) *Labour: A Tale of Two Parties*, London: Hogarth Press.

FIVE

Engendering the machinery of governance

Catherine Durose and Francesca Gains

Introduction

This chapter focuses on the opportunities taken by New Labour in power to engender the machinery of governance at national and local levels both in terms of representational policies and in changes to the organisation of the executive and other administrative policies. These types of policies are often described as the machinery of *government* (Massey 1995). Here we describe these changes as relating to the machinery of *governance* to reflect the devolved and distributed decision-making arenas of the contemporary British state (Flinders 2002). These administrative policies provide the context for policy-making in other substantive policy areas such as those discussed in Part Three of this book.

We begin by examining changes to the *representation policies* in the UK, Scottish and Welsh legislatures, in local government and the non-elected state. We then move on to explore the way in which *executive and administrative policies* under New Labour have been engendered not only through the establishment of a Women's Policy Unit and mainstreaming policies but crucially through the agency of individual policy actors in the Cabinet and the work of their departments.

We conclude that over the longer term there is some evidence from the experience of the national legislatures that a critical mass of women representatives will change the conduct of political business and place women's issues higher on the agenda. However, in any assessment of the impact of machinery of governance changes in New Labour's first two terms, we argue the focus only upon 'Blair's babes' misses an appreciation that the greatest impact on policy outcomes arises from the very local level in the work of social entrepreneurs in the non-governmental sector and individual feminist Cabinet members heading departmental resources and acting in allegiance with the core executive, notably with actors in the Treasury.

Women's formal representation in politics

Much of the now extensive literature about the role and position of women in politics focuses on the issue of representation. The arguments for better representation are set out in Chapter Two here (see also Childs 2002b). Although Britain has managed a gradual, if somewhat differentiated increased of women in political institutions, women still only constitute 19.8% of the British legislature, less than many other developed states and European partners (see Table 5.1). The Labour Party is the only political group hitherto to seek to increase levels of representation (see Chapter Four). The following section will discuss the representation policies adopted by New Labour in government and assess the success that they have had across all levels of governance.

Table 5.1: Representation of women in politics, 2004

Area	2004 % women
Members of Parliament	18.1
The Cabinet	27.3
Members of the House of Lords	17.7
Members of the Scottish Parliament	39.5
Members of the National Assembly for Wales	50.0
Local authority council leaders	16.6
UK members of the European Parliament	24.4

Source: EOC 2005

In accounting for this low level of representation Rao (2005, 328) suggests it is helpful to distinguish between factors that restrict the *demand* for women in political life (such as prejudice against women in politics, discriminatory practices, a lack of family-friendly arrangements and exclusionary male networks), and *supply* factors relating to both the circumstances and attitudes of the women themselves (for example, domestic responsibilities, self-esteem and self-confidence and political efficacy). The Fawcett Society considers time availability and the difficulty of maintaining a work–life balance as a particular constraint for women who often have primary caring responsibilities (Fawcett Society 2005).

UK Parliament – House of Commons

The 1997 British General Election saw a record number of women MPs returned to the House of Commons and in the PLP. Table 5.2

Table 5.2: Representation of women in the House of Commons, 1983 to 2005

Year	1983	1987	1992	1997	2001	2005
No. Labour MPs	209	229	271	418	412	356
No. Labour women MPs	10	21	37	101	95	98
% Labour women MPs	4.8	9.2	13.7	24.2	23.1	27.5
Total number MPs	650	650	651	659	659	646
Total number women MPs	23	41	60	120	118	128
% Total women MPs	3.5	6.3	9.2	18.2	17.9	19.8

Source: www.parliament.uk

shows that although both fell slightly in 2001, the composition of the 2005 House of Commons produced a small increase and women now constitute 128 of the 656 MPs – up from 118 in 2001 (CAWP 2006). The election of 'Blair's babes' was a visible statement of difference and to date has commanded the most sustained media and academic attention.

Since 1997, Labour governments have built on its experience in promoting representation in the party (see Chapter Four) in promoting parliamentary and procedural change to modernise Parliament. The Modernisation of the House of Commons Select Committee has made a number of recommendations including changes to working hours aimed at addressing the demand side restrictions on participation by women (Ross 2000, 5). The government also took action to clarify the legality of parties seeking to employ positive discrimination to select candidates. The decrease in the number of women MPs elected at the 2001 General Election was a consequence of the sex discrimination case won by a failed male Labour Party candidate which led to positive discrimination being ruled unlawful.

The government responded by introducing the Sex Discrimination (Election Candidates) Bill in 2002 which allowed political parties to introduce positive action in the selection of candidates. Although each of the main parties said that they wanted more women in Parliament and all of the main political parties undertook some equality promotion measures such as extra training for women, only the Labour Party used positive action using AWS in some seats (Fawcett Society 2005). Consequently, after the 2005 General Election women MPs constituted a higher proportion of the PLP than ever before.

The impact of the new intake of Labour women MPs in 1997 and whether these women were acting as and for women, rather than for themselves, their party, or their constituency, was soon questioned;

fuelled by the voting through of cuts to lone-parent benefit in the autumn of 1997. On this issue, which disproportionately affected women, only one of 65 new intake Labour women MPs rebelled.[1] This has become 'widely regarded as the moment when women MPs failed to act for women' (Childs 2002a, 143). The claim that 'descriptive' and 'substantive' representation are linked is, in this respect at least, discredited (2002a, 143).

However, by only taking account of these traditional measures of political efficacy is to neglect much of the work and impact of women MPs and the argument that women 'do politics differently'. Many women MPs believe that they have a different style of politics, that they are 'less combative and aggressive, more collaborative and speak in a different language compared to men' (Childs 2004, 365). In addition, they claim that they have articulated women's concerns through a range of not commonly discussed means, for example, through debates, select committees, signing Early Day Motions and in the PLP's women's group. Also, they have 'exerted power behind the scenes, lobbying, arguing, writing reports, bending ministers' ears ...' (Childs, 2001). Moreover, in constituencies their presence has enabled dialogue between women constituents, women's organisations and women representatives and the articulation of a feminised agenda (Childs 2002a, 143-4). However, the outcomes of 'doing politics differently' are hard to measure and consequently it is difficult to make an assessment of the impact of women MPs (Ward 2001a).

House of Lords

As with the House of Commons, the proportion of women in the House of Lords has now reached double figures (see Table 5.3). This is largely because of the reform of the House of Lords in 1999 which reduced the overall total membership by removing most of majority of hereditary, predominantly male peers (Ross 2000, 7). Further reforms

Table 5.3: Representation of women in the House of Lords (at July 2005)[2]

	Number of women peers	Total number of peers	% Women peers
Labour	52	215	24
Total	131	693	19

Source: CAWP 2006

that have been put forward by commentators, including direct election of the Lords and a quota-led Appointments Committee, may lead to a more socially representative House of Lords (see Russell 2005b for further detail).

Scottish Parliament and Welsh Assembly

The clearest opportunity to engender representation that the New Labour government had was in the creation of new decision-making arenas through devolution. In the campaigning that preceded the establishment of the devolved assemblies, 'there was always the proviso, particularly amongst New Labour pro-devolutionists, that it must usher in a new politics. Central to this new politics was to be substantial representation and influence from women' (Feld 2001, 74). Women's representation in the devolved institutions is much higher than in Westminster and in May 2003, the Welsh Assembly became the world leader on equal representation, with women constituting 50% of Assembly members (see Table 5.4). The establishment of new institutions permitted measures to tackle several of the demand restrictions listed earlier and both selection and electoral systems have been key factors for increases in representation.

All parties fielding candidates in these elections did use some sort of positive action with the Labour Party notable for the extent of its actions. Candidate selection for the Labour Party was organised through a system of 'twinning' where neighbouring constituencies are paired and it is ensured that at least one of the candidates is a woman. This has proven effective in terms of representation and also in avoiding

Table 5.4: Representation of women in the devolved assemblies, 2003

	Number of women representatives	Total number of representatives	% Women
Scottish Parliament			
Labour	27	50	54
Total	50	129	39.5
Welsh Assembly			
Labour	19	29	65.5
Total	30	60	50

Source: Fawcett Society 2005

the situation where women candidates are predominantly selected for marginal seats. In 2003, in both Scotland and Wales, AWS were used in some constituencies by the Labour Party.

The mixed electoral systems adopted in the devolved assemblies which combine FPTP with a list system have been key in establishing a 'new politics'. The outcome of the mixed system has effectively led to coalition governments and that no one party can hold an overall majority. Shephard and Cairney note that the Scottish Parliament appears to have more dialogue between the executive and legislature and a greater readiness to consult and take account of the views of the MSPs (2005, 317). This arguably makes the notion of women doing politics differently far more potent.

Finally, attempts have been made to establish institutions notably different from their Westminster counterpart with the responsibility to drive forward equality issues embedded in the working and objectives of the assemblies. This has been manifested in, for example, family-friendly working hours, childcare provision and gender neutral language although not all commentators agree these translate into substantive policy measures (Busby and MacLeod 2002, 41).

Consideration of the devolved assemblies therefore allows a more telling test of feminist arguments concerning the impact of representation. In an examination of policy debates in the first term of the National Assembly for Wales, Chaney argues that the link between descriptive and substantive representation is complex requiring not only a 'critical mass' but also the agency of 'equality champions', feminists with experience and expertise who can drive forward policy proposals (2006, 709). In the Scottish Parliament, which has far greater capacity to act than the Welsh Assembly, Mackay points to a broad consensus that higher representation has made a difference in Scotland suggesting most women MSPs feel 'empowered, effective and able to make a difference as backbenchers' (2002). However, also acknowledged is that it is 'difficult to disentangle differences that may be due to the "new politics" principles and the institutional design of the Scottish Parliament and the presence of women' noting that 'they work in ways that mutually reinforce one another' (Mackay 2002).

Regional and local representation

Increasing the diversity of representation at local level was an explicit aim of the government's reform agenda for the local and regional level. These aims were pursued through the creation of the Greater London

Authority and through a major shake-up in the political management arrangements in local government.

Women's representation is relatively high in the Greater London Assembly[3] following the 2004 election – with 36% women Assembly Members (see Table 5.5). However, it is notable that Labour, the Liberal Democrats and the Green Party have all achieved women's representation of more than a third. Even the Conservatives have a higher level than they have achieved at Westminster, 22% (Fawcett Society 2005).

Table 5.5: Representation of women in the London Assembly, 2004

	Number of women AMs	Total number of women AMs	% Women
Labour	4	7	57
Total	9	25	36

Source: Greater London Authority 2006

In local government as at the national level, women were under-represented when Labour came to power in 1997 (Stephenson 2001, 90). The proportion of women councillors had doubled from 12% in 1964 to 25% in 1999 (Stoker et al 2003a, Table 5.1). Ministers were keen that proposals for the modernisation of local government involving a reorganisation of political management arrangements should have a beneficial impact on diversity. 'We need', declared Local Government Minister Hilary Armstrong, 'people from all groups in our communities to come forward and offer their services as councillors. We need to break free from the pattern so often found today where many councillors are relatively old, few are women, and even fewer are drawn from ethnic minorities' (Armstrong 1999, 21).

Local government reforms included the abolition of the committee system and new roles for councillors as 'community champions'. The hope was that these features would attract new entrants previously put off by the style of local government decision-making. An early evaluation of the reforms found no difference in levels of representation by 2002 (Stoker et al 2003a), however, a small increase to 29% is now reported by the Fawcett Society, although this figure disguises a varied picture by type of authority and region (2005). Women are still acutely under-represented at senior levels as council leaders (17%) or as executive councillors (23%) (Ross 2000, 13; Stephenson 2001, 89; Stoker et al 2003a); and the turnover of women councillors is notably high with many lasting only one or two terms before resigning (Stephenson 2001, 89).

Explanations for this lack of success draw on the demand factors of local party political culture in recruitment and promotion and the lack of family-friendly practices as well as the supply side factors of the time constraints faced by women as working carers (Stoker et al 2003b).

The non-elected state

Appointed bodies and quangos

Public bodies have become increasingly important over the past 30 years raising the issue of fair and equal appointment of women (McRae 1996). Michael White noted in 1998 that 'white middle class men from the "quango establishment" are still chosen to fill thousands of posts in important public bodies largely because they "play golf and know the chairman of the board"' (White 1998, 11). New Labour sought to change this and to improve the diversity of the non-elected state as a key, but often neglected, aspect of public decision-making and influence. In 1999, as part of the Nolan Committee's work in examining standards of public life, Peter Kilfoyle, (then) Parliamentary Secretary for the Cabinet Office, set out government recommendations that all Departments 'continue their work towards the equal representation of women and men in public appointments' (Cabinet Office 2001). Yet, according to the Cabinet Office's report *Public Bodies 2001*, women held just under a third of appointments to these bodies at the UK level (Cabinet Office 2001). Len Peach, Commissioner for Public Appointments introduced only basic reforms, such as the requirement for most paid posts to be advertised.

The explanations for low representation here draw on similar supply and demands factors as other aspects of representation. More radical reform, however, has again been led by the devolved assemblies, perhaps because quangos have a particularly prominent role in Scotland and Wales with responsibility for many aspects of government. Reforms aim to 'ensure that the whole process of public appointments is open to scrutiny and is fully accountable' (Ron Davies quoted by Wolmar 1997: 12). Commentators have argued that 'what needs to be monitored and scrutinised more carefully is the relationship between applicants and appointees as well as the wider issue of attracting "non-traditional" members of the public to come forward to serve the public's interest' (Ross 2000: 20).

Women's informal participation in politics

For some commentators, the perceived lack of formal involvement in political decision-making ignores the location, nature and extent of women's participation in political life (Lovenduski and Randall 1993; Lowndes 2004). Research for the Joseph Rowntree Foundation has highlighted the critical role played by women in community life and contrasts between the genders in terms of activism (Andersen et al 1999). Women of all ages play a critical role in maintaining the social fabric of the neighbourhood and being actively engaged in the formal and informal organisations (Forrest and Kearns 1999). Traditional conceptions of political participation are perhaps not capable of capturing the form of women's participation which is often 'invisible' due to its highly localised and informal nature (see Lowndes 2004). As Patricia Hewitt, then Minister for Women and Equality noted, 'in local communities, voluntary organisations and faith groups, there are thousands and thousands of women engaged in small "p" politics and making a real difference ... All too often, they don't feel that they can or want to operate on that larger stage and I think it's a real challenge for Labour and the other parties – to make themselves much more welcoming' (Hewitt quoted by Happold and Katz 2003).

Further recent research suggests the value of informal participation may be underestimated with a reciprocal relationship between the informal civic participation and more formal political participation of women in need of further examination. Not only does the density of women in visible political positions act as a determinant for women's mass participation (Burns et al 2001; Childs 2004; Norris et al 2004), there is also evidence that the relationship works in the opposite way. Giddy argues that there is a strong link between the presence of women on a local council and the existence of a robust network of community groups focusing on and run by women; developing improved links with voluntary and community groups can be an important way to build links between the issues that engage women voters and the politics of the council (2000). There is also evidence that women's engagement can support a different type of politics: one that is rooted in trust and mutuality and builds on informal community connections (Lowndes 2004).

This examination of the impact of representational policies suggests that although the focus has largely been upon the activities and impact of women representatives in the House of Commons a focus solely on representation politics is not perhaps conducive to understanding either the role of women in politics or the impact that women's engagement may have on women's lives (Lovenduski and Randall 1993). A focus solely on a critical mass perspective 'fails to identify the multiple and complex determinants and configurations of feminist policy change' (Childs and Withey 2004). In a system dominated by a powerful executive and majority party rule, as in the UK, most contemporary policy analyses focuses on the operation of the executive. The following section of this chapter examines the organisation of the executive and the administrative policies established by New Labour and looks at the impact of administrative policies on engendering government.

Engendering in the core executive

As Chapter One argued, most public policy analysis in the UK examines the activities of the executive rather than the legislature in seeking to understand how the party in government seeks to develop its policy proposals into policy programmes. This literature suggests for policy change to be realised, actors in the core executive need to cooperate in power dependent networks to achieve shared goals (Thain and Wright 1995; Smith 1999; Richards and Smith 2004). The commitment of individual Ministers is key and they need to have the capacity to act and hold institutional resources (Gains 1999; Smith et al 2000; Flinders 2002). It is argued here that this literature has, with notable exceptions, paid insufficient attention to gender when there are three reasons why a gender focus is relevant. First, because of Blair's deliberate appointment of more female Cabinet Ministers. Second, because in power New Labour established a women's policy machinery by appointing a Minister for Women and establishing a Women's Unit to work alongside her to support mainstreaming initiatives across government. Finally, because of the possibility of policy advocacy coalitions operating at national level in pushing feminist policy aims (see Chapter Four). The rest of this chapter will examine each of these possibilities in turn, drawing on secondary analysis as well as making an assessment using the analytical themes suggested by the public policy literature.

Feminising the Cabinet

Alongside the iconic 'Blair's Babes' picture, Blair also symbolically granted his first five Cabinet ministerial appointments to women (Chittenden and Grice 1997). Three of these appointments were in spending ministries – and therefore directly able to command resources to direct the policy process. At the time this represented the greatest number of women in Cabinet ever (see CAWP 2006). However, following Blair's first reshuffle, although the number of women in Cabinet remained five, only one was in a spending ministry. It appeared that the women in Blair's first Cabinet were being used to do the backroom organisation and management (see Table 5.6).

The 2001 election afforded the opportunity for Blair to bring into the Cabinet new faces in new roles. At this stage, there were seven women Cabinet Ministers and five were in the spending ministries (Ward 2001b). During the ensuing reshuffles the cabinet maintained a level of women's representation of around 30% including five female Ministers with spending departments.

Table 5.6: Women Ministers since 1997

	Office	Women	Men	Women as % of total
1997	Cabinet	5	17	22
	Junior Minister	14	56	20
2001	Cabinet	7	16	30
	Junior Minister	23	44	34
2005	Cabinet	6	17	35
	Junior Minister	19	63	28

Source: CAWP (2006)

This proportion was not initially maintained in the 2005 Cabinet which began with six women Cabinet Ministers, only four in spending departments: and two further women in organisational roles. Following Blair's latest and possibly last reshuffle, there are now eight women in Cabinet with Margaret Beckett moving to be the first female Foreign Secretary (for a useful summary of all Cabinet Minister appointments and reshuffles see *Independent*, 6 May 2006, 3).

It is difficult to assess the impact of increased representation of female Cabinet Ministers. First, it is not possible to make the assumption that women will act for women. The women in Blair's Cabinets represent different parts of the Labour Party's broad church (Drucker 1979). There are feminists like Harman, Hewitt and Jowell who were part of the movement to feminise the party and its policy programme (see Chapter Four and Russell 2005a). There are also women like Margaret Beckett and Ann Taylor of a slightly older generation who connected with a more trade union base and according to Sieghart, 'were forced to be one of the lads' (2001).

Second, even where Ministers were avowedly feminist in their intentions, other constraints can curtail their ability to act. Perhaps the most telling example of this is how Harriet Harman when Secretary of State for Social Security and Minister for Women was bound to stick to the spending limits of the Conservative administration even though they entailed cutting benefits to lone parents, the majority of whom are women.

Finally, the link between being a woman and acting for women is not clearly shown when looking at the gender of Cabinet Ministers in policy areas which are seen to benefit women. Most commentators agree that the most successful policies in terms of benefiting women are policies coming out of the Treasury or Department of Health (DoH) such as the working family tax credit (WFTC), child tax credit and the Sure Start programme (Harman 2004; WEU 2005). The national minimum wage (NMW) although not stemming from a feminist agenda had a disproportionately beneficial impact on women, as two thirds of the one and a half million low-paid workers in receipt of it are women (Triesman 2002). Policy change to benefit women cannot be simply linked to the numerical proportions of women in the core executive.

However, insider accounts suggest that policy developments were seen where departments were headed by women or where women Ministers had an interest in gender mainstreaming (Veitch 2005). There are some indications that when women Cabinet Ministers cooperated they challenged the combative culture of Cabinet competition for resources (Sieghart 2001). Both Morris and Jowell report on how they cooperated to come to agreement about school sport. Jowell stated 'For the first time ever, we've put in a joint bid for these programmes, which is unheard of in the rivers where the testosterone flows and success is measured by how much money you get' (Bedell 2002; Ward 2002). However, reports of these individual indications of a different way of doing politics are far outweighed by reports of the laddish culture which surrounds New Labour's inner circle and Ashley argues New Labour has been more female-friendly in its policies than in its political culture (Ashley 2004; see also Bradberry 1998; Coote 1999; Harman 2004).

The establishment of gender policy machinery and gender mainstreaming policies

As Mazur points out much international feminist literature has focused on the operation of specific gender policy machinery (2003). Likewise following the Beijing Declaration at the UN's Fourth World Conference on Women in Beijing, 1995, there has been international interest in evaluating mainstreaming initiatives which aim to transform the policy process to ensure a gendered perspective in forecasting the implications of policies for equality of opportunity and outcomes. As discussed in Chapters One and Four the concept of gender mainstreaming can be used to describe in its broadest sense the adoption of a gendered awareness in all policy-making to ensure equality of outcome or in a narrower sense associated with more specific policy initiatives such as equal opportunity policies (Squires and Wickham-Jones 2002, 2004; True 2003; Veitch 2005).

In the UK, the work of Squires and Wickham-Jones (2002, 2004) has provided the key analysis of New Labour's gender policy machinery in examining the work of the Ministers for Women and Women's Policy Unit (later WEU) who were initially responsible for promoting gender mainstreaming in the UK Government. Harriet Harman was appointed the first Minister of Women, following through on New Labour's pledge in opposition to appoint a Minister for Women within the Cabinet (Benn 2000; see Chapter Four). Harman in the first government debate on the role of women stated, 'we are committed to building and sustaining a new habit of government that has women's voices and women's interests at its very heart' (Harman 1998). Harman was assisted in an unpaid capacity by Joan Ruddock, both located in the DSS where Harman was also Secretary of State. Shortly after these appointments, a Women's Unit was also established and located in the DSS absorbing some staff from the sex equality branch of the Department for Education and Employment (DfEE) (Squires and Wickham-Jones 2002, 65).

In early 1998, the government adopted a policy of mainstreaming which committed all departments to assess policies for their impact upon gender. The Women's Unit provided the policy guidelines on departmental implementation, established training and a network of officials responsible for this area of policy across Whitehall (Ward 1998; Squires and Wickham-Jones 2002, 59; 2004, 84; Veitch 2005). One critically decisive activity was to become involved more proactively, even if at a late stage, in ensuring equality issues were included in the first set of Treasury public sector agreements (PSAs) with departments (Veitch 2005, 601). PSAs set targets for departments to achieve as part of their budgetary negotiations and strengthen the incentives for departments to achieve key policy goals. However, these early steps towards providing an institutional focus for including a gender perspective on policy formation was politically undermined by the cut in lone-parent benefits to meet the previous Conservative government's spending priorities. Administratively, the Women's Unit was seen to be small, initially overwhelmed by ministerial correspondence, disconnected from the government's main policy agenda and with only a small budget (Bradberry 1998; Coote 2000, 41; Hill and Hinscliff 2000; Squires and Wickham-Jones 2002, 2004; Veitch 2005).

After only one year, both Harman and Ruddock lost their jobs and were replaced by Baroness Jay, Leader of the House of Lords assisted by Tessa Jowell, combining their roles with other jobs in government. The Women's Unit moved nearer to the centre of government both physically and metaphorically in moving to the Cabinet Office (Squires and Wickham-Jones 2004, 84). The work of the Women's Unit was centred around gathering statistical information and a 'listening to women exercise' and was seen as only having an indirect impact on policy (Squires and Wickham-Jones 2004, 84). Although the Women's Unit increased its staff slightly as the 2001 General Election drew near most commentators predicted its demise (Woolf 2001; Squires and Wickham-Jones 2002).

In fact, following the General Election, the Women's Unit was renamed the Women and Equality Unit and grew with an increased budget of £11 million (Squires and Wickham-Jones 2002, 57; 2004, 86). The Ministers also changed, with Patricia Hewitt in Cabinet taking over alongside her role heading the Department for Trade and Industry (DTI): assisted by Sally Morgan (subsequently Jacqui Smith from November 2001) as Deputy Minister for Women. The remit of the WEU also changed with responsibility for mainstreaming passed back to departments with the WEU involved in monitoring achievement of the relevant targets. Sally Morgan chaired a Cabinet committee to which departmental Ministers reported on their gender mainstreaming targets. This move to the management of mainstreaming initiatives through a Cabinet committee represents an embedding of the work of the WEU into the established Whitehall way of conducting business (Burch and Holiday 2004). The WEU set out a clear focus upon five priorities: reducing the pay gap; work–life balance; women in public life; domestic violence and public services (Squires and Wickham-Jones 2004, 86-7). With Hewitt – a former feminist like Harman – in charge, the women's policy machinery appeared to be having an impact and the WEU was moved to the DTI.

However, when the 2002 public service agreement targets were published, the women's budget group – a group of feminist academics and policy advisers committed to promote gender equality in economic policy – pointed out that women's issues were not visible in the targets set suggesting the policy of mainstreaming had not significantly impacted upon the work of departments and their negotiations with the Treasury. Media reports suggested the David Blunkett at the DfEE had blocked a target on equal pay (Ward 2002). And, Squires and Wickham-Jones report that where mainstreaming measures were implemented 'the primary agent has been the Government department most concerned' and not the WEU (2002, 65).

Nevertheless, in the intervening three years up to the 2005 General Election the WEU was clear about how it was contributing to the five areas listed above. The WEU is working with more and more departments to establish contributing targets to the cross–cutting gender equality public service agreement and lists the achievement of these targets in a progress report (WEU 2005). The WEU was able to strengthen gender equality targets established in the second round of public service agreements in 2003. The targets are a mix of milestone achievement and ongoing performance measurement targets. Some are internal, relating to government as employer, legislator or provider and some involve government working in partnership with other private and not–for–profit organisations. For example, targets involve better representation of women on public bodies and in the senior civil service; increases in usage by women as customers of government-sponsored business support services; the numbers of DTI employees reporting satisfaction with their work–life balance; working with the EOC to ensure large employers undertake pay reviews; the creation of new childcare places and taking action to reduce domestic violence. The incentive effect of targets on the attention given in departments' gender equality initiatives is now described as 'the most powerful gender mainstreaming tool' (Veitch 2005, 602).

Following the 2005 General Election, Tessa Jowell was initially appointed Minister for Women in the Cabinet alongside her role as Secretary of State for Culture, Media and Sport, assisted by an unpaid Parliamentary Secretary based in the Department for Productivity, Energy and Industry (the renamed DTI), Meg Munn. Jowell, like Hewitt and Harman, had a background in feminist activism and Meg Munn chaired the PLP women's group (Sieghart 2001; Branigan 2005). Finally, from 2006, Ruth Kelly took over as Minister for Women alongside her role as Secretary of State for Communities and Local Government. The WEU also moved from the DTI to the newly created Department for Communities and Local Government which will sponsor the Commission for Equality and Human Rights (CEHR) from 2007 (DCLG 2006). It is likely that the WEU will join the CEHR when it replaces the separate EOC, Disability Rights Commission and the Commission for Racial Equality (Squires and Wickham-Jones 2004, 87). Gender mainstreaming is now emphasised as being part of the public service modernisation agenda. A mainstreamed approach is one which ensures consultation with, recognition of and responsiveness to diversity among users, consumers and citizens (Veitch 2005).

Overall, the literature suggests that the women's policy machinery and the policy of gender mainstreaming has had only variable success. The WEU and gender mainstreaming initiatives suffered at various times from a lack of resources, and changing remit, the lack of a key ministerial policy advocate, its shifting and peripheral location within Whitehall and consequent lack of capacity to raise and deliver a mainstreaming agenda in many areas (Flinders 2002; Squires and Wickham-Jones 2002, 2004; Veitch 2005;). These resourcing constraints are identified by True in comparative studies of women's policy machineries (True 2003). Nevertheless, as True also notes the 'policy entrepreneurship of gender advocates' both politicians and officials in the executive, and is key in levering change through building networks and coalitions (2003, 372 and 379). The bureaucratic policy actors serving Ministers in the WEU were successful in creating a network of responsible civil servants which elsewhere has been found to extend the reach of mainstreaming policies. The WU and WEU were also able to recognise and exploit the institutional possibilities of the developing PSA incentives. The impact on policy has been strongest where the concerns of the Unit and New Labour in general have coincided, and in departments headed by sympathetic Ministers where women politicians were able to 'champion gender mainstreaming most effectively [is] where it can be shown to improve the efficiency and impact of policies in reaching significant sections of the electorate' (Veitch 2005, 605).

Policy advocacy coalitions in the core executive

Feminist policy advocacy coalitions are said to have influenced the adoption of domestic violence policies in two local areas and subsequently challenged the dominant PAC at national level (Arbrar et al 2000). As both Chapter Four and Russell (2005a) point out, a feminist policy advocacy coalition worked hard within the Labour Party in the 1980s and 1990s to see changes in the representational and substantive policies adopted within the party and in the 1997 election. What evidence is there now of feminist policy advocacy coalitions operating in New Labour's core executive? There are indications of networks of academics, policy activists, politicians and advisers operating to influence policy implementation in two areas. First, the creation of the WU, especially following its expansion in 2001, drew in staff from a wide variety of backgrounds from across the civil service and from the private and voluntary sectors (Squires and Wickham-Jones 2004, 86). Coupled with the establishment of a network of civil servants responsible for mainstreaming in departments, this indicates that there are possibilities for the type of feminist influenced networks advocating policy change both across government and in departments. However, as Chapter Two points out there are many feminisms and the demands of women are not uniform. For example, Veitch notes that policies like better legal rights for part-time employment can be viewed as reinforcing womens' gender roles (2005, 605).

Second, and much more clearly established, is the work of the Women's Budget Group (WBG) which brings together female economists, researchers, policy experts and activists to act in a network to promote gender equality (WBG, 2006) and has clearly contributed to the development of the cross-cutting PSA on gender equality (Himmelweit 2005). Himmelweit reports a close relationship between the WBG and the Treasury since 1997 although is cautious about the impact consultations have had on policy (2005, 112).

Networks, dependencies and trust in the core executive

Much of the reporting of the activities of women in the core executive is supportive of the more mainstream – but hitherto gender blind – public policy analysis of core executive power relations. Mainstreaming worked best in departments where the Minister was committed to gender equality indicating the importance of a key actor with resources and determination (Ward 1998; Gains 1999; Squires and Wickham-Jones, 2002, 2004). This would certainly appear to be the case with Patricia Hewitt at the DTI, for example. The WEU appeared to work best within the conventional Whitehall committee structures and New Labour networks. For example, Squires and Wickham-Jones point out that Jay and Jowell made alliances with non-feminist allies (2002, 66) and Jowell and Blunkett at the DfEE collaborated to bring in Sure Start (Hill and Hinscliff 2000). Finally, many policies which can be argued to benefit women stem from the Treasury which has extended its involvement in the shaping of social and fiscal policies impacting on low-paid workers and the benefit system. This assessment of New Labour's executive and administrative policy reforms points to the need for a gendered perspective to the examination of the core executive in Blair's government.

Conclusion

This chapter has reviewed the representational, administrative and executive changes which New Labour has made to engender the machinery of governance. These changes – policies in themselves – have the effect of framing the context for functional policy-making of the sort examined in Part Three of this book. In government, New Labour has taken several steps to improve the *representation* of women in the national, devolved and local governments and the non-elected state. The evidence reviewed here suggests the increase in representation at Westminster requires further positive discrimination policies before a tipping point is reached. Evidence for a critical mass is difficult to discern due to temporal delays. However, the experiences of the devolved governments provide a natural laboratory for future research. Although the mixed electoral system complicates investigation of causality. In local government, attempts to encourage participation have likewise not been very successful and the importance of participation at the very local and unelected level by local women policy actors is worthy of further policy and academic attention.

Also required is a greater focus on actors in core executive working with policy advocacy coalitions as a key determinant of policy change. In terms of the organisation of the executive and administrative policies, the conventional public policy approach set out in Chapter One provides a helpful framework. Electoral imperatives and the operation of networks within the core executive explain how committed feminist actors in spending departments have worked with the centre of government – notably the Treasury – to push through policy agendas directly impacting on the lives of women. Part Three of this book will compliment this review of the secondary data of how the centre of government works. The following policy chapters take a detailed empirical look at seven key economic, social and international policy initiatives to examine just how the first two terms of New Labour have met the feminist policy aims of the Party in opposition.

Notes

[1] Ann Cryer, MP, Keighley.

[2] Figures do not include the 26 peers spiritual, all of whom are men or the eight on leave of absence, one of which is a woman.

[3] Pimlott and Rao (2002) provide an excellent overview of the establishment of the Greater London Authority although the analysis does not refer to gender.

References

Andersen, H., Munck, R., Fagan, C., Goldson, B., Lansley, I., Novah, T., Melville, R., Moore, R., Bentowim, G. and Harrison. M. (1999) *Neighbourhood Images in Liverpool: 'It's all down to the people'*, York: Joseph Rowntree Foundation.

Arbrar, S., Lovenduski, J. and Margetts, H. (2000) 'Feminist ideas and domestic violence policy change', *Political Studies* 48, 239-62.

Armstrong, H. (1999) 'The key themes of democratic renewal', *Local Government Studies* 25(4), 19-25.

Ashley, J. (2004) 'Better Claire than the politics of yah boo', *Guardian*, 4 March.

Bedell, G. (2002) 'The trials of Tessa', *The Observer*, 19 May.

Benn, M. (2000) 'A short march through the institutions: reflections on New Labour's gender machinery', in A. Coote (ed) *New Gender Agenda*, London: IPPR.

Bradberry, G. (1998a) 'Blair's laddish culture: women in politics', *The Times*, 24 November.

Bradberry, G. (1998b) 'Blair's laddish New Labour', *The Times*, 28 November.

Branigan, T. (2005) 'Minister for Women to work unpaid', *Guardian*, 16 May.

Burch, M. and Holliday, I. (2004) 'The Blair government and the core executive', *Government and Opposition* 39(1), 1-21.

Burns, N., Schlozman, K.J. and Verba, S. (2001) *The Private Roots of Public Action, Gender Equality and Political Participation*, Cambridge, MA: Harvard University Press.

Busby, N. and McLeod, C. (2002) 'Maintaining a balance: the retention of women MSPs in Scotland', *Parliamentary Affairs* 55(1), 30-42.

Cabinet Office (2001) *Public Bodies 2001*, London: Cabinet Office.

CAWP (Centre for the Advancement of Women in Politics) (2006) www.qub.ac.uk/cawp (accessed 20 March 2006).

Chaney, P. (2006) 'Critical mass, deliberation and the substantive representation of women: evidence from the UK's devolution programme', *Political Studies* 54(4), 691-714.

Childs, S. (2001) 'In their own words: New Labour women MPs and the substantive representation of women', *British Journal of Politics and International Relations* 3(1), 175-90.

Childs, S. (2002a) 'Hitting the target: are women Labour MPs "acting for" women?', *Parliamentary Affairs* 55(1), 143-53.

Childs, S. (2002b) 'Concept of representation and the passage of the sex discrimination (Election Candidates) Bill', *Journal of Legislative Studies* 1(8), 90-108.

Childs, S. (2004) 'A feminised style of politics? Women MPs in the House of Commons', *British Journal of Politics and International Relations* 6(1), 3–19.

Childs, S. and J. Withey (2004) 'Women representatives acting for women: sex and the signing of Early Day Motions in the 1997 British Parliament', *Political Studies* 52(3), 552–64.

Chittenden, M. and Grice, A. (1991) 'Gentleman Tony calls women first to complete Cabinet team', *The Sunday Times*, 4 May.

Coote, A. (1999) 'It's lads on top sat Number Ten', *Guardian*, 11 May.

Coote, A. (ed) (2000) *New Gender Agenda*, London: IPPR.

DCLG (Department for Communities and Local Government) (2006) www.dclg.gov.uk (accessed 31 May 2006).

Drucker, H.M. (1979) *Doctrine and Ethos in the Labour Party*, London: Allen and Unwin.

Fawcett Society (2005) *Women's Representation in British Politics 2005*, www.fawcettsociety.org.uk (accessed 20 March 2006).

Feld, V. (2001) 'A new start in Wales: how devolution is making a difference', in A. Coote (ed) *New Gender Agenda: Why Women Still Want More?*, London: IPPR.

Flinders, M. (2002) 'Governance in Whitehall', *Public Administration* 80(1), 51–75.

Forrest, R. and Kearns, A. (1999) *Joined up Places? Social Cohesion and Neighbourhood Regeneration*, York: Joseph Rowntree Foundation.

Gains, F. (1999) 'Implementing privatisation policies in Next Steps agencies', *Public Administration* 77(4), 713–30.

Giddy, P. (2000) 'First thoughts: on attracting women into local politics – a woman's place is in the chamber', *Local Government Association*, www.lga.gov.uk (accessed 31 May 2006).

Greater London Authority (2006) www.london.gov.uk (accessed 13 July)

Happold, T. and Katz, L. (2003) 'Hewitt: extend positive action to councils', *Guardian*, 12 March.

Harman, H. (1998) Women (Government priorities) Debate, *Hansard*, 27 February 1998, Column, 608, www.parliament,gov.uk (accessed 24 July 2006).

Harman, H. (2004) 'Why the lobby needs women', *Independent*, 27 September.

Hill, A. and Hinscliff. G. (2000) 'On message with a mission', *The Observer*, 25 June.

Himmelweit, S. (2005) 'Making policy-makers more gender aware: experiences and reflections from the Women's Budget Group in the UK', *Journal of Politics and Policy* 27(12), 109–21.

Lovenduski, J. and Randall, V. (1993) *Contemporary Feminist Politics: Women and Power in Britain*, Oxford: Oxford University Press.

Lowndes, V. (2004) 'Getting on or getting by? Women, social capital and political participation', *British Journal of Politics and International Relations* 6(1), 45–65.

Mackay, F. (2002) 'Women in the Scottish Parliament: making a difference?', *Towards Equality*, London: Fawcett Society.

Massey, A. (1995) 'Ministers, the agency model and policy ownership', *Public Policy and Administration* 10(2), 71–87.

Mazur, A. (2003) *Theorising Feminist Policy*, Oxford: Oxford University Press.

McRae, S. (1996) *Women at the Top: Progress after Five Years*, London: Hansard.

Norris, P., Lovenduski, J. and Campbell, R. (2004) *Gender and Political Participation*, research report London: Electoral Commission, available at www.electoralcommission.org.uk.

Pimlott, B. and Rao, N. (2002) *Governing London*, Oxford: Oxford University Press.

Rao, N. (2005) 'The representation of women in local politics', *Policy & Politics* 33(2), 323–40.

Richards, D. and Smith, M.J. (2004) 'Interpreting the world of political elites', *Public Administration* 82(4), 777–800.

Ross, K. (2000) *Women at the Top 2000: Cracking the Public Sector Glass Ceiling*, King-Hall Paper No. 9, London: Hansard Society.

Russell, M. (2005a) *Building New Labour: the Politics of Policy Organisation*, London: Palgrave.

Russell, M. (2005b) 'The House of Lords and reform: a view from the outside', in N. Baldwin (ed) *Parliament in the 21st Century*, London: Politico's.

Shephard, M. and Cairney, P. (2005) 'The impact of the Scottish Parliament in amending executive legislation', *Political Studies* 53(2), 303–19.

Sieghart, M. (2001) 'The magnificent seven', *The Times*, October 15.

Smith, M.J. (1999) *The Core Executive in Britain*, London: Macmillan.

Smith, M.J., Marsh, D. and Richards, D. (2000) 'Re-assessing the role of ministers', *Public Administration* 78(2), 305–26.

Squires, J. and Wickham-Jones, M. (2002) 'Mainstreaming in Westminster and Whitehall: From Labour's Ministry for Women to the Women and Equality Unit', *Parliamentary Affairs* 55(1), 57–70.

Squires, J. and Wickham-Jones, M. (2004) 'New Labour, gender mainstreaming and the Women and Equality Unit', *British Journal of Politics and International Relations* 6(1), 81–98.

Stephenson, M. (2001) 'Quality and equality on the council: renewing local democracy', in A. Coote (ed) *New Gender Agenda: Why Women Still Want More?*, London: IPPR.

Stoker, G., Gains, F., Harding A., John, P. and Rao, N. (2003a) *Implementing the 2000 Act with Respect to New Council Constitutions and the Ethical Framework: First Report and Executive Summary*, London: ODPM and www.elgnce.org.uk.

Stoker, G., John, P., Gains, F., Rao, N. and Harding, A. (2003b) *Diversity under New Council Constitutions*, London: ODPM and www.elgnce. org.uk

Thain, C. and Wright, M. (1995) *The Treasury and Whitehall: The Planning and Control of Public Expenditure 1976–1993*, Oxford: Clarendon Press.

Triesman, D. (2002) Letter to the Editor, *Guardian*, 31 October.

True, J. (2003) 'Mainstreaming gender in global public policy', *International Feminist Journal of Politics* 5(3), 368-96.

Veitch, J. (2005) 'Looking at gender mainstreaming in the UK Government', *International Feminist Journal of Politics* 7(4), 600-6.

Ward, L. (1998) 'Women given Whitehall voice', *Guardian*, 19 May.

Ward, L. (2001a) 'Learning from the 'Babe' experience: how the finest hour became a fiasco', in A. Coote (ed) *New Gender Agenda: Why Women Still Want More?*, London: IPPR.

Ward, L. (2001b) 'Women emerge to take on big spending ministries', *Guardian*, 9 June.

Ward, L. (2002) 'Will admission of failure condemn women to political wilderness?', *Guardian*, 25 October.

WBG (Women's Budget Group) (2006) http://wbg.org.uk (accessed 31 May 2006).

WEU (Women and Equality Unit) (2005) *Delivering on Gender Equality: A Progress Report*, London: DTI.

White, M. (1998) 'Quango members are still "chosen at the 19th hole"', *Guardian*, 19 February, 11.

Wolmar, C. (1997) 'Quangos to offer jobs for the girls', *Independent*, 14 June, 12.

Woolf, M. (2001) 'Baroness Jay's decision to quit raises doubt over women's unit', *Independent*, 17 February.

Part Three
Engendering policy?

Two steps forward, one step back: the gender dimensions of Treasury policy under New Labour

David Coates and Sarah Oettinger

Introduction

Governing in a society that is heavily gendered inevitably gives the policy process gender consequences, but it also makes those consequences very difficult to isolate. For gender relationships in a society such as the UK's are not simply ubiquitous. They are also immersed, and sub-subsumed into wider relationships of class, ethnicity, region and age; and they are themselves in flux. Policy initiatives therefore not only impact on a stable and isolated set of gender relations. They also impact on what is essentially a moving and often an obscured target. To assess the importance and centrality of those policy initiatives to a world so gendered, it is essential first briefly to establish the nature of those movements and the character of that immersion.

The New Labour government inherited an economy in which more and more women carried the double burden of paid and unpaid work.[1] They also inherited a society in which the vast majority of lone parent families were headed by women,[2] and one in which women – either married or living alone – were significantly 'under-pensioned' relative to men.[3] A greater percentage of women worked outside the home, and for pay, than ever before; but they did so, in the main, from within family structures in which the distribution of domestic roles still left them with the bulk of responsibility for child rearing and the care of the old.[4] The rules governing paid work in most privately owned businesses, the length of the male working day in those businesses, and even the structure of the school calendar in the UK of the 1990s – all remained largely insensitive to the cross-pressures they inevitably created for women attempting to mix unpaid work inside the home with paid work outside it; so obliging large numbers of those women to settle for low-paid and part-time employment of an inherently unsatisfactory kind.[5] These cross-pressures of home and work then fell unevenly on women of different class and ethnic backgrounds. Traditional work roles were most heavily entrenched in Asian ethnic communities. Poverty and job insecurity were greatest among working class women. Access to public health and education were easiest for women (and children) in the middle class, and so on.

In consequence, New Labour policy was bound to have a differential impact across the whole range of gender relationships in the UK, and was bound to do so whether that impact was consciously planned or not. Decisions on the character and scale of public spending on education and health inevitably touched the lives of all UK citizens, but impacted on the lives of women more directly than those of men. Decisions on welfare rights clearly shaped the lives of poor women more directly than that of rich ones; and decisions on taxation fell differently on women no less than on men, depending on the target group at which they were aimed. New Labour came into power with sets of general commitments on public spending that had such differential consequences, and they came into power with specific policy initiatives – and policy silences – that were equally gender significant. To assess the impact of macro-economic policy on gender relationships in the UK, therefore, we need to examine both the generality and specificity of what New Labour has done, and the generality and specificity of what it has not.

Big ambitions

The Treasury has been the key department of government in all of this, because of the role Gordon Brown and his ministerial team came to play in the design and over-sight of the entirety of New Labour's domestic policy. Initiatives from the front-line departments of health, social security, education and industry often held the headlines, but the Treasury was a major designing force behind all of them, and the Treasury team had a view and an agenda of its own. It had a view on how best to trigger economic growth: combining a 'third way' enthusiasm for human capital development with a strict set of 'golden rules' on public spending (Coates 2005, 36-41, 53-6, 63). It had an agenda on employment. It had an agenda on welfare to work. It had an agenda on poverty reduction; and it had an agenda on competitiveness and growth. Each one of these agendas, as it was developed and implemented over time, had significant gender consequences.

New Labour's Treasury team was sensitive to at least some of those consequences from the very outset of its period in office. Indeed, even earlier, Gordon Brown had linked the need for new thinking in the Party to changing gender roles in the workplace. In 1994, he told a widely reported London conference that the time for 'patriarchal and class-bound Conservatism, the New Right or even past Labour' was now over: not least because 'for the first time the majority of women are in the labour force, demanding an economic policy built around the needs of women' (Brown 1994). New Labour entered office sensitive to those needs, but also keen to see that the labour force grew, not least because, although it had ambitious plans for public spending, it lacked any equivalent enthusiasm for the taxation hikes that traditionally had paid for them. In macro-policy terms New Labour entered office determined to avoid its 'tax and spend' past, primarily by widening the tax base itself: lowering the overall economic inactivity rate by raiding (and reducing) the UK's major pools of reserve labour. It entered office determined to get the unemployed back to work. By its third term in office, it was equally determined to flush out those hiding from work on disability benefit; and between those two initiatives, it worked steadily to facilitate the return of more and more women of child-bearing age to paid employment. This was a government that always set itself performance targets. Less than four in 10 lone parents were in paid employment in 1997. The current target is to have seven in every 10 lone parents so employed by 2010; and to raise the overall employment rate for people of working age from 70% to 80%. (It is currently just under 75%.)

New Labour's initial macro-policy stance was focused more on the employment than the gender dimensions of this labour market transformation. Yet even in 1997 the Chancellor was sufficiently sensitive to traditional feminist concerns, and sufficiently aware of the gendered nature of the UK labour market, to give high initial priority to the creation and funding of a national system of childcare. As he told the House of Commons in his first budget speech: 'from this budget forwards, childcare will no longer be seen as an afterthought or a fringe element of social policies but from now on – as it should be – an integral part of our economic policy' (Brown 1997). That first budget planned for 50,000 young people eventually to train as childcare assistants, as part of its New Deal for the young unemployed. It also allowed families receiving family credit, housing benefit or council tax benefits to have the first £100 of their weekly childcare costs disregarded in the calculation of their in-work benefits; and that was just a beginning. Each subsequent budget and pre-budget statement built on that 'first step', and did so in a steady, incremental and consistent fashion.

In budget after budget, the aim of policy was consistent – 'to enable parents and carers to balance work and family responsibilities' (Brown 1998c). And the response was equally consistent: 'extra help for childcare' in the form of funds for childcare places and changes in the tax code to give the poor and low paid easier access to them. Indeed, over time the Treasury became ever more inventive of ways in which public spending and welfare institutions could ease the cross-pressures experienced by parents in the UK's increasingly ubiquitous two-income families. Tax relief on expenditure for childcare was just the beginning. Public funding of wrap-around schooling followed, as did the 2000 Work–Life Balance Challenge Fund and the later consultation document on *Work and Families, Choice and Flexibility* (DTI 2005). From that consultation exercise came a Treasury commitment to the financing of a fairer, and less gendered, balance at the point of birth itself: increasing the level and duration of maternity pay and the length of maternity leave – and introducing two weeks' paid paternity leave and 26 weeks' paid adoption leave (both at the same level as maternity pay) – this latter in spite of opposition to such policy from some UK business circles.

Nor, given the disproportionate way in which poverty impacts on women in the contemporary UK, should we forget that this Treasury team, from the very outset, was highly sensitive to the particular difficulties experienced by families on low incomes; and was prepared directly to address issues of low pay through the introduction of an NMW and the resetting of the tax code to guarantee an improved (and steadily rising) minimum family income. As Dawn Primarolo later put it for the entire Treasury team: 'to help parents move into paid employment, and help them progress at work, we need to make sure that there is appropriate support available. From the Government's point of view this involves two key areas of work: first, our childcare strategy, and second, financial support for parents' (Primarolo 2004). Twice during New Labour's first two terms, the Treasury totally reset the tax system in an attempt to lift low-paid full-time working families with children out of poverty. Gordon Brown did so first through a significant increase in child allowances and the introduction of a new WFTC, which from October 1999 guaranteed to any family in which at least one person was working full-time a minimum income of £180 a month and a freedom from income tax until that income reached £220 a month. Then in 2002, Gordon Brown extended the WFTC to take in childless couples on low pay, and announced plans to introduce a new unified child tax credit from April 2003, to be paid on top of universal child benefit, to integrate all means-tested income-related support for children into one payment: and as such into a 'single, seamless system of income-related support for families with children'. Significantly for our concerns here, the Chancellor told the House of Commons in 2002 that all this support was 'to be paid to the main carer – normally the mother' (Brown 2002a).

As is also well known, New Labour came into power committed to the outgoing Conservative government's modest ceilings on public sector spending. It initially had things to prove – to the City in particular – about its financial prudence and its capacity to govern, which outweighed any pressure it felt to redistribute resources to the poor and the needy. But it is now clear that Gordon Brown and his ministerial team found those ceilings as irksome as did sections of the electorate who supported them, such that – as quickly as its commitment allowed – New Labour moved systematically to increase the percentage of Gross Domestic Product (GDP) going into health care and into education. Those increases in welfare provision touched the lives of everyone – men and women, young and old – but insofar as women still carried the bulk of private responsibility for caring roles within the family, this expansion of public provision in these key areas of social reproduction clearly impacted more directly on their lives than on those of their male partners. Over the first two terms of New Labour's period in power, the Treasury increased public spending on the health service at an average of 6.5% per year, and that on education at 5.2%. Through that period too, through its targeted help to those over 65 surviving on particularly small state pensions, the Treasury lifted 1.8 million people over the poverty line. Of those 1.8 million, an estimated 75% were women (Churchill and Mitchell 2005, 19).

Treasury Ministers also became increasingly aware over time of the tenacity of a set of glass ceiling issues, and directed at least a small part of their policy stance towards their diminution. Ministers were aware from the outset that a gender pay gap remained firmly in place, and, did eventually put the weight of public policy behind the Prosser recommendations for its removal.[6] Likewise, in relation to the small business sector and business start-ups, the Treasury eventually added a deliberate gender dimension to the relevant problem specification, policy paradigm and performance indicators. In characteristic New Labour fashion, the Treasury first issued a review of government services for small businesses (2002) and then set targets for an increase in the number of those businesses owned and led by women. The current target is a 2% increase (to 14%) by 2006, charged to the Small Business Service of the DTI, which now contains a cross-government women's policy enterprise group with its own 'strategic framework' geared to improving the business support environment for women. New Labour, that is, brought to the 'glass ceiling' question in the business sector its usual policy mix of solid research, small civil service-based task forces, formalised plans and targets, and tiny amounts of money for pilot projects.

Modest ambitions

The Treasury under Gordon Brown recognised the gender consequences of its policy initiatives, and sought means of eroding gender inequalities, in ways that previous Conservative administrations had not. It designed macro-economic policy in ways that were sensitive to the changing gender divisions in the new economy, and to the disproportionate burden of poverty carried by women at the bottom of the society whose economy it was managing. All that was to its credit; but there has been a debit side too. Policy here has actually been two-faced, because that same macro-economic policy has also been designed on the premise that the main route out of poverty, for the bulk and generality of those trapped within it, lies through entry into paid work. Since 1997 the UK has been led by a gender sensitive government. It has also been led by one heavily infused with a workerist ethic: one whose overall economic strategy has in practice required a generalised intensification of work processes – an intensification in direct tension with its professed commitment to the easing of the work–life balance (Coates 2005, 161-213). In any weighing of New Labour's performance, both sides of the ledger have to be read; when they are, in this area as in so many others, the positive scores are higher for aspiration than for performance.

This ongoing tension in Treasury policy between gender sensitivity and what we are terming here 'workerism' was clear even in Gordon Brown's first budget speech, when he launched a theme to which he would return on many subsequent occasions: the theme of lone parents and paid work. Amid a torrent of other early initiatives – so many in fact that this one went by initially largely unnoticed – New Labour's new Chancellor said that 'under the programme I am announcing today, when the youngest child is in the second term of full time schooling, lone parents will be invited for job search interviews and offered help in finding work that suits their circumstances'. A budget of £200 million was in fact set aside for that purpose alone (Brown 1997). It was and remains the Brown view that 'helping lone parents into work is the most effective long-term method of tackling family poverty' (Brown

1998a, 1); and that 'because women have suffered most from injustice in employment opportunities', the progressive thing to do is to push 'forward with a new programme of 'choices' for lone parents – to push up employment rates from just over 45% when we came to power to 70%, underpinned by a National Childcare Strategy' (Brown 2002b). Which is presumably why Harriet Harman, as New Labour's first Social Security Secretary, found herself under such pressure to cut the benefit to lone parents and to implement these 'job search invitations' in the winter of 1997/98, cuts that caused an early if rare rebellion among backbench Labour MPs.

The resulting political fall-out from the Harman affair clearly persuaded New Labour Ministers thereafter to turn this particular screw more slowly and in a less public way: but they did turn it nonetheless – and on a regular basis. In the 1998 budget, for example, the 'quarter-of-a-million women, who [were] partners of unemployed men' suddenly found themselves 'offer[ed] expert and personalised help to find work', 'expert help' that would also 'now be available on a national basis for all lone parents who want to work and whose children are at school'. That was also the budget after which 'partners of the unemployed under 25 without children, who [were] not allowed to register as unemployed, [would] now be given exactly the same opportunities for training and work that others under 25 now enjoy' (Brown 1998b). The experts and the invitations then came with progressively stronger incentives for compliance as budget followed budget. Lone parents with children over the age of five were 'invited' to work focused interviews (WFI) in 2000. A year later the invitation became a requirement; and currently (2006) the Chancellor is proposing to 'help lone parents back to work' by piloting 'personal action plans starting with compulsory interviews and an intensive work plan' (Brown 2005b): all this in pursuit of the already mentioned self-imposed target of 70% lone parent employment by 2010.

This has also been a Labour government willing to adopt only the most parsimonious interpretation of European labour law, even where that law favoured the rights of women workers. The years after 1997 have witnessed a generalised failure by New Labour Ministers to do more than marginally strengthen worker rights after the Thatcher onslaught upon them, or to reinforce the collective power of the main labour movement institutions capable of pushing for better conditions for women workers – namely trades unions. For all its years in office, the New Labour government has yet to reset the bargaining power of capital and labour even back to the unequal partnership of the 1970s, and has missed a golden opportunity directly to strengthen institutions of gender equality. Only very recently have Ministers even begun to introduce targets relating to gender issues in the PSAs that the Treasury negotiates across the public sector; and only now has the government legislated for a new 'gender duty' that will oblige public authorities from April 2007 to promote equality of opportunity across the sexes (Women and Work Commission 2006, 100). More normally, the Treasury under New Labour has pursued competitiveness, productivity and investment across the public sector through Private Finance Initiative (PFI) agreements whose terms have not included an explicit gender dimension. Data on the consequences of the PFI on gender inequalities in UK labour markets is not systematically available to us, but the anecdotal evidence seems clear enough: such schemes seem invariably to intensify the work process and erode the working conditions, rights and remuneration of the workers caught up in them – many of whom are women, and often poorly paid women at that.

In consequence, so far at least, there has been a near complete failure on income redistribution. Poverty has been eased at the bottom of the society, but income inequality has continued to grow because of the absence of any public constraints on salary growth at the top. That policy silence has helped the tiny number of female CEOs, but has done nothing to dent the persistent inequality of earnings between social classes in the UK, or between the genders. The poverty initiatives themselves have suffered from their stealth-like and complex nature, with their impact lessened by the resulting shortfall in take-up; and even the targeted help to poor pensioners – which has impacted positively on women among the aged poor – still leaves untouched the general vulnerability of women to poverty in old age: a vulnerability rooted in the systematic underpayment of women through the bulk of their working lives (see Chapter Nine). It is significant in this regard that the Brown Treasury – keen as it is on the targeting of programmes to specific groups of the poor – initially set its face firmly against the Turner Commission's solution to that general vulnerability: namely a generalised rise in the state pension for everyone, with the rate of pension increase tied to the growth rate of average earnings (Pensions Commission 2005). Gordon Brown and his Ministers relented eventually, agreeing to such a linkage from 2012; even giving their support to the extension of full state pensions to more than a quarter of a million women hitherto denied them because of career breaks linked to childcare. Yet for all New Labour's targeted help to the poorest pensioners, in a pension population two thirds of whom are women and half of whom are single, female single pensioners remain 'one of the poorest groups of the older population' with a median personal income that is 'only 56% of older men's' (Churchill and Mitchell 2005, 18-19). New Labour may be gender sensitive, but try telling that to the aged female poor.

Nor has gender discrimination in pay been significantly reduced by Treasury policy thus far (see Chapter Seven). While New Labour has been in office the gender pay gap for full-time workers had changed slightly. It stood at 20.6% in 1998, narrowed to 19.83% in 2000, remained almost unchanged until 2002, and then fell to 16.85% in 2005.[7] But lest that be thought of as a sign of any early removal of the gap itself, recent data also suggests that the pay gap for part-time work – and 44% of women remain locked in part-time employment – made no such change. It remains stubbornly entrenched at around 40%. The Prosser Commission found that, even for women working full time, the rate of change in the diminution of the gender pay gap 'has slowed in recent years' (Women and Work Commission 2005, 4). The Institute for Fiscal Studies (IFS) recently reported that the decision to have children continues to have a significant impact on the earning power of women relative to men over their working life as a whole. According to the IFS, for women working full time, hourly wage rates averaged 94% of those of men before childbirth, but only 74% when rearing children and 79% after the children had left home[8] (IFS 2006). Policy initiatives on the NMW helped here slightly. Its introduction in 1999 affected low-paid workers, two thirds of whom were women; but even then 'it only narrowed the gender pay gap by a little under one percent' (Metcalf 2003, 181). Treasury policy under New Labour is clearly helping to stop the gender pay gap widening; but policy has yet to be devised that can meet the Chancellor's commitment to end it for all time.

Employment patterns have also been affected, at the margin, by policy from this same source. Certainly job tenure for women having children has been strengthened under New Labour: both by the new set of maternity rights and by tax changes designed to facilitate access to childcare (see Chapter Eight). 'The percentage of women with young children and job tenure of more than five years rose from around 30% in 1990 to 39% in 2002' (Robinson 2003, 237), demonstrating an increasingly ability of women to combine work and home responsibilities. By 2005, indeed, the employed labour force in the UK, at 28.7 million, was two million larger than ever before, with just under 75% of the population of working age participating in some form of paid employment. Within those totals, as the Department for Work and Pensions (DWP) recently proudly proclaimed, 'the number of women in work has risen by one million since 1997. There are more women in work than ever before, and at 70% the UK has one of the highest female employment rates in the world' (DWP 2006, 25). A total of 12,446,000 women between 16 and 64 were engaged in paid labour in the UK in 2004: seven million of them working full time, the rest working part time or (in the case of a tiny minority) being self-employed. And among their number were lone parents, the percentage of whom combining childcare and paid work in 2005 stood at 54%. Only 42% of lone parents had been in paid work a decade before.

Activity rates among women (although not among men) are therefore

Table 6.1: Employment, unemployment and activity rates in Britain, 1996–2004 (thousands)

			Women				Men	
	1996*		2004		1996		2004	
	thousands	%		%		%		%
In employment	11,105	67	12,446	67	13,998	77	14,318	79
ILO unemployed	719	6.5**	561	4	1,418	9.2	752	5
Economically active	11,824		13,007	70	15,416		15,070	83

Notes: * Autumn 1996; **percentage of the economically active
Source: Employment Policy Institute 1998b, 3; EOC 2005a, 8

Table 6.2: Full-time and part-time employment: employees and self-employed aged 16 and over, 1997–2004 (thousands)

			Women				Men	
	1997*		2004		1996		2004	
	thousands	%		%		%		%
Full time	6,013	56	6,966	56	11,083	92	12,998	89
Part time	4,748	44	5,449	44	930	8	1,536	11
All employees and self-employed	11,618	100	12,539	100	14,411	100	14,543	100

Note: *Autumn 1997
Sources: Employment Policy Institute 1998a, 8; EOC 2005a, 8

rising – that much of Gordon Brown's underlying strategy is clearly bearing fruit – but that rise has been accompanied by significant shortfalls on related policy objectives elsewhere. There is extensive evidence, for example, of continuing problems with the cost and supply of high-quality childcare,[9] and of entrenched discrimination by UK-based employers against women of child-bearing age. The latest EOC data suggests some 93,000 women annually suffering financial loss or dismissal in the UK because of pregnancy (Hogarth and Elias 2005, iii). It is also clear that policy on improving the work–life balance for women (and indeed men) in families with children remains at best embryonic in design and effect, in spite of the emerging research evidence of a strong desire for an improvement in that balance in well over a third of the UK workforce (Fagan 2001). At best, after nearly a decade of New Labour in power, only one full-time worker in five in the UK enjoys even vestigial access to a flexible working week. The UK remains the only nation within the EU to allow its workers to exceed the 48 hours per week working hours limit set by the European Working Time Directive; and since 1998 'the number working more than forty-eight hours has doubled … from 10% to 26%' (Bunting 2004, 9). With positive implications for increasing gender equality but with negative implications for the quality of family life, the number of women working more than 48 hours a week has grown by 52% since 1992 (Bunting 2004, 9). The dichotomy between the need for more money to sustain family life and the need for time to enjoy that family life is striking in the statistics. In 1988, only 19% of mothers worked over 40 hours a week. A decade later that figure had risen to 33%; and by then a greater proportion of fathers than men without children were working more than 50 hours a week, week after week after week (Harkness 1999, 104). Little wonder then that Health and Safety Executive figures for 2002/03 suggest 557,000 people in the UK suffering from work-related stress and anxiety, at the cost of 12.8 million lost working days (EOC 2005c, 7): in an economy where macro-economic policy seems better designed to spread the growing burden of work more evenly between the genders than to reduce that burden on men and women alike.

Time to try again?

When Colette Fagan examined the relationship between the highly gendered sphere of work organisation and people's preferences on hours and timing of work, she found a considerable gap. People working long hours wanted to work fewer hours. People working part time (mainly women) wanted to work longer. She also found that 'recent reforms in family policy and working-time regulations [had] made only modest steps towards redressing this imbalance' (Fagan 2001, 260). And what she found about the impact of policy, the Prosser Commission found also: in its case, that there remain embedded gender inequalities in pay – gender inequalities that are still among the highest in Western Europe[10] – gender inequalities that have been moderated at the margin by enlightened policies since 1997, but inequalities that remain intact because those policies have proved insufficiently powerful to their task. Similar findings are to be found too in other recent reports on, among other things, gender discrimination through pregnancy and part-time working, and differential gender vulnerability to poverty in old age.[11]

All this suggests at least two possible further lines of inquiry: one optimistic, one rather less. The first is concerned with the adequacy of the policies so far pursued under Treasury leadership in a government led by Tony Blair but steered by Gordon Brown, and with the possibility that a change of leadership in that government might bring with it stronger policies. The second is concerned with the extent to which any such policy shift would be possible without a complete recasting of the growth model underpinning the Blair/Brown economic strategy as a whole. In relation to the first, the material now exists for policy redesign: recent months have seen a veritable explosion of proposals rooted in serious and extensive scholarship and research.[12] But strategic resetting is quite another thing. In its macro-economic policy, the New Labour government has thus far scored high on its intentions in relation to gender inequality. It has even scored moderately in relation to delivery and effect. But in the UK economy as a whole, full-time hours of work remain excessive; incomes remain unequal; skills remain under-developed and productivity is unimpressive. Entrenched inequalities of that scale rarely vanish in the face of incremental change. They have not yet in the gendered world of paid and unpaid work under New Labour; and they will not until policy-makers address their place in this wider scheme of things. For all Gordon Brown's fine words, a long-hours, low-investment economy is not the best environment for a gender revolution at home and work; and because it is not, if New Labour Ministers really want to trigger that gender revolution, they also need to find, and to find as a matter of urgency, a macro-economic policy strong enough fundamentally to change that environment.

Notes

[1] 46% of the labour market is now female, and that includes 67% of all women aged between 16 and 64. 44% of women in the labour market have part-time jobs. The equivalent figure for men is 10% (EOC 2005a, 8). For the data on the double-burden, see note 4.

[2] 'In 1998 25% of all families with dependent children were headed by a lone parent, over 90% of whom were women.' (EOC 2001, 3).

[3] For the data on this, see the Pensions Policy Institute Report (2003), and Chapter 8 of *Pensions: Challenges and Choices*, the first report of the Pensions Commission chaired by Adair Turner (Pensions Commission 2004).

[4] The most recent comprehensive data on the persisting (but changing) gender division of labour within the child-rearing home is available in EOC 2005b. The Women and Work Commission Report, Shaping a Fairer Future, also reports that 'women are ... most likely to care for elderly or disabled relatives and friends ... a quarter of all women aged 50 -59 provide unpaid care, compared to about one in six men' (2006, 28).

[5] On the under-utilisation of skills by as many as 5.6 million part-time workers in the UK, see EOC 2005c.

[6] '... because women's rights and women's equality have been unacceptably neglected for far too long, we are even now studying recommendations from Margaret Prosser, chair of the Women and Work Commission. Our aim: to move to ending once and for all the gender pay gap' (Brown 2005a). The Woman and Work Commission's report, initially delayed, was eventually published in February 2006; and drew from Gordon Brown – in his 2006 Budget Statement, a commitment to follow its recommendations, and to address what he then termed 'the unacceptable discrimination in women's pay'.

[7] But not apparently for women in executive positions, where the EOC continues to report a 27% gap in average earnings between men and women (*The Observer*, 4 June 2006, 18).

[8] At existing levels of gender inequality in pay, a low-skilled mother of two can still expect to earn £250,000 less than she would if she had remained childless over the course of a working lifetime (Women and Work Commission 2005, 29), with serious consequences for, among other things, the strength of her claim on a pension later. In fact, because of this impaired access to a strong full-time wage over the course of their working lifetime, currently 'only 16% of recently retired women

have an entitlement to a full basic state pension on the basis of their own contributions' (EOC 2005c, 6).

[9] The Daycare Charity Trust reported in February 2006 that childcare bills had risen by 27% since 2001, and drew attention to the gaps in affordable provision experienced by families on low incomes and by parents wishing to train rather than work.

[10] 'When both part-time workers and full-time workers are included, the UK has the largest gender pay-gap in the EU. When only full-time workers are considered, the UK ranks 12th out of 15 countries' (this, in the pre-expansion EU, from Walby and Olsen 2002).

[11] On the pregnancy job barrier, see the report by the Recruitment Employment Federation, reported in the *Guardian*, 25 November 2005; on the under-utilisation of women part-time workers, see EOC (2005c); on the one in five single women pensioners still at risk of poverty in old age, see the EOC Women's Pension Network data, February 2006.

[12] Not least Walby and Olsen 2002; and Women and Work Commission 2005, 2006.

References

Brown, G. (1994) 'New policies for the global economy', speech to the Annual Conference.

Brown, G. (1997) speech to the House of Commons, 12 July.

Brown, G. (1998a) *Putting Fairness into Practice*, London: Tribune.

Brown, G. (1998b) speech to the House of Commons, 17 March.

Brown, G. (1998c) speech to the House of Commons, 3 November.

Brown, G. (2002a) speech to the House of Commons, 18 April.

Brown, G (2002b) *The Social Priorities of Labour's Second Term*, London: Bevan Society.

Brown, G. (2005a) speech to the Trades Union Congress, 14 September.

Brown, G. (2005b) speech to the House of Commons, 5 December.

Bunting, M. (2004) *Willing Slaves*, London: Harper Perennial.

Coates, D. (2005) *Prolonged Labour: The Slow Birth of New Labour Britain*, Houndsmill: Palgrave.

Churchill, N. and Mitchell, M. (2005) *Labour's Pension Challenge*, London, Catalyst.

DTI (Department of Trade and Industry) (2005) *Work and Families: Choice and Flexibility: Government Response to Public Consultation*, October, London: DTI.

DWP (Department for Work and Pensions) (2006) *Five Year Strategy*, London: DWP.

Employment Policy Institute (1998a) *Employment Audit* 7, Spring, 8.

Employment Policy Institute (1998b) *Employment Audit* 9, Autumn, 3.

EOC (Equal Opportunities Commission) (2001) *Women and Men in Britain: The lifecycle of inequality*, London: EOC.

EOC (2005a) *Facts about Men and Women in Britain*, London: EOC, 8.

EOC (2005b) *Time Use and Childcare*, London: EOC.

EOC (2005c) *Britain's Hidden Brain Drain*, London: EOC.

Fagan, C. (2001) 'Time, money and the gender order: work orientations and working-time preferences in Britain', *Gender, Work and Organization* 8(3), July, 260.

Harkness, S. (1999) 'Working 9 to 5?', in P. Gregg and J. Wadsworth *The State of Working Britain*, Manchester: Manchester University Press.

Hogarth, T. and Elias, P. (2005) *Pregnancy Discrimination at Work: Modelling the Costs*, London: EOC.

IFS (Institute for Fiscal Studies) (2006) 'Newborns and new schools: critical times in women's employment', cited in P. Barkham, 'Stuck on the 'mummy track' – why having a baby means lower pay and prospects', *Guardian*, 20 January.

Metcalf, D. (2003) 'Trade unions', in R. Dickens, P. Gregg and J. Wadsworth *The Labour Market under New Labour: The State of Working Britain*, Houndsmill: Palgrave.

Pensions Commission (2004) *Pensions: Challenges and Choices: The First Report of the Pensions Commission*, London: The Stationery Office.

Pensions Commission (2005) *A New Pension Settlement for the Twenty-First Century: The Second Report of the Pensions Commission*, London: The Stationery Office.

Pensions Policy Institute (2003) *The Under-Pensioned: Women*, London, Pensions Policy Institute.

Primarolo, D. (2004) Speech to a conference on childcare, Worklife and Employers: Achieving the Work–Life Balancing Act, 26 October.

Robinson, H. (2003) 'Gender and labour market performance in the recovery', in R. Dickens, P. Gregg and J. Wadsworth *The Labour Market under New Labour: The State of Working Britain*, Houndsmill: Palgrave.

Walby, S. and Olsen, W. (2002) *The Impact of Women's Position in the Labour Market on Pay and Implications for UK Productivity*, London: WEU.

Women and Work Commission (2005) *A Fair Deal for Women in the Workplace: An Interim Statement*, London: The Stationery Office.

Women and Work Commission (2006) *Shaping a Fairer Future*, London: The Stationery Office.

SEVEN

New Labour policy and the gender pay gap

Damian Grimshaw

Introduction

This chapter explores the effects of labour market policy under the New Labour government on women's pay. Long-run trends towards a closing of the gender pay gap in the UK have stagnated in recent years and this has provoked considerable debate about the role of labour market policy interventions to improve women's earnings position. As argued elsewhere in this book, the appointment of a Women's Minister, the establishment of the WU (renamed as the WEU), the campaigning role of the WBG and an apparent concern within New Labour to appeal to women voters have led some observers to proclaim a feminisation of the policy platform. In this new 'gender sensitive' environment, this chapter explores a range of policy interventions that have directly or indirectly shaped women's pay. Certain policy changes have been presented by government as beneficial – namely, the NMW, strengthened employment protection for part-time workers, extended maternity leave provision, Working Tax Credits, gender pay reviews in the public and private sector and new harmonised systems of pay setting for public sector workers. But in practice, the government's policy interventions have only made a small contribution to closing the gender pay gap, and the marginal improvement in the relative position of low-paid women workers has been far less than anticipated.

The chapter begins with a brief review of empirical trends in women's relative pay. Against a backdrop of limited improvement in gender pay equality, we then analyse the government's response along three dimensions: the role of the WEU and special review bodies; specific labour market policy (both direct, such as the new gender duty in local government, and indirect, such as the NMW); and changes in public sector pay.

Trends in the gender pay gap

Analysis of earnings data over the last 20 years provides an essential backdrop to the question of how effective the New Labour government has been in closing the gender pay gap. Since the early 1980s, the UK has witnessed a narrowing of the gender pay gap among employees. Taking the average hourly pay of women in full-time *and* part-time work and comparing this to men's average full-time hourly earnings, women's relative pay increased from 66% in 1984 to 73% in 2003. And the new source of earnings data (Annual Survey of Hours and Earnings (ASHE) ONS 2006b) shows a trend increase from 74% in 1997 to 77% in 2005. Progress has clearly been slow. And, as Figure 7.1 demonstrates, it has not been at a steady pace. Between 1984 and 1987 there was very little change in the gender pay ratio. The next

Figure 7.1: The gender pay ratio, 1984–2005

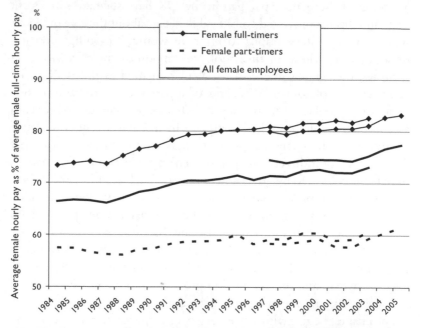

Note: The methodology for collecting earnings data changed in 2003. Data for 1984–2003 are from the New Earnings Survey and data for 1997–2005 are from the ASHE (which has been projected backwards to 1997). For both, the figures refer to average gross hourly earnings for female employees (full time, part time) as a share of average gross hourly earnings of male full-time employees. Earnings include overtime and cover employees on adult rates whose pay for the survey period was not affected by absence. For the 1984–2003 trend line, average pay for all female employees is calculated using employment data for female full-timers and part-timers from the Labour Force Survey data (because of inaccuracies in the New Earnings Survey coverage of female part-timers).

Source: ONS 2006a, 2006b, various years

eight years was a period of relatively significant progress, with close to one percentage point shaved off the pay gap in some years, raising women's pay from 66% of men's to 71%. But during 1995 to 2002 this trend halted: instead, the gender pay ratio fluctuated, with a widening of the gap recorded in 1997, 1998, 2001 and 2002. On average, the pay gap closed by a little more than a tenth of a percentage point per year during this period, arriving at just 72% by 2002. Thus, the election of New Labour in 1997 was not a catalyst for rapid improvements in women's pay; more damning, women's gains were far more substantial under the Conservatives during the 1987-95 period. Fortunately, there is evidence of progress during the latter period, 2002-05; the new source of earnings data points to significant gains in women's relative pay during these three years, from 74% to 77%, narrowing the gap with men by an average of one percentage point per year.

A further discomforting piece of empirical evidence for the New Labour government is the poor position of the UK with respect to its European partners. The two main sources of harmonised earnings data – the European Community Household Panel and the European Structure of Earnings Survey – both rank the UK bottom among member states surveyed (see Figure 7.2).

Use of headline average indicators in a country like Britain marked by high levels of fragmentation and inequality can only be a starting point in an analysis of women's pay. As such, the average gender pay ratio is a very crude indicator of the inequality in women's and men's pay.

Figure 7.2: The gender pay ratio in 15 EU member states

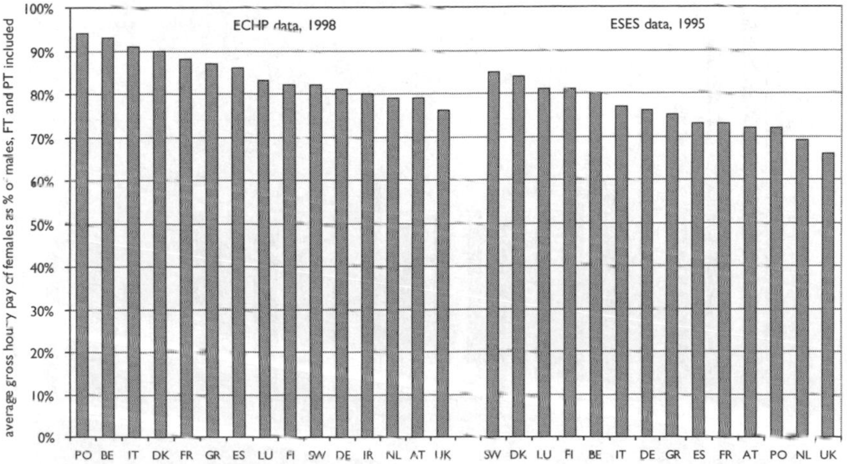

Source: Eurostat 2006a, 2006b

One important line of segmentation concerns the fortunes of women in full-time and part-time employment. Figure 7.1 above shows that improvements in gender equality have not been equally shared. Over the 20-year period, whereas women in full-time jobs closed the pay gap by 10 percentage points (73% to 83%), women in part-time jobs benefited from a trivial four-point improvement (58% to 62%). The widening division is shown in Figure 7.3. This compares the average pay of female part-timers to average female full-time pay. Again, the year 1997, or subsequent years (allowing for a policy lag effect), does not stand out as a significant point in altering this pattern.

Another crucial line of segmentation involves the overall dispersion of the pay structure. One of the important questions addressed in many studies during the 1990s and 2000s is how women's pay has fared in a context of a rapid increase in wage inequality (Harkness 1996). It is well known that the gulf between the lowest paid and highest paid widened considerably during the 1980s and 1990s. Hourly pay for the highest decile group of employees was around three times the pay of the lowest decile in 1985 (2.88), but this widened to a multiple of close to four (3.75) by 2003 (New Earnings Survey data).[1] This widening gap says nothing, of course, about the even greater increase in inequality of total income in the UK, including income from interest, rent and profit, as well as from wages (Atkinson 1998). It is

Figure 7.3: Relative average hourly pay of female part-timers compared to female full-timers

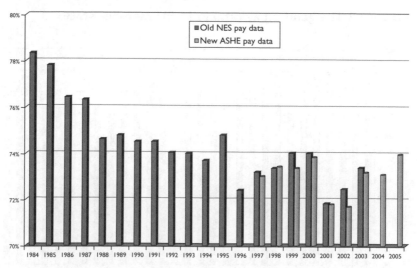

Note: see notes to Figure 7.1 for details on pay data.
Source: ONS 2006a, 2006b

less well known that wage inequality has followed a different path for men and women from 1997 to 2005 – relatively stable for women, but continuing to widen for men (ASHE data). For women in full-time employment, the highest paid 10% earned between 3.45 and 3.50 of the hourly pay of the lowest paid 10% throughout the period, and for women in part-time employment the ratio fluctuated between 2.97 and 3.11 with no clear trend direction. By contrast, male full-timers experienced a clear widening of the inter-decile pay ratio from 3.72 to a multiple of nearly 4 (3.95).

The highly differentiated wage structure imposes a severe penalty on those workers at the bottom and the vast bulk of these low-wage workers are women. Adopting the widely accepted Organisation for Economic Co-operation and Development (OECD) definition of low pay (two thirds of median earnings for all full-time employees) means that in 2005 more than half of all female part-timers in the UK were low paid and more than one in four female full-timers (compared to around one in seven male full-timers).

Figure 7.4 shows the position of lowest decile pay and median pay compared to the low-wage threshold (at 1.00 on the vertical axis) for women and men, distinguishing between full-time and part-time work for women. Lowest decile pay for female employees in both part-

Figure 7.4: Lowest decile and median pay relative to the OECD low-wage threshold for female part-timers, female full-timers and male full-timers

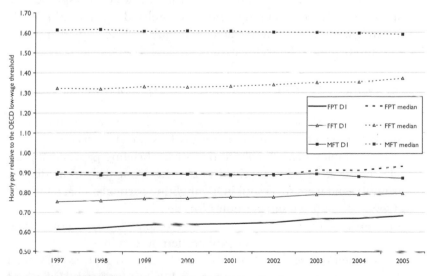

Source: ONS 2006b (gross hourly pay including overtime)

time and full-time employment actually improved during the period shown, whereas for men there was a slight decline. Thus, levelling down of men's pay at the bottom of the wage structure contributed to the narrowing of the gender pay gap from 2003 to 2005. A second observation is that median pay for female part-timers (the point below which half of all female part-timers are paid) is very similar throughout the period to the level of pay for the lowest decile of male full-time employees, and both fall below the low-wage threshold. And thirdly, the very low relative pay at the lowest decile for female part-time workers deserves emphasising. Throughout the entire period, this group of female workers (numbering some 500,000 women) earned at most two thirds of the OECD low-wage threshold for the UK. In 2005, this translated as an hourly rate of £4.91 compared to a low-wage threshold of £7.19.

The New Labour government response

The poor performance of the UK government in addressing the problem of gender pay inequality has been the focus of concern among many bodies, including the EOC, the Fawcett Society and the government's WEU (within the DTI, formerly the Cabinet Office WU). Moreover, the European Council of Ministers in its recommendations relating to member states' National Action Plans for Employment has repeatedly singled out the UK to take action to meet the target of 'a substantial reduction in the gender pay gap'.[2]

So what has the New Labour government done in response? We divide our attention among three inter-related agendas: the WEU, research and special reviews; direct and indirect labour market policy and improving public sector pay.

The Women's Equality Unit, research and special reviews

Since its establishment, the WEU has been an important instrument for the government to commission a series of research reports on women's pay and employment. Thanks to the WEU's briefing papers and press releases, several studies received public attention (in the media, for example) and were successful in highlighting particular characteristics of women's employment position. Notable examples include: the report on 'women's incomes over the lifetime' (Rake 2000), demonstrating the 'gender gap' and 'mother gap' of lifetime earnings between men and women differentiated by low-, medium- and high-skill levels; a study on the impact of the pay gap on UK productivity (Walby and

Olsen 2002) that highlighted the gendered nature of skills deficits and labour market failures affecting the UK's poor productivity record; an analysis of the UK pay gap as part of a six-country study, focusing on the obstacles among target groups of teaching associates, food processing workers and engineering professionals (Metcalfe and Korou 2003); and a detailed study of the 'part-time pay penalty' experienced by women workers (Manning and Petrongolo 2004), calling for policy measures to ease women's transitions from full-time to part-time work without downgrading status. Other WEU activities include the annual 'gender briefings' providing statistical information on women's position in the labour market and individual incomes, consultations on improving equal value tribunals and dissemination of equal pay questionnaires to help potential equal pay complainants.

The extent to which the findings and policy recommendations of the WEU's research find their way onto Ministers' desks is unclear (see Chapter Five). However, one might anticipate a relatively strong connection between special reviews of the pay gap commissioned by the government and government policy action. Remarkably, the New Labour government has funded three separate reviews on the causes of the gender pay gap and policy recommendations in a space of just four years, 2000-04 – illustrative, it would seem, of the Labour government's preference for review over policy action when faced with challenges to its record.

The first review was undertaken in 2000/01 by the 'Equal Pay Task-Force' and coordinated by the EOC. Unlike the WEU, the EOC is a non-departmental body and said to be independent, although it relies primarily on government funds and is answerable to the Cabinet Minister with responsibility for women and equality. The Taskforce undertook an 18-month campaign of consultation and research, resulting in two reports and a set of recommendations to government, employers and unions (EOC 2001; Grimshaw and Rubery 2001; Morrell et al 2001). However, the New Labour government rejected the recommendations of the EOC's Equal Pay Taskforce to introduce compulsory equal pay audits by employers (aimed to make the pay process transparent and root out inequality).

Instead, following the 2001 General Election, it chose to commission a second review on the gender pay gap, coordinated by Denise Kingsmill (a former deputy chair of the Competition Commission). This report was closer to government thinking, emphasising a voluntary approach to addressing inequities in pay structures ('focused on actions that work with the grain of the market', Kingsmill 2001, 9). Nevertheless, the government still watered down the Kingsmill proposals. The main examples include:

- The government was asked to monitor progress of voluntary pay reviews by private sector employers (with a view to considering future legislation if required), to which the response was to request the EOC (and other 'partners' of the government such as the Chartered Institute of Personnel and Development (CIPD), Fair Pay Champions and Opportunity Now) to act as monitor, specifically by funding the EOC's 'Equal Pay Review Kit'. Government subsequently set itself a target of 45% of large employers completing a pay review by April 2005; this was then adjusted to 45% by 2008. Data from the EOC suggest that while there was a substantial increase in activity between 2003 and 2004 (from 14% to 33% completing a review), this stalled during 2005 with only 34% of large (500+ employees) private sector employers having carried out an equal pay review (Adams et al 2006). Jenny Watson, Chair of the EOC, has called for a 'fresh approach' (EOC 2006).
- Government rejected a requirement for public sector bodies to report human capital management information in their annual reports in favour of monitoring progress related to the Company Law Review and considering further development for both public and private sector bodies.
- Government implemented a legal requirement for public sector organisations to conduct pay reviews but only for the civil service (see below), with a commitment to encourage pay reviews in other parts of government.
- Government rejected the recommendation that private sector bidders for public services work ought to be required to offer the same terms and conditions where these have been established through a pay review.

It is perhaps no surprise, then, that the government faced ongoing challenges from equality bodies on its record on the pay gap. In July 2004, gender equality issues (among others) were debated at the policy forum between unions and government held at Warwick University. And, as an outcome of the so-called Warwick agreement, the government commissioned a third review on the gender pay gap. In October 2004, it set up the Women and Work Commission and this time it appointed a former trade union official to chair the commission – Baroness Margaret Prosser, former deputy general of the TGWU and, incidentally, involved in the previous two reviews. The Commission appointed a tripartite mix of members (including a further four trade union officials of the 14 members).

Like the Kingsmill report, this third review presented recommendations that 'work with the grain of the market'. Surprisingly, however, given its leadership by a former trade union senior official, it presented a thoroughly unambitious set of challenges to government that did not reflect the scale of the problem facing women at work. It focused largely on how government bodies, voluntary sector organisations and public and private sector employers could implement new practices to help women make better choices in the world of work. For example, a key concern was the failure of girls at schools to break away from career choices that led them into low-paid women's jobs; here, the commission recommended better career advice in schools to tackle gender stereotypes, as well as new gender sensitive teaching methods. Also, despite a valuable review of evidence that points to the undervaluation of women's part-time work, low pay and the concentration of women's part-time jobs in a handful of occupations (in retail, caring, catering and cleaning) (Women and Work Commission 2006, 27-37), the commission dodged much needed policy recommendations, instead requesting a paltry £5 million initiative within the DTI to improve the quality of part-time work 'aimed at achieving a culture change so that more senior jobs ,,, are more open to flexible and part-time working' through identifying senior role models, job sharing, or web-based matching services, for example (Women and Work Commission 2006, 27-37). The problem is that while the commission is right to call for 'a culture change' that will reduce the level of sex segregation across UK workplaces, it does not address the employer strategies and institutional inadequacies of the labour market that both sustain old forms of pay discrimination against women at work and generate new forms. Writing in the *Guardian*, Polly Toynbee argued the approach was largely the result of the way the Commission was constituted:

> The commission was a careful mix of government, unions and employers, including the acerbically rightwing deputy director of the CBI, John Cridland. Instructed only to recommend what they could all agree, timidity was guaranteed. So they all agreed women themselves must be thoroughly re-educated and retrained.... Low pay is their own fault; if only they would aim higher and try harder, they would be paid more. So what they really need is more guidance. (Toynbee 2006)

One of the more interesting recommendations concerns procurement policy so that public sector organisations 'ensure their contractors promote gender equality in line with the public sector Gender Duty and equal pay in line with the current Equal Pay legislation' (Women and Work Commission 2006, 95). Gordon Brown has hinted he will accept this so that all contractors to the public sector must demonstrate an equal pay policy. We discuss policy action on public sector contracting below.

Direct and indirect labour market policy

Direct government policy action that explicitly targets the reduction of the gender pay gap has been limited during New Labour's term of office. The various narrowly focused pieces of legislation are as follows:

- 2001: funding for training trade union representatives on equal pay negotiations and pay review methodology.
- 2003: the legal right for an individual to obtain information from the employer on which an equal pay case could be based (under the 2002 Employment Act).
- Legislation to reduce inequality in the numbers of men and women elected to public office.
- 2003: extended maternity pay from 18 to 26 weeks and increased leave to one year (under the 2002 Employment Act).
- 2003: the right for male and female employees with young (under the age of 6), or disabled (under the age of 18), children to request to work flexibly (under the 2002 Employment Act July).
- Requirement for the civil service to undertake pay reviews from April 2003.
- 2005: a new framework of principles to underpin public sector pay negotiations that includes a commitment to eliminate the gender pay gap.
- A legal 'gender equality duty' for public bodies to come into force in April 2007 that requires public authorities to promote gender equality and eliminate sex discrimination with regard to employees and service users.

Direct policy action on pay inequalities is not the only, or necessarily the most effective, means of closing the gender pay gap. Injustices and deficiencies that characterise wide-ranging dimensions of the model of employment organisation in the UK can all contribute to gender inequality in pay. In practice, this means progressive policy action to reduce the share of low-paid workers or to strengthen employment rights for part-time workers can have an enormously beneficial impact on women's pay, due to their over-representation among these two groups. Conversely, privatisation of public services jobs through outsourcing and the promotion of tax credits to subsidise low-paid jobs are likely to harm women's pay prospects. Thus, for example, the New Labour government is correct, in principle, to claim that its introduction of the NMW contributed to improving women's relative earnings (although see below). But it is inconsistent by not recognising the potentially negative gender pay impact of privatisation and tax credits (see Chapter Six).

As women are concentrated in low-paid jobs, minimum wage regulation plays a valuable role in improving gender equality; but the beneficial impact obviously depends on the relative and absolute level at which it is set. The New Labour government is very proud of its introduction of minimum wage legislation (for example, it was the first in the list of achievements in Blair's speech to the TUC in 2004) and it is often rolled out as evidence of its commitment to improving women's employment position. But most commentators now agree that it was initially pitched far too low to make a significant impact and this problem has not yet been remedied, despite increases above average earnings growth for most years.

When first introduced at £3.60 per hour in April 1999, the NMW was just 39.7% of the median hourly pay for male full-time employees (excluding overtime). The first up-rating was characterised by a long 18-month wait and then a trivial 10 pence increase to £3.70 in October 2000; the result was that by April 2001, the annual UK earnings survey revealed a fall in the relative level to just 37.6% (Table 7.1).[3] Despite a relatively generous increase the following year, by April 2003, four years after its introduction, the NMW was only at its starting level of 39.7% of male median earnings. It was only during the fifth and sixth years of the NMW that its relative level improved against the median, up to 43% by April 2005. However, no further improvement was witnessed during 2006. Measured against women's median earnings, the NMW is obviously slightly higher because of the gender pay gap. But even compared to women's median pay it still has not yet reached 50%.

Whatever the comparator, it is clear that the UK minimum wage falls a long way behind the OECD's definition of low pay as two thirds of the median pay for all employees; it also falls substantially below the threshold of half male median earnings which is the target for the major public services trade union, Unison. Ranked against other countries, the UK was 16th out of 21 reported in the OECD Minimum Wage

Database for 2005 (with Ireland, Australia, New Zealand and France scoring the highest relative levels of 48%-53%, compared to 35% for the UK) (Immervoll 2007). So why was it pitched so low? A major problem was the reliance by the Low Pay Commission (LPC) on the Treasury's macro-economic model which had an inbuilt bias against wage-led inflation, thus countering a high level with the prediction that it would lead to job losses. Nevertheless, the orthodox economic model still allowed for a massive two million workers to be covered and this was the main target said to justify the initial rate of £3.60 (Bain 1999). But the model relied on accurate pay and employment data and it is arguable that there was insufficient attention at the time among members of the commission to the quality of the data underpinning these grandiose claims. We now know that the data were

Table 7.1: The relative level of the National Minimum Wage, 1999–2005

	April 1999	April 2000	April 2001	April 2002	April 2003	April 2004	April 2005	April 2006
Adult NMW (as of *April* each year)	£3.60	£3.60	£3.70	£4.10	£4.20	£4.50	£4.85	£5.05
Male median hourly wage	£9.07	£9.35	£9.84	£10.26	£10.58	£10.96	£11.29	£11.71
Female median hourly wage	£7.58	£7.83	£8.23	£8.67	£9.04	£9.37	£9.82	£10.24
NMW *as a % of:* Median male wage (%)	39.7	38.5	37.6	40.0	39.7	41.1	43.0	43.1
Median female wage (%)	47.5	46.0	45.0	47.3	46.5	48.0	49.4	49.3

Note: the sample for the earnings data is collected in April each year while the NMW was introduced in April 1999 and up-rated in October of subsequent years; all earnings data refer to full-time employees and exclude overtime pay and hours worked.

Source: ONS 2006b, various years

riddled with errors. Revised estimates of the numbers of employees suggest only between 850,000 (Dickens and Manning 2003) and 1.2 million (LPC 2003) workers had their earnings uplifted to the new NMW. In response to this scandal, the then chair of the LPC claimed that had the commission received accurate data the initial level would have been £3.90 rather than £3.60 (Bain 2002), which would have represented 43% of the male full-time median – exactly the level the NMW reached by April 2005, a full six years later.

Studies of the impact of the NMW on the gender pay gap suggest it has been limited. Robinson's (2002) study found it had only 'a moderate effect' precisely because it was set at too low a level. Between 1998 and 1999, the share of female workers paid less than the minimum wage fell from 13% to 9% (6% to 4% for female full-timers and 22% to 16% for female part-timers), compared to a fall from 9% to 6% for men (not adjusted for inflation). However, while the overall distribution curve for women's wages did shift to the right slightly, the location of the peak (mode) of the curve did not change significantly from 1998 to 1999, so that 'for many low-paid women, the introduction of the NMW had little impact' (Robinson 2002, 431). Robinson's simulations show that a slightly higher level would have made a significant difference: an initial level of £3.70 instead of £3.60 would have improved the gender pay ratio from 73.7% to 74.3% in 1999 (2002).

The continuing problem is that the government retains the right to accept or reject the recommendations made by the LPC and there is no mention of using the NMW to bring workers above a defined low-pay threshold. This is surprising for a government that sets targets in many areas of economy and society from school performance and hospital cleanliness to fiscal rules for the economy. John Monks, former General Secretary of the TUC, has pointed to the inconsistency of the government's approach and warned of the dangers of politicising NMW up-ratings:

> The government earned widespread praise for taking decisions over interest rates away from politicians. The Low Pay Commission offers the same potential for the minimum wage. The danger is we go down the US road where the minimum wage is a political football used for electoral reasons. Instead a regular uprating fixed through a process of social partnership offers a much better prospect for the low paid, employers and economic stability. (TUC 2001)

But the NMW is not only an instrument for providing a floor to wages, it is also an essential prop for Gordon Brown's cherished policy of Working Tax Credits (WTCs). Without the NMW, wages could fall to a very low level and make the top-up, in-work benefits paid by government unaffordable. The WTCs are an important tool in the effort to reduce poverty; estimates suggest that a combination of increased employment and more generous in-work benefits will have lifted around one million children out of poverty between 1997 and 2003/04 (Sutherland et al 2003). However, it presents a major conflict with efforts to improve women's pay for two reasons. First, it conflicts with the principle of equal pay for equal work since it links pay to household income needs (Rubery and Rake 2000). Tax credits treat couples as a unit rather than as two individuals so that pay prospects for second earners, typically women, are very poor (Brewer and Shephard 2003). The need to individualise access to tax credits fits logically with the already individualised system of income tax and would establish women's right to a wage on the same footing as men's. Promoting a dual breadwinner model would also avoid the risk of unfair competition between subsidised and non-subsidised low-paid workers.

Second, like the early 19th century Speenhamland Law, tax credits reduce pressures on employers to raise low wages and lessen the incentive for workers to bargain for higher wages.[4] Tax credits keep afloat 'parasitic employers' (Figart et al 2002) by removing their need to pay for the social costs of their workforce. Moreover, workers face disincentives from moving into higher pay brackets because high effective marginal tax rates claw back additional earnings in reduced benefits and increased tax. There is therefore a danger that a strong line of segmentation will become established between a minimum wage labour market and a decent wage labour market, as suggested by a growing spike in the wage distribution at around the minimum wage.

Improving public sector pay

Progress towards equal pay has been stronger for the public sector workforce both because it is more highly unionised than in the private sector and because the New Labour government has been able to address gender inequality in its role as an employer without stepping on the toes of private sector business interests. This is a significant area of progress because the public sector has long been an important source of employment for women, both in providing relatively well paid manual jobs and good prospects in professional jobs. Since 1997, there have been several positive examples of change in public sector pay policy that have improved prospects for women's relative pay, although there has not been consistency of approach across departments.

In two departments – health and local government – the New Labour government has introduced new national frameworks for pay structures, in both cases designed to meet the principle of equal pay for equal work (using a complex job evaluation), harmonising terms and conditions especially among manual and non-manual groups of workers, and marking a welcome reversal (from a gender pay equity perspective) of previous policies under the Conservative government which sought to break up national agreements in favour of local pay structures. For local government, a national framework was agreed in 1997 and local authorities were given until 2007 to implement a new pay structure. For the NHS, record increases in spending in the DoH have enabled a more rapid transition; a comparison of real spending growth on healthcare shows average annual growth of just 1.3% during 1993/94 to 1999/2000, compared to 8.4% during 1999/2000 to 2003/04 (Grimshaw and Carroll 2007). Agreed in 2004, NHS trusts were given two years to implement the new pay structure. The agreement reduces the weekly hours of manual workers (many of whom are women in part-time jobs) from 39 to 37.5 in line with nursing staff, which has the automatic effect of increasing hourly rates. It lifts minimum basic rates for all groups of staff – for example, a cleaner on the old pay scale in 2003/04 saw basic hourly pay increase from £4.76 to £5.52 on the new pay scale in 2004/05 (a rise of 16%) and a newly recruited healthcare assistant experienced a rise from £5.32 to £5.90 (a rise of 11%). And, if sufficient investment is provided for the parallel policy of a 'skills escalator', it should provide better prospects for women (and men) to move up into higher paid jobs (DoH 2001).

However, there have been problems. Because the new basic pay rates also consolidate a large proportion of the old enhancements to pay (especially the extras for working unsocial hours, overtime and shifts), the increase in basic rates is not a true reflection of the net change for NHS workers. The new pay structure intended to abolish the long-standing custom of paying double time, time and a half or time and a third for the various types of unsocial hours worked and to replace this with a less generous sliding scale that would pay 9% to 25% of the basic wage as an enhancement depending on the proportion of the week worked during unsocial hours. Although original estimates suggested most workers would still benefit, in practice there has been a great deal of dissatisfaction among staff and the issue has been put on hold.[5] Unison only agreed to recommend the new pay structure once the employers had agreed to decouple unsocial hours from the package (Grimshaw and Carroll 2007). NHS workers therefore moved on to the new basic rates, but retained their old entitlements to pay enhancements thanks to an effective trade union campaign to review problems with the new proposals; new recommended conditions are expected in April 2007. Thus the prospects for women's pay in the NHS do not look as bright as anticipated, but a strong union campaign has, to date, managed to protect a slide into a worse position for many women working unsocial hours.

While there has been some progress on matching systems of pay determination with principles of gender equality, a serious contradiction in New Labour's ability to improve women's pay in its role as an employer is its ideological commitment to expanding the role of the private sector in delivering public services – veiled behind the often repeated slogan, 'what matters is what works' (OPSR 2001, 26). As is now well known, under New Labour, the outsourcing of public services to the private sector was accelerated. In the NHS, for example, by 2001 one third of total spending on ancillary services had been outsourced (£1.1 billion), in education the outsourced market amounted to some £2.5 billion in 2001 (including 37% of school meal services) and in the largest area of social services spending, elderly care, two thirds of provision came from outside the public sector (HM Treasury 2003; Burkeman 2001; IPPR 2001).

The bulk of outsourcing and privatisation of public services delivery has involved the transfer of public sector workers to the private sector. Groups of women workers affected involve a range of occupations from hospital cleaners and catering assistants to supply teachers in schools and IT workers in the civil service. Terms and conditions related to pay are protected at the point of transfer from the public sector to the private sector thanks to European legislation in the form of the 1981 Transfer of Undertakings (Protection of Employment) Regulations (TUPE). Pensions are not protected, however, and unions have been campaigning for many years for the Labour government to extend TUPE to protect pensions. At present government guidance requires private sector contractors to offer 'broadly comparable' pensions but it is looking at this issue as part of a review of TUPE legislation during 2006. In addition, the legislation does not provide cover for new recruits to private sector contractors and this has led to the widely publicised problems of the 'two-tier workforce' where two groups of workers carry out similar tasks for very different rates of pay.

Here, again, however, strong trade union campaigns have forced a reluctant policy shift from government. In local government, strikes and a high-profile living wage campaign in East London led to new statutory provisions in 2003 requiring private contractors to provide all employees with terms and conditions 'no less favourable' than conditions set out in the local government collective bargaining agreement. And in the National Health Service (NHS), a long campaign directed mainly at the outsourcing of staff under the new private sector led hospital building programme, the notorious PFI, finally led to an announcement by Patricia Hewitt in late 2005 that from October 2006 most workers transferred would be entitled to 'terms and conditions no less favourable than' the collectively bargained pay structure for NHS workers. Workers covered include female-dominated groups (so-called 'soft facilities management' staff), such as cleaners, catering assistants, laundry staff, as well as the male-dominated group of porters. Excluded from the new agreement are the 'hard facilities management' workers, largely men, employed in estates and maintenance. Around the same time, there was also a removal of the obligation for non-supervisory staff to transfer as part of PFI contracts with an innovative policy (known as 'retention of employment') whereby the private sector manages ancillary staff but the NHS remains their employer; the main reason for this policy was to protect NHS pensions for these low-paid workers.

Despite some welcome policy reforms, the broad thrust of privatisation remains central to Labour policy. This means that more and more women workers formerly working for the public sector will be subject to employment practices of the private sector and, even if they do not transfer employers, their working conditions will be subject to cost-cutting pressures resulting from the obligation of all public sector bodies to 'test' wage and non-wage conditions against the market. Part-time workers – most of whom are women – have borne the brunt of market tendering exercises. While policy reforms now oblige private sector contractors to retain similar basic hourly rates of pay, they are still free to cut weekly hours of part-time workers, resulting in a significant reduction in weekly earnings. Research on part-time catering assistants in schools, for example, shows that with each round of market tendering, even local authority employed women workers faced cuts in hours with the same volume of work, resulting in greater work intensity and lower weekly earnings (Beynon et al 2002; Rubery et al 2005).

Conclusion

Progress in closing the gender pay gap under a Labour government in office since 1997 has been slow. Only since 2002 can a significant improvement be identified, suggesting a serious problem of policy lag. Of course, the average gender pay gap is only one headline indicator of women's progress in the labour market. Other indicators suggest more significant improvement, especially the lifting of the relative position of the lowest-paid women in part-time employment. However, their relative level is still very low. Too many women workers in the UK remain trapped below the international definition of a low-wage threshold, despite two and a half terms of a Labour government.

So why has the Labour government failed to meet expectations? Four key factors appear to be significant. First, there has been a lack of a sustained, serious commitment to gender mainstreaming involving interrogation of labour market policies for their impact on women's relative position. Second, it is only in the third term of office that the Labour government has established a more cooperative position with trade unions in an effort to improve the position of low-paid workers; the failure to respond to evidence-based trade union campaigns during the late 1990s against the injustices of a two-tier workforce, for example, delayed much needed improvements in pay (and job security) for many women in part-time work, especially. Third, policy action to improve women's pay has faced a conflict with other key areas of government policy, especially the use of means-tested tax credits to subsidise low paying firms and the privatisation of public services. And finally, in the absence of a more sustained effort to halt the widening of wage differentials (especially at the top end), the relative position of women concentrated among the low paid is unlikely to improve significantly. Greater wage equality has been rejected since it 'implies a zero-sum trade-off between the interests of rich and poor which New Labour considers misguided' (Glyn and Wood 2001, 22). But the characteristics of low-wage work in the UK – especially the high volume of women workers involved and the very low relative level of pay – are the result, in part, of political decisions. New Labour must decide whether the current state of women's employment is appropriate to the norms and values of 21st-century UK society. The evidence from the bulk of social science research suggests a radical shift in policy is needed.

Notes

[1] The highest decile pay is the rate of pay at which 10% of all employees in the UK earn more and the lowest decile pay is the level at which 10% earn less.

[2] Critical gender assessments of National Action Plans for the UK government have found very limited evidence of new policy initiatives.

For example, in her assessment of the 2002/03 UK National Action Plan, Jill Rubery (the then coordinator of the EC's group of experts on women and employment issues) found the policy response to have been 'very inadequate', with 'no new policies of substance and no reports of outcomes of policies with respect to the gender pay gap' (Rubery 2003, 21-2).

[3] The manner in which the relative level of the NMW is reported in Table 7.1 is unorthodox, but reflects more accurately the real significance of the minimum wage for low-paid workers. There is no perfect method for comparing average earnings and the NMW rate for each year because the earnings survey is undertaken in April of each year while the NMW is up-rated in October. What this means is that the NMW for 2004, for example, was £4.50 from January to September and then £4.85 from October to December. Despite the fact that the up-rated NMW only applies to the last three months of 2004, government reports present this as the 2004 rate and compare this figure with the previous April earnings data. Instead, Table 7.1 reports the October 2003 rate as the rate for 2004 since it is what applies at the time the earnings data are collected.

[4] Speenhamland established inwork benefits based on the notion of a 'right to live'. Subsidies in aid of wages were commonly granted in accordance with a scale linked to the price of bread, with additions for the worker's family. While universally popular at first, among parents, workers and employers, in the long run it led to the pauperisation of the workforce (Polanyi 1957).

[5] Calculations show that employees working a high load of unsocial hours lose out the most under the new system. For example, a healthcare assistant working nights would earn £8.35 per hour on old rates (basic plus enhancements) but only £7.96 on the new rate, despite receiving the maximum 25% enhancement (Grimshaw and Carroll 2006).

References

Adams, L., Carter, K. and Schäfer, S. (2006) 'Equal Pay Review Survey 2005', *EOC Working Paper Series*, No 42, Manchester: EOC.

Atkinson, A.B. (1998) 'The distribution of income in industrialised countries', *Symposium Proceedings*, Kansas City, MO: Federal Reserve Bank of Kansas City.

Bain, G. (1999) 'The National Minimum Wage: further reflections', *Employee Relations* 21(1), 15-28.

Bain, G. (2002) *Financial Times*, 11 November.

Beynon, H., Grimshaw, D., Rubery, J. and Ward, K. (2002) *Managing Employment Change*, Oxford: Oxford University Press.

Brewer, M. and Shephard, A. (2003) *Has Labour Made Work Pay?*, York: Joseph Rowntree Foundation.

Burkeman, O. (2001) 'Next stop, schools', *Guardian Education*, 26 June, 2-3.

DoH (Department of Health) (2001) *Working Together, Learning Together*, London: DoH.

Dickens, R. and Manning, A. (2003) 'Minimum wage, minimum impact', in R. Dickens, P. Gregg and J. Wadsworth (eds) *The Labour Market Under New Labour: The State of Working Britain*, London: Palgrave.

EOC (Equal Opportunities Commission) (2001) *Just Pay: The Final Report of the Equal Pay Taskforce*, Manchester: EOC.

EOC (2006) Press release, www.eoc.org.uk (accessed 30 May 2006).

Eurostat (2006a) European Community Household Panel 1998, http://ec.europa.eu/comm/eurostat/ (accessed 30 May 2006).

Eurostat (2006b) European Structure of Earnings Survey 1995, http://ec.europa.eu/comm/eurostat/ (accessed 20 May 2006).

Figart, D.M., Mutari, E. and Power, M. (2002) *Living Wages, Equal Wages – Gender and Labor Market Policies in the United States*, Routledge: London.

Glyn, A. and Wood, S. (2001) 'New Labour's economic policy', in A. Glyn (ed) *Social Democracy and Economic Policy*, Oxford: Oxford University Press.

Grimshaw, D. and Carroll, M. (2007: forthcoming) 'Improving the position of low wage workers through new coordinating institutions: the case of public hospitals', in C. Lloyd, G. Mason and K. Mayhew (eds) *Low-wage Employment in the UK*, New York, NY: Russell Sage Foundation.

Grimshaw, D. and Rubery, J. (2001) *The Gender Pay Gap: A Research Review*, EOC Research Discussion Series, Manchester: EOC.

Harkness, S. (1996) 'The gender earnings gap: evidence from the UK', *Fiscal Studies* 17(2), 1-36.

HM Treasury (2003) *PFI: Meeting the Investment Challenge*, London: The Stationery Office.

Immervoll, H. (2007) 'Minimum wages, minimum labour costs and the tax treatment of low wage employment', *OECD Social, Employment and Migration Working Papers*, No 46, Paris: OECD.

IPPR (Institute of Public Policy Research) (2001) *Building Better Partnerships: The Final Report of the Commission on Public Private Partnerships*, London: IPPR.

Kingsmill, D. (2001) *Report into Women's Employment and Pay*, London: DTI.

LPC (Low Pay Commission) (2003) *The National Minimum Wage: Building on Success, Fourth Report of the Low Pay Commission*, Cmnd 5768, London: HMSO.

Manning, A. and Petrongolo, B. (2004) *The Part-Time Pay Penalty*, Report to Women and Equality Unit, London: DTI.

Metcalfe, H. and Korou, A. (2003) *Towards a Closing of the Gender Pay Gap: UK Country Report*, Report to Women and Equality Unit, London: DTI.

Morrell, J., Boyland, M., Munns, G. and Astbury, L. (2001) *Gender Equality in Pay Practices*, EOC Research Discussion Series, Manchester: EOC.

OECD (Organisation for Economic Co-operation and Development) (2000) *Labour Market Statistics Database*, www.oecd.org (accessed May 2006).

ONS (Office for National Statistics) (2006a) New Earnings Survey (1984-2003), www.statistics.gov.uk (accessed May 2006).

ONS (2006b) Annual Survey of Hours and Earnings UK (1997-2005), www.statistics.gov.uk (accessed May 2006).

OPSR (Office of Public Services Reform) (2001) *Reforming our Public Services*, report by The Prime Minister's Office of Public Services Reform, www.pm.gov.uk/files/pdf/Principles.pdf (accessed Feb 2006)

Polanyi, K. (1957) *The Great Transformation The Political and Economic Origins of our Time*, New York, NY: The Free Press.

Rake, K. (ed.) (2000) *Women's Incomes over the Lifetime*, London: The Stationery Office.

Robinson, H. (2002) 'Wrong side of the track. The impact of the minimum wage on gender pay gaps in Britain', *Oxford Bulletin of Economics and Statistics* 64(5), 417-48.

Rubery, J. (2003) *Gender Mainstreaming and Gender Equality in the UK National Action Plan for Employment*, October, EC's Expert Group on Gender and Employment, European Commission.

Rubery, J. and Rake, K. (2000) *Gender Impact Assessment in the UK*, Report to the European Commission's Expert Group on Gender and Employment, DG Employment, European Commmission.

Rubery, J., Ward, K. and Grimshaw, D. (2005) 'The changing employment relationship and the implications for quality part-time work', *Labour and Industry* 15(3), 7-28.

Sutherland, H., Sefton, T. and Piachaud, D. (2003) *Poverty in Britain: the Impact of Government Policy Since 1997*, York: Joseph Rowntree Foundation.

Toynbee, P. (2006) 'It really won't do to blame women for Britain's pay gap', *Guardian*, 28 February.

Trade Union Congress (TUC) (2001) Press release, 21 June, www.tuc. org.uk (accessed Feb 2006).

Walby, S. and Olsen, W. (2002) *The Impact of Women's Position in the Labour Market on Pay and Implications for UK Productivity*, Report to Women and Equality Unit, London: DTI.

Women and Work Commission (2006) *Shaping a Fairer Future*, London: WEU.

EIGHT

New Labour: family policy and gender

Karen Clarke

Introduction

This chapter examines the coherence of New Labour's approach to the family and the implications for gender roles of its policies. Family policy is a notoriously difficult concept to define. At its most general it is 'everything the state does to and for the family' (Kamerman and Kahn 1978, 3) whether or not the family is the explicit object of those state activities. Under a more limited definition family policies may be defined as 'policies that identify families as the deliberate target of specific actions and where the measures initiated are designed to have an impact on family resources and ultimately on family structure' (Hantrais 2004, 132). Within this broad field, the specific focus of this chapter is on those policies which have implications for parents and for the division of responsibilities for children, both between mothers and fathers, and between parents and the state.

After a brief discussion of family policy in Britain before 1997, the chapter outlines the policies introduced by the New Labour governments. It examines their effects on gender divisions in paid work and unpaid care, and their differential impact on partnered and lone mothers, and on women of different social classes. It raises some questions about the overall coherence of these policies and identifies a number of different notions of parental responsibility that underlie the policies on parenting in relation to pre-school and older children.

Family diversity and family policy

Before the early 1990s, UK governments avoided adopting any kind of explicit family policy (Kamerman and Kahn 1997); so that although policies affecting the family were informed by a set of normative values and assumptions about the family, gender roles and the relative responsibilities of state and family, these were implicit rather than explicit. There was a view, shared across the political spectrum, that the state should not interfere in the private sphere of the family, except where necessary to protect children from harm. Policies were based on an increasingly inappropriate 'male breadwinner' model of the family, according to which, the man provided material support and the woman was the carer. Apart from the provision of maternity leave, Britain had no state policies – such as childcare provision – to support maternal employment, or to facilitate greater paternal involvement in caring for children. Childcare arrangements were seen as a private matter, which parents should be left to make for themselves. As a consequence, although maternal employment increased throughout the 1980s and 1990s, employed mothers were concentrated in part-time employment. The lack of public childcare resulted in increasing divisions between partnered and lone mothers and between highly qualified and less well-qualified mothers in terms of economic activity and hours of work (Brannen et al 1997).

This position began to change from the late 1980s because of the rapid growth in the numbers of lone parent families during the 1970s and 1980s. The number of lone parent families rose from 570,000 in 1971 to 1.3 million in 1991. Over 90% of lone parent households were headed by women and an increasing proportion were wholly dependent on welfare benefits for their financial support. This was seen as posing serious problems for the welfare state, both financially and morally. The increase in the number of lone mothers dependent on Income Support had substantial implications for the social security budget. Expenditure on welfare benefits for lone parents rose from £1.4 billion in 1980/81 to £3.2 billion in 1988/89.

Rising lone parenthood was also seen by the New Right as posing various threats to social order and to the two-parent norm (Lister 1996). The 1989 Children Act and the 1991 Child Support Act both sought to define the responsibilities of parents. The 1989 Children Act represents an important acknowledgement of the diversity of family forms and a shift from *marriage* as the assumed basis of the family, to *parenthood* regardless of the particular formal and informal context in which it is exercised. However, the 1991 Child Support Act reflected a strongly gendered notion of parental responsibility, with the role of absent parents (overwhelmingly fathers) restricted to providing financially for their children and for the support of the 'parent with care' (overwhelmingly mothers). The policies of the 1990s Conservative governments increasingly sought to move lone mothers into the labour market, so that responsible motherhood for this group involved both paid work and unpaid caring. For the first time it was acknowledged that this could not be achieved without some childcare assistance from the state. This represented an important move away from the idea that childcare was the private responsibility of parents, although it was restricted to a particular subset of families. Lone mothers on Family Credit received a childcare disregard so that the cost of childcare was effectively subsidised for this group of low-income employed mothers. Thus in the 1990s, before the election of New Labour there had already been some tentative moves towards acknowledging family diversity and supporting maternal employment, although only for lone mothers. In other respects, however, the Conservative administration was strongly resistant to introducing a more explicit set of family policies originating in the EU and aimed at promoting greater gender equality in relation to paid and unpaid work (Lister 1996).

Supporting Families: *A new approach to family policy*

The New Labour government broke with the long-standing implicit approach of UK governments when, early in its first term, it published a consultative paper, entitled *Supporting Families* (Home Office 1998) and produced its proposals for a National Childcare Strategy (DfEE 1998). A number of further policy documents since then have developed the proposals set out in these initial publications, including *Every Child Matters* (HM Treasury 2003) and the 10-year childcare strategy (HM Treasury 2004a).

It is notable that all these policy documents have been cross-departmental, involving various combinations of the Home Office, the DWP, the DTI, the DfES, the Treasury and other departments, providing evidence of the government's recognition of the cross-cutting nature of family policy. One consequence of this cross-departmental approach has been a concentration of policy influence in the Treasury; due to its control over the associated spending allocation across departments. The biennial spending reviews have been used to direct family policy firmly towards the 'adult worker' model and to promote a social investment conceptualisation of childcare services and education (Dobrowolsky and Jensen 2005). The Treasury's influential role in shaping family policy is indicated by the fact it is the publisher of a number of the key policy papers in this area.

Further aspects of New Labour's approach to the family are contained in the policies that have been developed to address various forms of youth misbehaviour, in which parents are identified as the principal agents for ensuring children and young people's good behaviour. The *Respect and Responsibility* White Paper (Home Office 2003) and the *Respect Action Plan* (Home Office 2006) set out how parents' role is conceptualised in terms of their accountability to others for their children's actions. Some of the different notions of parental responsibility that run through these policies, and their consequences for women and men, are considered later in this chapter.

Supporting Families was produced by an inter-departmental ministerial group on the family, chaired by Jack Straw, then Home Secretary. It set out proposals for the role of the state in relation to parents, covering five broad areas: services and support for parents bringing up children; financial support for families; work–home balance; support for marriage; and support for families with serious problems (education, youth offending, teenage parenthood and domestic violence). The paper acknowledged the sensitivity and novelty of its topic: 'governments have to be wary about intervening in areas of private life and intimate emotion' (Home Office 1998, 4), but also justified the focus on developing an explicit family policy on the grounds that 'in almost everything that government does, we can help families, neglect them or even do them active harm' (Home Office 1998, 5). It stated three principles on which the proposals were based. These were: first, that the interests of children were paramount; second, that marriage was the 'surest foundation for raising children' and that therefore the government's aim was to strengthen marriage; and third, that state intervention in the family should be minimal, with the role of government being to support parents rather than substituting for them (1998, 4). These principles show a strong degree of continuity with the principles of the previous Conservative governments. What is new is the breadth of the interpretation of what constitutes 'support' in terms of the policy measures that it proposed and that have subsequently been introduced. These measures fall into three broad areas: employment-related support (including both services and financial support); advice and support on parenting; and policies in relation to adolescent misbehaviour and parents' responsibility for controlling their children. They represent a new conceptualisation of the respective roles of parents and the state in relation to children, and embody some contradictory norms about maternal and paternal roles.

Employment-related family policy

New Labour's policies in relation to parental employment are underpinned by their more general adult worker approach to welfare, encapsulated in the 1998 welfare reform Green Paper slogan of 'work for those who can; security for those who cannot' (DSS 1998). This has been framed within the constraints of a liberal economic policy, which gives a key role to the market and a commitment not to increase direct taxation. In practice, the principal emphasis of policy has been on 'work for those who can', although two important changes to welfare benefits for families with children were introduced early on in the first administration: Child Benefit was significantly increased and there was a substantial up-rating of Income Support for younger children. This compensated, to some extent, for the announcement in 1997 that benefits to lone parents were to be cut.

The policies introduced can be seen as deriving from two different but overlapping concerns. The first is a commitment to greater gender equality and the second is the commitment to eliminating child poverty by 2020 (Blair 1999). The principal mechanism for achieving the latter objective is paid work, in particular through a reduction in the number of workless households, among which lone-mother households are disproportionately represented. This has therefore meant addressing the obstacles to women's labour market participation. Arguably, the objective of eliminating child poverty, rather than that of increasing gender equality, has been the stronger driver of policy in this area.

A number of important measures were taken to encourage and support parental employment. The WFTC and the Childcare Tax Credit, introduced in 1999, were both intended to make the financial rewards of paid work significantly greater than the income from welfare benefits. The Childcare Tax Credit provided a subsidy for the costs of childcare that extended a considerable way up the income scale. At the same time the government addressed the shortage of childcare places through its National Childcare Strategy by extending the role of local authority Early Years Development Partnerships to review childcare provision and identify needs, and by providing subsidies for the capital costs of expanding provision (DfEE 1998).

Lone parents, over 90% of whom are lone mothers, have been the focus of specific policies aimed at increasing lone mothers' employment to 70% by 2010. A combination of sticks and carrots has been used to promote paid work. In addition to the measures in support of parental employment, the New Deal for Lone Parents, introduced in 1998, provides lone mothers with individual advice on employment opportunities, childcare and training from a personal adviser. While the government has stopped short of requiring lone mothers to enter the labour market, it has made attendance at an interview with a personal adviser a condition of claiming welfare benefits, with benefit penalties applied to those who do not attend (Joyce and Whiting 2006). The 2006 welfare Green Paper proposed to increase the pressure on lone parents to enter paid work, by increasing the frequency of these WFIs to quarterly for lone parents with children aged over 11 and six-monthly for those with younger children (DWP 2006a; also see Chapter Three). Incentives to enter the labour market include a complete disregard of child support payments in calculating WFTC (now WTC) entitlement. In other respects, despite some changes to the legislation, New Labour has left the principles underlying child support largely unchanged, so that they continue to uphold the role of the non-resident parent (predominantly fathers) as the provider of financial support for the resident carer, although she is now expected to be in paid work too. The administration of the Child Support Agency (CSA) has been hugely problematic, with £3.5 billion of maintenance uncollected and a backlog of over 300,000 cases in 2006 (National Audit Office 2006). The government has now announced that the Agency is to be replaced and greater encouragement given to parents to arrive at voluntary agreements on maintenance (DWP 2006b).

New Labour has also introduced a number of policies more specifically aimed at gender equality in the labour market, by increasing women's labour market security in pregnancy and early motherhood. The most significant of these are the extension of maternity rights to all pregnant employees, extension of the period of paid maternity leave (to six months from 2003), an increase in the level of maternity pay and the extension of maternity leave from six months to 12 months after the birth. Current proposals include increasing the period of *paid* leave to nine months and eventually 12 months, with some of this to be transferable between mothers and fathers.

Fathers' involvement in early childcare and the needs of working parents have also been addressed. The 2002 Employment Act introduced a statutory right to two weeks' paternity leave, paid at a flat rate of £100 a week. Since 1999 either parent has also had the right to take a period of three months' unpaid parental leave and to take unpaid time off for family emergencies (such as a breakdown of childcare arrangements, or child illness) (Smeaton and Marsh 2006, Appendix 1).

Other measures with implications for the gender division of paid and unpaid work derive from European Directives on Working Time and on Part-time Work. The working time legislation sets a maximum working week of 48 hours (although with numerous exceptions) and provides a statutory entitlement to paid holidays. Under the legislation relating to part-time work parents of children under the age of six are entitled to request a reduction in their working hours, although it is at the employer's discretion to agree this. The introduction of an NMW in April 1999 had a disproportionate impact on women

(Low Pay Commission 2000), because of women's concentration in low-paid occupations, and was therefore also an important gender equality measure.

Taken together, the policies outlined above represent a substantial raft of measures to promote maternal employment, particularly among poor families where lone mothers are concentrated, and, to a lesser extent, to encourage and support greater involvement by fathers in caring for children.

Parenting and family support

Another major strand in New Labour's family policy has been the provision of advice and support for parents on the care and upbringing of children. Parenting is conceived of as a 'difficult job' in many New Labour policy documents and policy pronouncements (see for example Home Office 1998; Blair 2005), in which the state can play a role by providing professional advice and support. One of the proposals in *Supporting Families* was the establishment of a National Family and Parenting Institute (NFPI). The NFPI is involved in a wide range of activities aimed at parents and policy makers, and acts as a lobbying and campaigning group on issues related to parenting and family policy (NFPI 2006).

While the NFPI is a national organisation providing information and advice to parents on a universal basis, the principal focus of New Labour's family support policies has been poor families, through the Sure Start programme, announced in 1998. From the initial 60 'trailblazer' projects started in 1999, the programme has been successively extended. By 2004, there were over 500 Sure Start Local Programmes (SSLPs) covering approximately one third of children living in poverty, and providing a variety of universal and targeted services and resources for parents and their children under the age of four, covering parent and child health, early education and childcare, at a cost of £760 million (National Audit Office 2004, 17). Sure Start was a central plank in the government's longer-term strategy for tackling social exclusion, with its principal aim being to break 'the cycle of disadvantage' by ensuring that children reached school ready to learn, and seeking to reduce the social class developmental divide apparent in children by the age of 22 months (HM Treasury 2004b, 50). Parents are the focus of Sure Start policies because they represent the means of achieving particular outcomes for their children, in particular better educational outcomes, so that these children will be better equipped to compete in the labour market.

From April 2006, Sure Start has been converted into a national programme of Children's Centres, which will eventually have universal coverage, rather than being specifically targeted on the poorest geographical areas. Children's Centres will provide a similar range of support services for families with children below school age, although it has been argued that there will be a stronger emphasis on their role in supporting parents in paid work (Glass 2005).[1]

These family support initiatives mark a clear departure from the position of previous governments which largely saw early infancy and childrearing as private matters, where the state had no role apart from maintaining minimum standards of care through the child protection system. 'Parenting' under New Labour has become the subject of scrutiny and concern, with parents seen by policy-makers as being in need of advice, support and guidance in a task which has been identified as difficult, demanding and of great long-term significance for the state, both economically and socially.

Parental accountability

While policies directed at parents of pre-school children have focused on providing support and advice for parents, primarily those living in poverty, those directed at parents of older children have identified the principal problem as one of insufficient parental control of children; and the solution as lying in intervention with parents to ensure school attendance and children's orderly behaviour. The 1998 Crime and Disorder Act, later extended by the 2003 Anti-Social Behaviour Act, introduced parenting orders, under which parents can be required to attend parenting programmes or can be required to exercise control over a child's behaviour, as a consequence of various forms of misbehaviour by their children. These forms of misbehaviour include persistent truancy, being convicted of a criminal offence or being made the subject of an anti-social behaviour order. Failure to comply with a parenting order is a criminal offence which carries a maximum fine of £1,000, or imprisonment.

This approach to the problem of youth behaviour frames the problem as a lack of parental skill in controlling children and also perhaps a failure to appreciate parental responsibilities. It takes a fairly simple view of the role of parents in solving the problem, as a speech by Tony Blair made clear:

> Parenting orders offer a programme of activity to support parents, they define their rights and responsibilities. For

example a parenting order can make clear to parents their responsibility to ensure that their child attends school, that the child takes part in literacy or numeracy clubs, or that they attend programmes dealing with problems as varied as anger management, or drug or alcohol mis-use. Parenting orders can also stop children visiting areas such as shopping centres, ensure a child is at home being supervised at night where that is necessary. Parents themselves can be forced by the order to accept support and advice on how to bring discipline and rules to their child's life. (2005)

As this section has shown, New Labour's policies on parenting involve a new definition of the relative responsibilities of the state and of parents, with the acceptance of greater state responsibility for facilitating parental employment and for providing support to parents. At the same time parents' responsibilities have been more explicitly defined as including paid work and conforming to certain parenting norms, promulgated by the state in the form of advice to parents; through Sure Start, and more coercively through training in parenting skills under a parenting order.

Gender impact of New Labour's family policies

What changes have occurred since the introduction of these policies and what has been their impact on the division of paid and unpaid labour between mothers and fathers? The various measures to promote parental employment were introduced in a context where maternal employment was already increasing, so a continuing rise cannot necessarily be attributed to these measures. Although there remains a gap between the employment rates of mothers with dependent children and those without: 67% and 73% respectively (Walling 2005), this gap has steadily reduced over the past 20 years. There remain significant differences between the employment rates for women who are married/cohabiting and those for lone mothers. In 2004, 71% of cohabiting/married mothers were in employment, compared to 53% of lone mothers. Table 8.1 shows the changes in employment rates for married/cohabiting mothers and for lone parents[2] between 1994 and 2004. Despite the changes to maternity rights and the substantial increase in childcare provision, mothers with pre-school children are still less likely to be in employment than those with a child of school age.

Table 8.1: Employment rates for married/cohabiting mothers and lone parents, 1994–2004

	Age of youngest child					
	0–4		5–10		11–18	
	Couple mother	Lone parent	Couple mother	Lone parent	Couple mother	Lone parent
1994	51	23	70	45	77	64
1997	58	29	72	47	78	63
2000	61	33	76	52	78	68
2004	59	34	77	57	80	67

Source: adapted from Walling 2005, Table 6

There has been a striking increase in the percentage of lone parents in employment over this period, especially among lone parents with younger children, although the gap between lone parents and married/cohabiting mothers remains substantial. Gregg and Harkness (2003) estimate just under half of the increase in lone parents' employment rates in the period 1992–2002 can be attributed to policy reforms in this period. They suggest, however, that the rate of increase is unlikely to be sufficient to allow the government to reach its target of 70% of lone parents in employment by 2010. The most recent figures from the DWP show that by 2005 the percentage of lone mothers in employment had further increased to 56.6% (DWP 2006a, 52).

Despite these increases there remain substantial gender differences in parental employment, particularly in the balance between full-time and part-time work, as Table 8.2 shows.

In 2004, 87% of married/cohabiting fathers worked full time, compared to 28% of married/cohabiting mothers. Only 4% of

Table 8.2: Full-time and part-time parental employment rates, 1994–2004

	Married/cohabiting mothers		Lone parents		Married/cohabiting fathers	
	Full time	Part time	Full time	Part time	Full time	Part time
1994	24	40	21	21	84	2
1997	26	42	22	23	86	3
2000	28	42	25	26	87	3
2004	28	42	28	26	87	4

Source: adapted from Walling 2005: Table 4

married/cohabiting fathers worked part time, compared to 42% of married/cohabiting mothers. Although in the 10 years from 1994 to 2004 there was a bigger increase in full-time than in part-time working among mothers in two-parent households, still only 40% of all mothers work full time, compared to 95% of fathers. At this level at least, New Labour's family policies have had relatively little impact on the distribution of paid and unpaid work between mothers and fathers, and this has important implications for women's long-term financial security in the context of high levels of separation and divorce.

The National Childcare Strategy has had a substantial effect in increasing the number of places in formal childcare. According to the government, the net number of childcare places increased by over 500,000 in the six years from 1998 to 2004 (HM Treasury 2004b, 3). The ratio of places to children for children under the age of eight increased from one place for every eight children in 1997 to one for every four children in the age group by 2004 (EOC 2005, 16). Nevertheless, informal care by family members remains the most common childcare arrangement. Formal provision is used primarily for younger children, especially those under the age of five (Lyon et al 2006). The expansion in the number of nursery class places means that by April 2004 there was an early education place available for all three- and four-year-olds whose parents wanted one (HM Treasury 2004b, 51) and about 90% of three- to four-year-olds were attending a nursery class. However, the majority of these places are part time, and therefore from a childcare point of view generally have to be supplemented with some additional form of day care to enable parents to work, even part time. Despite these increases in provision, the availability of childcare remains an issue for a substantial proportion of families. One third of those in the Families and Children Study 2004 thought there was not enough childcare in their area, with the proportion rising to 40% among families with children under the age of five. A third of lone parents and a quarter of couples thought that childcare in their local area was 'not at all affordable' (Lyon et al 2006, Table 16.11).

Evidence from the most recent survey of maternity and paternity rights and benefits (Smeaton and Marsh 2006) indicates that the increases in maternity leave and pay introduced in 2003 have enabled mothers to take longer periods of leave. The average period of leave increased from four to six months between 2002 and 2005. The percentage of mothers returning to work within 17 months of the birth was unchanged at 80%, but mothers reported that there was greater flexibility and fewer obstacles to their return, including more opportunities to work part time. There was a 50% drop in the proportion of mothers who changed employers on their return to work (from 41% to 20%). Money was the principal reason given for returning to work and the increase in the period of leave taken reflects the extension in the period of *paid* leave in 2003. The survey showed that women in higher earning jobs were able to exercise greater choice over the period of leave that they took. This reflects both their own higher income and the fact that they were likely to have a higher earning partner than women in less well-paid occupations.

The introduction of Statutory Paternity Leave and Paternity Pay in 2003 appears to have affected fathers' behaviour too. Fathers in 2005 took more time off than at the time of the previous survey in 2002; 36% took more than the statutory two weeks, using a combination of paternity and other leave. The survey also found that almost three quarters of fathers made some change to their working arrangements after the birth. Just under a fifth worked shorter hours, over a quarter adjusted their hours to fit with those of their partner and more than a third worked more regular hours. According to fathers, the opportunities for various forms of flexible working (part-time work, flexi-time and working at home occasionally) had approximately doubled since 2002, with about half of all fathers having access to at least one of these forms of flexible working. However, a tiny percentage of fathers had taken up the opportunity to work part time, with only flexi-time and working at home taken up by fathers to any significant extent (Smeaton and Marsh 2006).

The introduction of the right to up to three months' unpaid parental leave during the child's first five years (or 18 weeks in the first 18 years for the parents of a disabled child) has had relatively little effect. Only 11% of mothers and 8% of fathers in Smeaton and Marsh's survey had used parental leave, and most had taken only short periods of time off (2006).

New Labour's investment in family support services in the form of the 500+ SSLPs has provided substantial additional services and support for many of the poorest families with children under the age of four. At the national level, the aims of the programme reflect an individualised and strongly instrumental conception of the parental role. Despite the generally gender neutral language of parenting, Sure Start is primarily focused on promoting a particular style of mothering, based on a strongly middle-class norm (Clarke 2006). However, in practice, at the level of individual SSLPs there is great variety in the kinds of services provided and evidence that in many local programmes these have been important in empowering and supporting mothers in a fairly non-prescriptive way (NESS 2005). Sure Start has had much less success in engaging with and involving fathers (Tunstill et al 2005). This partly reflects the fact that a high proportion of families in Sure Start areas are headed by lone mothers – 25% of births in Sure Start areas were to lone mothers compared with 15% nationally (Barnes et al 2003) and that in practice it is women who have the principal, and often sole, responsibility for caring for children. The strong emphasis within Sure Start on the individual behaviour of parents as shaping children's early development, together with the fact that for practical and ideological reasons this responsibility is associated predominantly with women, has the consequence that Sure Start tends to reinforce a strongly maternal view of 'parenting'.

Policies to address juvenile disorder by holding parents responsible for their children's actions have also in practice had a greater impact on mothers than fathers, and on lone mothers in particular. Despite the gender neutrality of 'parenting orders', the majority of those made subject to such orders have been mothers. An early evaluation of parenting orders found that three quarters of those made the subject of a parenting order were mothers (Holdaway et al 2001). The authors comment: 'This is likely to reflect a number of factors, including fathers who are not present in an offender's family, fathers absenting themselves from responsibility for parenting, and assumptions about female roles and responsibilities made by courts and by professionals' (2001, 100).

Discussion

New Labour's family policies have had mixed effects as far as women are concerned. Policies introduced to support and promote parental employment have had different impacts on mothers in different circumstances. There remain substantial social class differences in the extent to which women are able to take up the extended rights to maternity leave, so that those in the most favourable position in the labour market are most able to exercise choice over when to return to work. Lone mothers have been pushed and cajoled into the labour market in increased numbers, but they are predominantly in lower level jobs, dependent on state supplements to low earnings, and subject to intense time pressure in combining paid and unpaid work. As Levitas et al point out, '[p]aid work is likely to increase time stress for lone parents, without necessarily lifting them out of poverty and thus constrain rather than promote social participation' (2006, 416).

The increasing dominance of the 'adult worker' model leaves those lone mothers unable or unwilling to enter paid work at an increased risk of exclusion, as they become an increasingly small minority of mothers. Although there have been some changes in paternal behaviour around childbirth, mothers retain principal responsibility for the care of children and this is reflected in their concentration in part-time work. One of the consequences of greater gender equality for some parents as a consequence of these policies would therefore appear to be greater differentiation *between* mothers, according to educational and family status, with lone mothers facing a particularly intense combination of responsibility for children, both in making material provision through paid employment, and in providing care.

Despite New Labour's acknowledgement of family diversity, the two-parent, dual earner family is the norm that its family policies promote. Paid work is seen as having a moral as well as a social and economic value, both for children (by providing a role model for the future) and for parents in fulfilling their responsibilities as citizens. There is no real policy space left which allows for alternative models of parenting and family life, in which there may be different underlying gendered moral rationalities about what constitutes a good parent (Duncan and Edwards 1999) or which acknowledge significant material constraints that prevent parents from following this norm. There is evidence from a number of studies that many mothers do not share the citizen worker norm so strongly promoted by New Labour (Lyon et al 2006; Meadows and Garbers 2004), but the scope to depart from it is limited. In the process of emphasising the importance of paid work, the value of unpaid caring work and the time necessary to do it, are in danger of being overlooked, except in the context of pathologised families, who are seen as needing to be trained in parenting skills.

New Labour's policies on parenting and parents' responsibilities, represented by Sure Start on the one hand and parenting orders on the other, reflect two alternative conceptualisations of responsibility. As Eekelaar (1991) has pointed out there is an ambiguity in the term parental responsibility between parents' responsibilities *to* their children (meeting children's needs) and parental responsibility *for* children (parents' accountability to others, and in particular to the state, for their children's actions). There is little acknowledgement in the policies introduced that the particular interpretation that has been placed on responsible parenting (the responsibilities that parents owe *to* their children) and that now involves paid work, may be incompatible with fulfilling the requirement to supervise and control (and so be responsible *for* children). In the context of an increasingly flexible labour market with extended working hours, still inadequate childcare provision, especially for older children (in terms of both the quantity of provision and its acceptability to young people), how are parents, especially lone mothers, to both be responsible as workers and maintain the sort of control and supervision over adolescents that parenting orders require? Seaman et al (2005) illustrate the difficulty for working parents of monitoring and controlling young people. Parents faced problems both in relation to the working hours demanded by the only jobs available in the area and their incompatibility with being there for children before and after school: 'For this parent, as with many others, there was a palpable sense of guilt about her need to work and she felt constrained by the fact that only family unfriendly hours were available to her' (2005, 14).

In relation to parents of older children, policies have emphasised the accountability of parents for the behaviour of their children, through measures such as parenting orders and in the rhetoric of the Respect Agenda. This impacts more on mothers than fathers, despite the acknowledgement that involving fathers is desirable, with the result that the responsibilities of both aspects of women's dual role, as carers and as workers, have been extended, with little acknowledgement of the time constraints and conflicts this involves, particularly for lone mothers. Although extended school hours are an attempt to respond to the need to provide supervised activity for older children, it remains to be seen how acceptable such provision is for the children themselves, who, unlike younger children, are able to express their preferences by voting with their feet. Sure Start and policies on juvenile crime both recognise rhetorically the critical importance of the unpaid care done by mothers, but at the same time make it increasingly difficult for that work to be the principal form of parental activity.

Much of New Labour's policy discourse on families is expressed in the gender neutral language of 'parents' and 'parenting', as if the use of gender neutral language might help to bring about a more equal sharing of caring for children. There is also explicit recognition scattered throughout policy documents of the importance of securing greater paternal involvement with children, particularly in relation to the fathers of children in lone mother households. However, the impact of the policies introduced has been primarily on mothers, facilitating their entry into the labour market, at the same time as reinforcing their primary responsibility for caring for children, and, arguably, increasing the dual burden that working mothers bear. Policies to increase and encourage men's unpaid caring work have been more limited and tentative, and, despite indications that there have been some changes in men's involvement in care, the degree of change in fathers' domestic involvement remains limited and is likely to remain so while the costs of unpaid care are borne largely by individual families.

Conclusion

New Labour's approach to the family has two distinct and somewhat contradictory elements. The first is concerned with promoting women's participation in the labour market on a more equal basis with men; the second is concerned with social order and promoting greater parental control of children as the means for bringing this about. There are a number of different drivers for the policies introduced. While the commitment to gender equality has been important, and has resulted in real improvements for women in the labour market, the concern to promote an adult worker welfare model and the wish to contain what is seen as an increasing problem of disorderly youth, consequent upon the breakdown of the two-parent family norm, have arguably been more important. One consequence of this is that lone mothers face the strongest pressures both to enter paid work and to exercise supervision and control over their children, and divisions between women – based on educational qualifications, earning capacity, and whether or not they have a co-resident partner – have increased. Women with partners in higher level jobs now have greater choice and flexibility in how they organise the balance of paid and unpaid work. Less well-qualified lone mothers face increased pressure to juggle paid and unpaid work in such a way as to meet state expectations about their responsibilities to and for children. Despite the inclusive and gender neutral language of parenting, men's roles in two-parent and one-parent families have been much less strongly targeted by the policies introduced and their role in providing care for children remains a relatively peripheral one.

Notes

[1] As part of the national childcare strategy announced in 2004, the government has also committed itself to ensuring that all parents of children aged 5-11 will have access to affordable school-based childcare between 8am and 6pm and that all secondary school would be open between 8am and 6pm throughout the year, offering a range of extra-curricular activities to occupy older children (HM Treasury 2004a, 33).

[2] Walling (2005) gives figures for lone parents rather than lone mothers. However, since less than 10% (173,000) of the 1.9 million lone parents are lone fathers, the figures for lone parents broadly reflect the picture for lone mothers.

References

Barnes, J., Broomfield K., Frost, M., Harper, G., McLeod, A., Knowles, J. and Leyland, A. (2003) *Characteristics of Sure Start Local Programme Areas: Rounds 1 to 4. National Evaluation Summary*, London: DfES Sure Start Unit.

Blair, T. (1999) 'Beveridge revisited: a welfare state for the 21st century', in R. Walker (ed) *Ending Child Poverty – Popular Welfare for the 21st Century?*, Bristol: The Policy Press, 7-18.

Blair, T. (2005) Speech on improving parenting, given at Meridian Community Centre Watford, 2 September, www.number10.gov.uk/out[ut/Page8123.asp (accessed 13 April 2006).

Brannen, J., Moss, P., Owen, C. and Wale, C. (1997) *Mothers Fathers and Employment: Parents and the Labour Market in Britain 1984–1994*, DfEE Research Report 10, London: The Stationery Office.

Clarke, K. (2006) 'Childhood, parenting and early intervention: a critical examination of the Sure Start national programme', *Critical Social Policy* 26(4), 699-721.

DfEE (Department for Education and Employment) (1998) *Meeting the Childcare Challenge*, Cm 3959, Sudbury: DfEE.

Dobrowolsky, A. and Jensen, J. (2005) 'Social investment perspectives and practices: a decade in British politics', in M. Powell, L. Bauld and K. Clarke (eds) *Social Policy Review 17*, Bristol: The Policy Press, 203-30.

DSS (Department of Social Security) (1998) *New Ambitions for our Country: A New Contract for Welfare*, Cm 3805, London: The Stationery Office.

Duncan, S. and Edwards, R. (1999) *Lone Mothers, Paid Work and Gendered Moral Rationalities*, London: Macmillan.

DWP (Department for Work and Pensions (2006a) *A New Deal for Welfare: Empowering People to Work*, Cm 6730, London: The Stationery Office.

DWP (2006b) *More Streamlined and Tougher Child Support System to Replace CSA*, DWP press release, 24 July.

Eekelaar, J. (1991) 'Parental responsibility: state of nature or nature of the state?', *Journal of Social Welfare and Family Law* 37(1), 37-50.

EOC (Equal Opportunities Commission) (2005) *Facts About Women and Men in Great Britain 2005*, Manchester: EOC.

Glass, N. (2005) 'Surely some mistake?', *Guardian*, 5 January.

Gregg, P. and Harkness, S. (2003) *Welfare Reform and Lone Parents Employment in the UK*, Centre for Market and Public Organisation (CMPO) Working Paper Series No. 03/072, Bristol: CMPO, University of Bristol.

Hantrais, L. (2004) *Family Policy Matters: Responding to Family Change in Europe*, Bristol: The Policy Press.

HM Treasury (2003) *Every Child Matters*, London: The Stationery Office.

HM Treasury (2004a) *Choice for Parents, the Best Start for Children: A Ten Year Strategy for Childcare*, London: The Stationery Office.

HM Treasury (2004b) *Child Poverty Review*, London: The Stationery Office.

Holdaway, S., Davidson, N., Dignan, J., Hammersley, R., Hine, J. and Marsh, P. (2001) *New Strategies to Address Youth Offending. The National Evaluation of the Pilot Youth Offending Teams*, RDS Occasional Paper No 69, London: Home Office.

Home Office (1998) *Supporting Families*, London: The Stationery Office.

Home Office (2003) *Respect and Responsibility – Taking a Stand Against Anti-social Behaviour*, Cm 5778, London: The Stationery Office.

Home Office (2006) *Respect Action Plan*, London: Home Office.

Joyce, L. and Whiting, K. (2006) *Sanctions: Qualitative Summary Report on Lone Parent Customers*, Leeds: Centre for Development Studies, University of Leeds.

Kamerman, S. and Kahn, A. (1978) *Family Policy: Government and Families in Fourteen Countries*, New York, NY: Columbia University Press.

Kamerman, S. and Kahn, A. (eds) (1997) *Family Change and Family Policies in Great Britain, Canada, New Zealand, and the United States*, Oxford: Clarendon Press.

Levitas, R., Head, E. and Finch, N. (2006) 'Lone mothers, poverty and social exclusion', in C. Pantazis, D. Gordon and R. Levitas (eds) *Poverty and Social Exclusion in Britain*, Bristol: The Policy Press, 405–27.

Lister, R. (1996) 'Back to the family: family policies under the Major government', in H. Jones and J. Millar (eds) *The Politics of the Family*, Aldershot: Avebury, 11–31.

Low Pay Commission (2000) *The National Minimum Wage: The Story so Far*, Cm 4571, London: The Stationery Office.

Lyon, M., Barnes, M. and Sweiry, D. (2006) *Families with Children in Britain: Findings from the 2004 Families and Children Study (FACS)*, DWP Research Report No 340, Leeds: Centre for Development Studies, University of Leeds.

Meadows, P. and Garbers, C. (2004) *Improving the Employability of Parents in Sure Start Local Programmes: National Evaluation Summary*, London: DfES Sure Start Unit.

National Audit Office (2004) *Early Years: Progress in Developing High Quality Childcare and Early Education Accessible to All*, London: The Stationery Office.

National Audit Office (2006) *Child Support Agency – Implementation of the Child Support Reforms*, HC 1174 Session 2005–2006, London: The Stationery Office.

NESS (National Evaluation of Sure Start) (2005) *Variation in Sure Start Local Programmes' Effectiveness: Report of the NESS Programme Variability Study*, London: DfES Sure Start Unit.

NFPI (National Family and Parenting Institute) (2006) www.nfpi.org. uk (accessed 13 April).

Tunstill, J., Meadows, P., Allnock, D., Akhurst, S. and Garbers, C. (2005) *Implementing Sure Start Local Programmes: An Integrated Overview of the First Four Years*, London: DfES Sure Start Unit.

Seaman, P., Turner, K., Hill, M, Stafford, A. and Walker, M. (2005) *Parenting and Children's Resilience in Disadvantaged Communities*, London: National Children's Bureau.

Smeaton, D. and Marsh, A. (2006) *Maternity and Paternity Rights and Benefits: Survey of Parents 2005*, London: DTI.

Walling, A. (2005) 'Families and work', *Labour Market Trends*, July, 275–83.

NINE

Caring, citizenship and New Labour: dilemmas and contradictions for disabled and older women

Kirstein Rummery

Introduction

Many of the case studies in this book look at policies aimed at groups of women whom New Labour has specifically targeted: working women, mothers, lone parents, and women living in poverty in particular. Policies aimed at these groups of women have clearly followed the overarching theme of making work pay and enabling women who were previously excluded from the labour market because of childcare duties to participate in paid work (see Chapters Six, Seven, Eight; Rake 2001). However, for some groups of vulnerable women at risk of or living in poverty, engagement in paid work is of much lesser significance. Older women, if they have been engaging in paid work are usually retired from doing so by the age of 60, and younger disabled women have a much lower rate of economic participation than the population generally and than non-disabled women particularly. In examining how far any government has managed to engender politics and policy, we therefore need to be aware that it is necessary to look critically not just at the position of women as a group in relation to men, but also to look at social divisions within the category of women, and particularly to look at groups of women for whom the intersection of social categories (such as gender, age and disability) has a significant impact on their citizenship (Jordan 2004; Lister 2003).

This chapter therefore looks at the area of caring and citizenship, and examines areas of policy which particularly affect disabled and older women's lives. It critically examines areas which have a significant impact on disabled and older women, contrasting areas where New Labour has taken a gender aware approach (such as pensions) with those in which a gender blind approach to policy has been adopted (such as the New Deal for Disabled People, direct payments and health and social service reorganisation), and discusses the effects these approaches have had on disabled and older women's lives and their citizenship status. It draws the conclusion that New Labour has favoured the worker-citizen over the carer-citizen, and examines why that is the case, and what that means for disabled and older women.

Formulating the policy problem

Caring and citizenship

An uneasy tension has long existed in both feminist scholarship and mainstream policy in the UK between seeing women's route to empowerment as being primarily through engagement in the public sphere of paid work on the one hand, and through acknowledging and valuing women's role as carers in the domestic, private sphere on the other (Pateman 1988; Lewis 2001; Lister 2002a; Millar 2004). While many scholars looking at the tensions and dilemmas in women's citizenship have focused on the issues raised by combining paid work with raising and caring for children, the issue of caring for spouses and other adult relatives is arguably of equal significance, particularly given the rate at which the UK population is ageing (Ungerson 1997; Daly 2002; Boneham and Sixsmith 2006).

Since the inception of the post-war welfare state in the UK, successive governments have attempted an uneasy balancing act between viewing citizenship as being a status accorded to those engaged in paid work and trying to support those who undertake unpaid caring work. The breadwinner model of welfare recognises the value to society and the economy of unpaid caring work, but has the disadvantage of reinforcing gendered divisions of labour and underpinning women's economic dependence, while more individualistic models of citizenship fail to support the value of unpaid caring work adequately.

Since coming to power in 1997 New Labour has explicitly favoured the worker-model of citizenship, with Blair's repeated mantra of 'work for those who can' and 'no rights without responsibilities' setting the policy tone (Rake 2001). Policies such as the New Deal (particularly for lone parents and disabled people) have stressed the importance of paid work not just as a route out of poverty and dependency on state benefits, but also as a badge of citizenship and fulfilment of obligations to society. However, this emphasis on paid work as the route to citizenship has several drawbacks. First, no matter how much support individuals get to overcome the barriers to paid employment (such as assistance with childcare and aids and adaptations for disabled people), it still relies on a favourable economic climate and full employment, conditions which some commentators argue will never fully be in place, and even if they were, would still lead to the fragmentation of the labour market and the marginalisation of some sectors of workers at the expense of others (Lister 2001; Craig 2004). Second, as Craig puts it, 'stressing the primacy of paid work devalues the status of those millions who undertake, often on an unpaid basis, caring work, looking after older or dependent friends and relatives, or voluntary community work' (Craig 2004, 96). Reform to the welfare state to take into account this work has resulted in a gendered division of citizenship — as it is overwhelmingly (but by no means exclusively) women who undertake the bulk of such work, women have generally been accorded a kind of second-class citizenship, with rights mediated by men, or the state (Dean and Melrose 1999; Lister 2001). Dean and Melrose (1999) also point out that while a gender neutral conception of citizenship tries to ignore social divisions and ends up exacerbating them, a differentiated notion of citizenship also has the result of increasing social divisions, not just along gender lines, but also those of race, disability and age.

As Craig (2004), Hills et al (2002), and others have pointed out, New Labour has focused on tackling social exclusion through the means of engagement in paid work — 'work for those who can' at the expense of 'security for those who cannot'. This has left largely unexplored the issue of citizenship for those who are either removed from the labour market by the barrier of the retirement age, or by the social, environmental and attitudinal barriers that discriminate against disabled people, which has an impact on older and disabled people. It has also left underdeveloped the issue of those people who are fulfilling their citizenship duties by engaging in *unpaid* work (usually childcare and/or caring for ill, frail or disabled friends and relatives), which has a particular impact on women. Moreover, what policy attention has been focused on older people has been largely to do with overhauling the pensions system, which is about ensuring that people fulfil their citizenship duties by saving appropriately for their retirement through paid work; and does not address the issue of unpaid work either over the life course or engaged in after retirement age.

This chapter will now examine some of the policy issues around citizenship and caring that have put in place, or reinforced, by New Labour since 1997 and critically discuss the impact of the 'deep normative core' (Sabatier 1986) of those policies on older and disabled women. Although it will be shown that the policies in question were varied in how gendered they were in their formulation, both their theoretical underpinnings and their implementation have led to outcomes that have been differentiated along lines of gender, disability and age, particularly for older and disabled women.

Balancing rights, duties and needs: the perspectives of disabled and older women

Disabled and older people have traditionally been viewed within policy terms as being largely passive, recipients of welfare assistance, rather than active and engaged citizens. One of the writers who was a key influence on the architects of the British welfare state, T.H. Marshall, defined citizenship as being 'a status bestowed on those who are full members of a community' (Marshall 1992, 18). He divided citizenship into three elements: the civil, the political and the social, which he felt evolved from each other as society developed over time. He defined these elements thus:

> *The civil element* is comprised of the rights necessary for individual freedom — liberty of the person, freedom of speech, thought and faith, the right to own property and conclude valid contracts, and the right to justice ... By the political element I mean the right to participate in the exercise of political power, as a member of a body invested with political authority or as an elector of the members of such a body ... By the social element I mean the whole range from the right to a modicum of economic welfare and security, to the right to *share in the full social heritage and to live the civilised life according to the standards prevailing in society*. (Marshall, 1992, 8, emphasis added)

Most commentators on citizenship have noted that it entails a balance of rights and responsibilities, which Marshall defined thus:

> If citizenship is invoked in defence of rights, the corresponding duties of citizenship cannot be ignored ... [such as] the general obligation to live the life of a good citizen, giving such service as can promote the welfare of the community ... of paramount importance is the duty to work. (Marshall 1992, 41–4)

What Marshall refers to as 'giving such service as can promote the welfare of the community' covers the kind of unpaid work (such as childcare and caring) that still have gendered dimensions in their distribution (Lister 2002b; Rake 2001; Pascall and Lewis 2004). However, Marshall's insistence that 'of paramount importance is the duty to work' hides his unspoken, and gendered, assumption that work meant engagement in *paid* work, or what feminist and other scholars refers to as the materialistic, public sphere of the economy (Petersen 2002), neglecting the arguably just as important private sphere in which unpaid caring work takes place (Ungerson 2000). This unspoken but gendered assumption framed the formation of the welfare state and still resonates soundly in New Labour's policy and practice.

However, older people above retirement age are not usually engaged in paid work, and due to mandatory retirement ages and pension provision are not expected to be. Employment rates prior to New Labour coming to power among younger disabled men were estimated to be at around 40%, around 35% for working-age disabled women (Burchardt 2000), as compared to just over 80% for working-age non-disabled men and 75% for working age non-disabled women. New Labour's own figures suggest that since 1998, 0.75 million disabled people have entered the labour market who were previously unemployed as a result of policies such as the New Deal for Disabled People, but that employment rates, although improving, have remained steadily low at 48% for disabled men and 45% for disabled women, compared to 86% of non-disabled men and 79% of non-disabled women (ONS 2005). However, given that women generally are over-represented in part-time and low-paid work, and disabled women are even less likely than their non-disabled counterparts to be working at all, paid work is only a small part of the way in which disabled women discharge their obligation to 'give such services as promotes the welfare of the community'.

Historically, the focus on disabled women (and some older women) as the *recipients* of care has overshadowed the role they play themselves as carers. In fact, most studies of disabled women's lives and experiences have shown how they view themselves not just as passive recipients of care but as part of reciprocal networks of care – as mothers, daughters, spouses, friends and relatives who give and receive support in a variety of ways, much as non-disabled women do (Campling 1981; Hillyer 1993; Morris 1993; Grue and Laerum 2002). Moreover, studies of older people's views of their lives and citizenship obligations show that removal from the obligation of engagement in paid work by no means signifies the end of active engagement in the community (Russell and Kendig 1999). Indeed, for many older women who had engaged in paid work only part time, or with gaps over their life course due to caring or other commitments, retirement from paid work simply meant more time to fulfil these other obligations as more time and energy was devoted to grandparenting, caring for ageing or frail relatives or spouses, or engaging in voluntary or other unpaid work (Crossman et al 1981; Rummery 2002; Craig 2004).

Policy developments under New Labour have failed to allow for the complexity of considerations around citizenship, ageing, gender and caring that are crucial to the ways in which disabled and older women have sought to play their role in society (Gilbert and Powell 2005). The next section will examine the development and function of some of these policy developments and discuss why this is the case.

New Labour's response: Citizenship policies for older and disabled women

'Work for those who can': New Deal for Disabled People

The New Deal for Disabled People, like other New Deal programmes, aims to help into paid work unemployed people who face particular barriers to employment, by allocating disabled job seekers dedicated Job Brokers to help them navigate their way into employment. In 2004, over three million people were claiming disability benefits, and 77% of those had been claiming for two years or more, as compared to 8% of unemployed people claiming unemployment benefit for two years or more (DWP 2005).

Unlike other New Deal programmes that did have an explicitly gendered focus (such as the New Deal for Lone Parents, which focused on enabling lone parents to find suitable childcare), provisions under the New Deal for Disabled People made no explicit allowance to enable disabled people with caring responsibilities to combine caring and work – instead, much of the focus was on accessing aids and adaptations through statutory, voluntary and other sector providers to help disabled people overcome the physical barriers to work. And despite the financial incentive of getting disabled people off long-term sickness and disability benefits, only £30 million was allocated to the New Deal for Disabled People in 2002/03, as compared to £80 million on the New Deal for Lone Parents (HM Treasury 2003). If we assume that disabled mothers follow the same pattern as non-disabled mothers in having more caring responsibilities for children than fathers do, and the problems discussed below about both cash benefits and services being geared towards providing physical care for the disabled person rather than recognising the disabled person's role in providing care for others, then the gendered disparity in employment rates is easily explained.

It is clear from the way in which the New Deal for Disabled People has been formulated and implemented that it was never intended to have a gender aware dimension: disabled people are conceived as being potential workers with structural help, aids and adaptations needed to participate in paid work. Very little account is given to the way in which disabled people, and disabled women in particular, combine receiving and giving care, support and parenting as well as paid work. This is probably due to a combination of factors including the lack of attention given by the WEU to women as carers (rather than parents) generally, the overarching role of the DWP in this area (and therefore by definition a concentration on the role of paid work) and an assumption that the needs of disabled women are limited to receiving, rather than giving, care and support.

'Security for those who cannot': Pensions and benefits for disabled and older women

Clearly, as so many disabled and older women are not engaged in full-time paid work, the issue of pensions and benefits, particularly given the link between poverty and social exclusion, is a vital one in citizenship terms. Because they are more likely than men to be working part time or in low-paid jobs, disabled women are less likely than disabled men to qualify for insurance based income replacement benefits should they fall sick and be unable to work (Smith et al 2004). Similarly, because their patterns of work over their life-course are more likely to have periods of withdrawal from paid work and working part time because of caring commitments, or working in low-paid jobs, older women are much less likely than older men to have adequate pension provision and are consequently at much greater risk of poverty (Joshi 1992). Women's average income in retirement is around 53% of men's (Bennett 2005).

In some respects, this is where the situation regarding gender aware policy diverges between younger disabled women and older women. The Commission on Social Justice, set up by the late John Smith MP, argued for key changes in social security, particularly pensions, to address the income gap between men and women, particularly older men and women (Commission on Social Justice 1994). However, when it came to power in 1997, New Labour largely abandoned a systematic gender focus on social security reform (Bennett 2005). Instead, it has focused on ways of increasing private sector involvement in the provision of pensions and reducing the role of the state pension – a move which commentators have argued will inherently disadvantage women still further (Davies and Ward 1992). For single women over retirement age, state benefits make up 60% of their income, as compared to 52% of men's income – the figures for couples are 46% for women and 32% for men respectively (WEU 2004) – any erosion of state benefits will therefore have adverse effects on disproportionate numbers of older women as compared to older men. In seeking to reduce women's risk of poverty in later life, New Labour's policy seems to be to rely on women's increased labour market participation, with the government predicting that by 2025 99% of women will have some kind of basic entitlement to a pension in their own right (Bennett 2005).

Gender aware changes to the pension system to take into account the impact of women's caring responsibilities, with 'second tier' rights to state pensions being extended to those who have spent time away from the labour market to undertake caring duties, and provisions to count only 20 years of working life in assessing contributions, rather than the full number, thus allowing women to discount any years not engaged in paid work due to caring commitments (DWP 2006). Changes to means-tested benefits for pensioners have also benefited women, who are more likely than men to be in receipt of them (DWP 2006). However, Ginn (2004) and others have noted that reliance on means-tested benefits to tackle poverty have a chequered history, and means-tested benefits are more likely to be stigmatising, divisive and consequently have a lower take-up than contribution-based benefits. It is therefore welcome that the latest proposals from the Turner Commission include a return to earnings-related increases in the basic (non-means tested) state pension, as these will benefit the poorest retired women the most – however, these changes are not due to be implemented for several years and therefore will not benefit older women currently (DWP 2006). Women are also more likely than men to be in receipt of attendance allowance (a benefit designed to help meet the costs of disability for older people) but when the differences in longevity and incapacity rates are controlled for this difference disappears (Bennett 2005).

In contrast, policies around social security benefits for younger disabled women have not benefited from an explicit gender aware focus. New Labour has concentrated on tightening rules for incapacity and other disability-related benefits, and through New Deal for Disabled People (see above) encouraging those on long-term sickness benefits to return to work. There has been no explicit policy focus on addressing income gaps between younger disabled women and men. Since 1997, not much progress has been made in recognising the role that working-age women play in providing care for adults. Rates of benefit allowance for younger carers (who are overwhelmingly women) have remained low, dependent on people caring for someone in receipt of disability benefits and providing over 35 hours of care a week, and when carers reach retirement age are mainly cancelled out by means-testing rules applied to the provision of pensions (Bennett 2005). In fact, apart from the Carers Act, passed under the previous Conservative administration (see below), there have been no significant improvements in provisions for carers since married women won the right to Invalidity Care Allowance over two decades ago.

The complexity of citizenship: Community care and health policies

The ability to give 'such service as can promote the welfare of the community' is for many older and disabled women contingent not just on access to income (either through paid work or through benefits), but also on access to services and support. Statutory intervention in this area in the UK is commonly the result of health and community care policies. In health policy, New Labour has presided over one of the most fundamental structural reorganisations the NHS has experienced, giving Primary Care Trusts a pivotal role in commissioning and providing health care. It has also focused on older people's services, investing in rehabilitation and intermediate care services, which are primarily designed to reduce use of acute hospital services and aid hospital discharge for those patients who are too frail to return to their own homes. However, this investment has not necessarily focused on increasing older people's autonomy and ability to 'share in the full social heritage and to live the civilised life according to the standards prevailing in society' nor is it designed to increase older people's capacity to give 'such service as can promote the welfare of the community'. Instead, it carries forward a programme of reform centred on the introduction of managerialism and market mechanisms into the public sector that was begun under the previous Conservative administration and which has echoes across several 'Third Way' type regimes. Several commentators have noted that these reforms, particularly the introduction of market mechanisms, have served to reinforce divisions of gender and class rather than ameliorate them, mainly through increased reliance on community-based unpaid or low-paid care workers (Hammer and Osterle 2003).

Within UK policy, community-based care work has fallen under community care, rather than health policy, and is thus largely the responsibility of local, rather than national government. However, while decisions about the range and type of services available, and the eligibility criteria to access them are made locally, community care policy generally is governed by national policy. Given the rapid and sometimes dizzying rate of reform of the social security, health and other welfare systems, it is surprising that community care policy has remained largely untouched under New Labour. The most fundamental recent development in community care has been the implementation of the 1990 NHS and Community Care Act, which introduced a mixed economy of care, giving local authorities the duty to involve the private sector in the provision of community-based and residential care services for disabled and older people. Lewis and Glennerster (1996) and others have argued that the 'deep normative core' (Sabatier 1986) of this policy was the need to curb rising expenditure on community care services caused by rising demand and runaway expenditure on residential care services due to benefits rules which allowed the costs of care to be offset against benefit income.

The 1990 NHS and Community Care Act also gave local authorities the responsibility to assess the needs of disabled and older people and to put together 'packages of care' (usually a mix of statutory, voluntary and family-provided support) to suit people's needs. They were also given the discretion to decide what level of needs they would meet (and following several legal challenges were given explicit direction that they had to take resources into account when deciding what needs to meet) and what the criteria would be for accessing their services. Given the 'deep normative core' of curbing rising expenditure on services, this has largely turned into a rationing exercise, with local authorities redefining the criteria for accessing services more and more tightly and targeting services on those at risk of entering residential or hospital care. Such services have tended to be concentrated on the personal tending side of care – washing, dressing, feeding and so on. One criticism of community care policy is that such targeting of services on those with the highest needs has meant a lack of investment in low-level preventative services (Clarke et al 1998). Disabled mothers and older women with caring responsibilities have noted particularly that the focus on providing personal care has meant that there are very few services available which are designed to support them in carrying out their caring roles (Rummery 2002). Community care services have also been criticised for being unreliable, of poor quality, and out of the control of users, leading to social exclusion – definitely not enabling people to 'share in the full social heritage and to live the civilised life according to the standards prevailing in society' or to give 'such service as can promote the welfare of the community'.

Arguably, this is in part to do with the way disabled and older people generally have been conceived within policy to be the passive recipients of care. The 1995 Carers Act gave carers of adults the right to ask for an assessment of their own needs, separate from the person they were caring for, but did not allocate any specific funds for this and did not give carers the right to access any particular services. Implementation of this has been patchy, which is not surprising given the competition for resources in this area (Scourfield 2005). Research has shown that in practice local authorities have not been able to find ways of adequately handling the kinds of complex, reciprocal and interconnected ways in which disabled mothers and older disabled carers, particularly women, give and receive support and care, preferring to make binary distinctions between 'users' and 'carers' (Grue and Laerum 2002). A seemingly gender neutral policy has failed to take into account lessons from feminist social policy about the complexity of people's lives, particularly because it has undervalued engagement in unpaid caring work as a means of discharging citizenship obligations (Crossman et al 1981; Gilbert and Powell 2005).

One policy development which has enabled disabled and older women to combine receiving and giving care, help and support has been the introduction of Direct Payments. Like the policies referred to above, this was an initiative started as part of the marketised reforms of community care policy by the previous Conservative administration. Prior to 1996 it was illegal for local authorities to give disabled and older people cash instead of services to meet their needs, but the introduction of Direct Payments has made this a possibility. It has been universally welcomed by disabled activists as research has shown that by purchasing their own care (usually through the employment of a personal assistant) disabled people can exercise more choice and control over the help and support they receive and can tailor it more effectively to meet their needs. By doing so, they have been able to move from being the passive recipient of services to being actively engaged in giving 'such service as can promote the welfare of the community', through paid work, parenting, caring, volunteering, political activism and other means (Rummery 2006).

The only real involvement New Labour has had in Direct Payments is in extending them to older people and carers of disabled children, and removing the discretion local authorities had in whether or not to offer them to their citizens. From a gendered perspective there are two important points to be made about Direct Payments. First, on a positive note, the increased choice and control that users have been able to exercise with them have enabled them to combine giving and receiving help and support in a way that is much more in line with what feminist social policy scholars have noted are the kind of complex, reciprocal networks particularly common to women's lives: it has facilitated a much more gender sensitive conception of citizenship rights and duties to be evolved and used by disabled women themselves (Rummery 2006). Second, on a more worrying note, Direct Payments have worked because they have relied on market mechanisms and the ability of disabled users to directly employ workers at relatively low rates of pay with relatively poor working conditions: such workers are much more likely to be women than men, and are more likely to be open to abuse and exploitation than workers in higher paid, more regulated working situations (Ungerson 1999).

The outcome

Work versus care: The failure to engender citizenship policy

Overall, very few of the policies referred to above have had a specifically gender aware focus. Instead, they have been largely the result of other driving forces in policy which might, on first glance, appear gender neutral: carrying on the Conservatives' legacy of managerialism and private sector involvement in the provision of public services, tackling poverty and social exclusion primarily through the facilitation of paid work, and moving services towards primary and community settings. However, being 'gender neutral' has meant that policy has failed to take on important lessons learned about women's lives from feminism, and thus policy outcomes have had a differentiated impact upon women and men, usually to the detriment of women, which has had profound implications for their citizenship status, particularly that of older and disabled women.

First, in drawing up the balance between duties and rights, and in deciding how citizens should both fulfil their citizenship duties and be socially included in society, New Labour has clearly come down in favour of paid work above all else. Correspondingly, although relying on unpaid care work (particularly unpaid care of adults – investment in community-based services to support carers has not increased at anything like the level that investment in childcare services has) the state simultaneously undervalues that work as a badge of citizenship in comparison to paid work. As women are over-represented among unpaid carers of adults this policy direction has clearly gendered implications.

Second, in several areas of policy, New Labour has opted for binary distinctions in citizens' identities that do not correspond to the complexity of women's real lives, particularly those of disabled and older women. People are either workers or non-workers; users or carers; disabled or able bodied; younger (working, or should be) or older (retired, and not working). However, women's lives, particularly disabled and older women's lives, are usually much more complex than these either/or distinctions allow. Younger disabled women are often combining paid work with giving and receiving care and support from a partner and parenting, as well as sometimes giving support and care to older relatives (Grue and Laerum 2002). Older women, while not usually engaged in paid work, are often engaged in work in its wider conception – voluntary work, community work, caring for older relatives, disabled spouses or disabled children, grandparenting – as well as, if they are frail or disabled themselves, receiving support and care from spouses, children, friends, relatives, statutory, voluntary and private health and social care services (Crossman et al 1981; Russell and Kendig 1999; Boneham and Sixsmith 2006). Women's lives in general, and disabled and older women's lives in particular, tend to involve complex networks of carrying out duties and receiving help, support and services, in ways which are simply not accounted for in the binary distinctions favoured by New Labour's citizenship policies.

Third, even where New Labour has had an overtly gendered approach to policies that affect disabled and older women's lives – most notably pensions policy – these policies have also favoured paid work as a route to ending social exclusion – in the case of pensions, *future* social exclusion caused by poverty and inadequate income in later life. Those changes to the pensions systems which have tried to take into account the ways in which most women combine paid and unpaid work over their lifetime have accorded a 'second-class citizenship' to those who have favoured caring over paid work. These policies do little to address the risk of poverty that older women are facing today, or to compensate for the ways in which younger disabled women are excluded from the labour market generally, particularly from the higher income, full-time sectors of the labour market that will lead to higher pensions provisions and therefore lower risk of poverty in later life.

Conclusion

It would be too damning to dismiss New Labour as having failed disabled and older women. Clearly, there are some areas of policy innovation or extension that have had significant benefits for these groups of women. The changes to community care support and the extension of direct payments has had a demonstrable impact on the ability of disabled and older women to combine giving and receiving care and support, for example. The recently announced changes to the pensions system, while falling short of adequately compensating women for time away from paid work engaged in caring, do at least firmly recognise and therefore value care as work.

However, there does not appear to be any evidence of a sustained commitment to tackling the problems of poverty and social exclusion experienced by disabled and older women, for several reasons. First, there has been no committed or unified policy process or actor that has focused on these groups. The DoH has never had an overtly feminist leadership or agenda: instead, it has focused on fundamental restructuring of the health service and social care services which has been done under the auspices of 'modernisation' (the extension of new public management, partnership working and the involvement of the private and third sector in the delivery of welfare) rather than with any overt or covert mission to address women's issues (Newman 2001). Any gains for women are therefore subsidiary results of policy action with a different purpose, rather than as a result of a feminisation of the policy process. The DWP has benefited from a feminisation of the policy process, but only to the extent of aiming to address the income disparity between men and women as paid workers, not to the extent addressing the undervaluation of caring.

Second, New Labour has fetishised paid work to the exclusion of all other routes to citizenship, whether this is in the area of poverty, class, disability, age or gender, and this has profound consequences for the kinds of policy problems that can be seen to be legitimate (Lister 2002b). Supporting the complexity of women's lives as carers and the receivers of care has simply not registered on the policy agenda either for New Labour generally, or more specifically for the feminist policy actors who might have been able to pursue more innovative and responsive policy solutions that have not focused on paid work as the route out of poverty. However, for most disabled and older women, paid work is not readily available as a way of tackling poverty and social exclusion.

If New Labour is going to protect the citizenship status of disabled and older women, and enable them to avoid social exclusion by helping them to 'share in the full social heritage and to live the civilised life according to the standards prevailing in society', then it has to meet the challenge of recognising the work that women do in giving 'such service as can promote the welfare of the community' in ways that include, but are no means limited to, engagement in paid work. A gender sensitive citizenship policy needs to end the over-reliance on paid work as the only means of fulfilling citizenship duties and needs to take into account the complex, interconnecting networks of help and support that communities in general, and disabled and older women in particularly, contribute to and get help from in order to help society thrive (Lister 2002b; Jordan 2004; Williams 2005). Engendering citizenship policy would mean really valuing care as work, and would ensure that caring citizens should not be second-class citizens: a challenge New Labour does not seem able to face.

References

Bennett, F. (2005) *Gender and Benefits*, Manchester: EOC.

Boneham, M.A. and Sixsmith, J.A. (2006) 'The voices of older women in a disadvantaged community: issues of health and social capital', *Social Science and Medicine* 62(2), 269-79.

Burchardt, T. (2000) *Enduring Economic Exclusion*, York: Joseph Rowntree Foundation.

Campling, J. (1981) *Images of Ourselves: Disabled Women Talking*, London: Routledge and Kegan Paul.

Clarke, H., Dyer, S. and Horwood, J. (1998) *That Little Bit of Help: The High Value of Low-Level Preventative Services for Older People*, Bristol: The Policy Press.

Commission on Social Justice (1994) *Social Justice: Strategies for National Renewal*, London: Vintage.

Craig, G. (2004) 'Citizenship, exclusion and older people', *Journal of Social Policy* 33(1), 95-115.

Crossmann, C., London, C. and Barry, C. (1981) 'Older women caring for disabled spouses: a model for supportive services', *Gerontologist* 21(5), 464-70.

Daly, M. (2002) 'Care as a good for social policy', *Journal of Social Policy* 31(2), 251-70.

Davies, B. and Ward, S. (1992) *Women and Personal Pensions*, London: EOC Research Series.

Dean, H. and Melrose, M. (1999) *Poverty, Riches and Social Citizenship*, Basingstoke: Macmillan.

DWP (Department for Work and Pensions) (2006) *Security in Retirement: Towards a New Pensions System*, Cm 6841, London: DWP.

Gilbert, T. and Powell, J.L. (2005) 'Family, caring and ageing in the United Kingdom', *Scandinavian Journal of Caring Sciences* 19(1), 53-7.

Ginn, J. (2004) 'European pension privatisation: taking account of gender', *Social Policy and Society* 3(2), 123-34.

Grue, L. and Laerum, K.T. (2002) '"Doing motherhood": some experiences of mothers with physical disabilities', *Disability and Society* 17(6), 671–83.

Hammer, E. and Osterle, A. (2003) 'Welfare state policy and informal long-term caregiving in Austria: old gender divisions and new stratification processes among women', *Journal of Social Policy* 32(1), 37–53.

Hills, J., LeGrand, J. and Piachaud, D. (eds) (2002) *Understanding Social Exclusion*, Oxford: Oxford University Press.

Hillyer, B. (1993) *Feminism and Disability*, Norman, OK: University of Oklahoma Press.

HM Treasury (2003) www.hm-treasury.gov.uk/budget/bud_bud03/bud_bud03_index.cfm (accessed November 2005).

Jordan, B. (2004) *Sex, Money and Power: The Transformation of Collective Life*, Cambridge: Polity.

Joshi, H. (1992) 'The cost of caring', in C. Glendinning and J. Millar (eds) *Women and Poverty in Britain: The 1990s*, Hemel Hempstead: Harvester Wheatsheaf.

Lewis, J. (2001) 'The decline of the male breadwinner model: implications for work and care', *Social Politics* 8(2), 152–69.

Lewis, J. and Glennerster, H. (1996) *Implementing the New Community Care*, Buckingham: Open University Press.

Lister, R. (2001) 'Citizenship and changing welfare states', in J.G. Andersen and P. Jensen *Changing Labour Markets, Welfare Policies and Citizenship*, Bristol: The Policy Press.

Lister, R. (2002a) 'Sexual citizenship', in E.F. Isin and B.S. Turner (eds) *Handbook of Citizenship Studies*, London: Sage.

Lister, R. (2002b) 'The dilemmas of pendulum politics: balancing paid work, care and citizenship', *Economy and Society* 31(4), 520–32.

Lister, R. (2003) *Citizenship: Feminist Perspectives* (2nd edn), Basingstoke: Palgrave Macmillan.

Marshall, T.H. (1992) 'Citizenship and social class', in T.H Marshall and T. Bottomore *Citizenship and Social Class*, London: Pluto.

Millar, J. (2004) 'Squaring the circle: means-testing and individualisation', *Social Policy and Society* 3(1), 67–74.

Morris, J. (1993) *Independent Lives: Community Care and Disabled People*, Basingstoke: Macmillan.

Newman, J. (2001) *Modernising Governance: New Labour, Policy and Society*, London: Sage.

ONS (Office for National Statistics) (2005) Labour Force Survey, Spring 2005 dataset, London: The Stationery Office.

Pascall, G. and Lewis, J. (2004) 'Emerging gender regimes and policies for gender equality in a wider Europe', *Journal of Social Policy* 33(3), 373-94.

Pateman, C. (1988) *The Sexual Contract*, Cambridge: Polity Press.

Peterson, V.S. (2002) 'Rewriting (global) political economy as reproductive, productive and virtual (Foucauldian) economies', *International Feminist Journal of Politics* 4(1), 1-30.

Rake, K. (2001) 'Gender and New Labour's social policies', *Journal of Social Policy* 30(2), 209-31.

Rummery, K. (2002) *Disability, Citizenship and Community Care: A Case for Welfare Rights?*, Aldershot: Ashgate.

Rummery, K. (2006) 'Disabled citizens and social exclusion: the case of direct payments', *Policy & Politics* 4(4), 633-50.

Russell, C. and Kendig, H.L. (1999) 'Social policy and research for older citizens', *Australasian Journal on Ageing*, 18(3), 44-9.

Sabatier, P.A. (1986) 'Top-down and bottom-up approaches to implementation research', *Journal of Public Policy* 6, 21-48.

Scourfield, P. (2005) 'Implementing the Community Care (Direct Payments) Act: will the supply of personal assistants meet the demand and at what price?', *Journal of Social Policy* 43(3), 469-89.

Smith, N., Middleton, S., Ashton-Brooks, K., Cox, L. and Dobson, B. with Reith, L. (2004) *Disabled People's Costs of Living: More Than You Might Think*, York: Joseph Rowntree Foundation.

Ungerson, C. (1997) 'Social politics and the commodification of care', *Social Politics* 4(3), 362-81.

Ungerson, C. (1999) 'Personal assistants and disabled people: an examination of a hybrid form of work and care', *Work, Employment and Society* 3(4), 583-600.

Ungerson, C. (2000) 'Thinking about the production and consumption of long-term care in Britain: does gender still matter?', *Journal of Social Policy* 29(4), 623-43.

Williams, F. (2005) 'New Labour's family policy', in M. Powell, L. Bauld and K. Clarke (eds) *Social Policy Review 17: Analysis and Debate in Social Policy*, Bristol: The Policy Press.

WEU (Women and Equality Unit) (2004) *Individual Incomes of Men and Women 1996/7 – 2002/3*, London: DTI.

TEN

New Labour and 'lesbian- and gay-friendly' policy

Angelia R. Wilson

Introduction

This chapter considers a range of policies championed by New Labour which have made an impact on the lives of lesbian and gay citizens. The inclusion of this chapter in this collection may appear rather odd to some as it relates not just to 'women'. Nevertheless, its placement here bares witness to the contested terrain of gender, sexuality and hetero-normativity and the impact of policies based upon stereotype and binary understandings of gender and sexual orientation. The level of cultural and political hostility toward lesbians and gay men prior to the election of New Labour and the overwhelming changes in policy since 1997 raises the question 'Why is New Labour "lesbian- and gay-friendly"?' The account below considers each policy in turn exploring the larger context of political culture, economic focus that underpinned the whirlwind 'triumph' of social justice.

Without a doubt, New Labour has been the most lesbian- and gay-friendly government in our history. Of course, such a statement must be understood in the historical context. For example, criminal law and public policy tended to be most concerned with the threat of male homosexuality to social morality (Weeks 1981, 85; Herman 1993, 253-4). Henry VIII in 1533 declared buggery with man, woman or beast a criminal offence punishable by death. In 1861 the death penalty was replaced by life imprisonment. In 1885, the Criminal Law Amendment Act made all male homosexual acts short of buggery, for example, kissing, oral sex, and mutual masturbation, committed in public or private illegal, labelling these 'gross indecency'. This 'blackmailer's charter' resulted in a number of famous trials including that of Oscar Wilde and Sir John Gielgud. During the Second World War and the post-war period 'gross indecency' charges rose significantly and by 1955 over 2,322 men were arrested under this Act, many of whom were prominent public figures

(Hyde 1970; Weeks 1990). The offence of 'gross indecency' remained on the statute books until the 2003 Sexual Offences Act.

The 1957 Wolfenden Report and subsequent 1967 Sexual Offences Act decriminalised homosexual acts in private between consenting men over 21 who were not members of the armed services. It did not, as popular opinion might suggest, 'legalise' homosexuality. Neither did it grant equality to homosexuals. The Wolfenden Committee comments set the socio-political tone for the next 40 years warning that 'any form of ostentatious behaviour now or in the future would … make the sponsors of the Bill regret that they have done what they have done' (Hyde 1970, 274). Of course, what followed surely caused them regret. The sexual revolution and birth of the Gay Liberation Front in November 1970 gave opened up space for 'gay pride' and burgeoning 'lesbian feminist' and 'gay' political activism. The advent of HIV/Aids in the late 1980s however, saw a backlash against gay men and anyone outside hetero-normativity. The embodiment of this was the Thatcher government's attempt to restore the moral value of heterosexuality and the nuclear family (see Weeks 1990; Jeffrey-Poulter 1991). Section 28 of the 1988 Local Government Act stated that a 'local authority shall not intentionally promote homosexuality or publish material with the intention of promoting homosexuality; promote the teaching in any maintained school of the acceptability of homosexuality as pretended family relationship'. While, it added that this did not prohibit work regarding the treatment or prevention of disease, the ethos of the legislation undermined HIV/Aids public awareness campaigns and education within schools. This chapter will consider the impact of Section 28 in relation to education in more detail. However, it is worth giving this brief policy history to set the stage for the election of New Labour in 1997 and to keep in perspective any feelings of gratitude or claims of the advent of a British lesbian and gay utopia.

I promise to …

In response to the homophobia surrounding Aids in the late 1980 and subsequent passage of Section 28, gay men and lesbians became more politically sophisticated, either through radical in-your-face activism of ActUp! and Lesbian Avengers or through the more traditionally organised campaign organisation Stonewall. These very different, but complementary, political approaches managed to keep gay and lesbian concerns on the political agenda through the years of the Major government and, by the election campaigns of the late 1990s New Labour specifically targeted the 'gay vote'. Some surveys report that

46% of lesbian and gay voters supported New Labour in 1997 with only 12% and 11% voting Liberal Democrat or Conservative, respectively (StormBreak 2000/01, 10). The election of openly gay candidates such as Stephen Twigg and Ben Bradshaw was followed by the Cabinet appointments of Peter Mandelson, Chris Smith and Nick Brown. These 'positive images' clearly signalled the changes ahead.

In October 1997, the government made concessions for unmarried partners in the immigration regulations opening the door for same-sex partners of British nationals to become eligible for residency status and in 2000 these concessions became an Immigration Rule. This fairly low-key and easy policy win, fuelled belief that New Labour would deliver on campaign promises in a timely fashion.

Until 1994, *being* homosexual in the military was a criminal offence. The 1994 Criminal Justice and Public Order Act decriminalised homosexuality in the military but it remained grounds for discharge. The Major government continued to defend the ban of 'gays in the military' citing the 1996 Homosexuality Policy Assessment Report which 'found' heterosexuals armed service personnel with 'negative' attitudes towards homosexuals; thus 'proving' that lifting the ban would 'upset' troops. Nicholas Soames, Conservative MP and Minister of State for the Armed Forces, admitted, however, that it would 'not be sensible, economic or efficient use of resources to identify those who were homosexual and wish to keep it to themselves' (1996). New Labour was not proactive in challenging the ban, but it found discrimination difficult to argue in court. Rank Outsiders, a campaign group for armed services personnel, and Stonewall supported a number of legal challenges to the ban on homosexuals in the military, one of which successfully convinced the European Court of Human Rights in 1999 to denounce UK ban as unlawful.

Stonewall also campaigned to lower of the age of consent for homosexuals to 16, in line with that of heterosexuals and their lobbying paid off in the 2000 Sexual Offences Amendment Act. The threat of intervention by European courts also played a part in this debate, as recent decisions had forced the Republic of Ireland to decriminalise homosexuality and equalise the age of consent (see *Norris v. Ireland*;[1] the 1993 Criminal Law (Sexual Offences) Act). Just before the June 2001 General Election, the Home Office revised the Criminal Injuries Compensation Scheme to include long-term same-sex partners. This was an attempt to show responsiveness to their 'gay' constituency who were outraged by the Soho bomb in 1999 and the inequalities facing surviving partners in its aftermath. For some, these achievements were perceived as a move toward equality; others saw it as 'policies for the boys' as gay men appeared to be those most benefiting from policy successes of the first term of New Labour. For example, importantly, New Labour was unable to fulfil one key election promise, the repeal of Section 28. Moreover, legal discrimination in employment remained.

Forsaking all others ...

Following the election in 2001, New Labour implemented wide-ranging 'friendly' policies in the areas of civil partnership, parenting and education; each of which is discussed here in turn. It is worth noting beforehand a larger socio-political climate that made such changes possible. First, movement in the EU towards equality had an impact on the general political climate and presented New Labour with opportunities to allow lesbian and gay policies to slip in the back door or wait until the eventual EU 'knock-on' effect. For example, the 1997 Treaty of Amsterdam, Article 13 committed member states to combating discrimination based on sexual orientation leading to the 2000 Directive requiring EU member states to ban such discrimination. While New Labour was privy to these discussions since the beginning, it took five years before putting the 2003 Employment Equality (Sexual Orientation) Regulation in place in the UK. Given Brown's focus on employment, one would think New Labour would have been keener to secure lesbian and gay taxpayers in work.

Second, in answering the question 'Why?': follow the money. In 1970, the Spartacus *Gay Guide* listed around 200 gay venues in the UK. In 2006 the value of the 'pink pound' is estimated at around £70 billion annually in the UK. In 1994, 19 Fortune 500 brands were said to be active in the gay consumer market and in 2006 that number is 150. A report by Out Now Consulting shows the average income for gay men and lesbians in full-time employment at £34,168 and £24,783 respectively (2005). Most surveys assume 6% of the population, around three million, are lesbian or gay (DTI 2005). So, once gay men and lesbians were free to 'come out' without the risk of prosecution or unemployment, capitalists have been able to identify a sizeable, relatively prosperous market. The economic growth of the 'pink pound' motivated social and political change and presented more opportunities for New Labour's 'friendly policies'. The economic impact on relevant policy developments is twofold as the free-market requires the state to minimise legislation hampering capitalist development and as lesbian and gay constituents can be construed as market forces with high disposable incomes.

Finally, the collapse of the Thatcher government put the brakes on the moralising about the family and homosexuality that had led to Section 28. New Labour came to power claiming the ethical high ground and vowing to fight social exclusion. In terms of lesbian and gay voters, this was articulated through the promise to repeal the homophobic Section 28. This reflected a cultural shift in attitudes towards gay men and lesbians from the rise of 'lesbian chic' in the mid-1990s, more positive representations in media and, unsurprisingly given the previous discussion, targeted advertising. In this apparently less threatening culture, gay and lesbian activism became both more concentrated and less angry. With Stonewall cuddling up to New Labour and a few more radically minded activists making the occasional headline, most gay men and lesbians got on with their daily lives. This decline of oppositional politics and the expectation of changes ahead, affected what it meant to 'be political'– during a march calling for the repeal of Section 28 in 2000 one protester commented 'it's just not as fun without Maggie'. The 'sexual-political' culture in the 1990s had changed beyond recognition. The EU, market forces, and, to some extent, cultural attitudes presented New Labour with a clear opportunity to move 'gay- and lesbian-friendly' policies forward. The next section reviews a few of these, not in chronological order, but thematically and selectively concentrating on policies regarding issues at the heart of what were previously known as 'pretend families'.

I now pronounce you ...

The first signal of change was the 1997 recognition of same sex partners in immigration matters but it took seven years before 2005 Civil Partnership Act finally gave legal recognition to same-sex couples. According to the government, civil partnership is 'similar' to marriage including joint treatment for income-related benefits, state pensions and recognition for immigration purposes. The government is absolutely clear, however, that civil partnerships are 'not marriage' and should not be labelled as such. Relatedly, the Church of England will not allow vicars to 'marry' or 'bless' a civil partnership but they are allowed to 'pray' with the couple. Such articulations have not stopped Stonewall celebrating a huge political victory. Moreover, gay and lesbians are jumping at the chance to declare their commitment publicly: from the first possible date 21 December 2005 until the end of January 2006 3,684 couples (2,510 male and 1,138 female) registered their partnership – approximately 121 per day (General Register Office 2006). The 'gay wedding' industry is predicted to be worth £600 million by 2010 (Matheson 2006). Of course, not everyone is celebrating. The failure to use the term 'marriage', linguistically marginalises all other 'relationships' as 'not marriage'. For example, there is no legal requirement of sexual intercourse – consummation does not legitimate the couple as it does for heterosexuals. So, it is possible for any two distantly related adults of the same sex (and not otherwise legally 'partnered/married') who wish to form a legal partnership to do so. It is not, using Pateman's term, a 'sexual contract' (1988).

For some, then, 'civil partnerships' perpetuate second-class citizenship status maintaining an 'us and them' divide between the heterosexual and non-heterosexual other. In June 2006, British university professors Sue Wilkinson and Celia Kitzinger who were married previously in Canada challenged in court the downgrading of their Canadian marriage to a 'civil partnership' in the UK (Wilkinson and Kitzinger 2005). Activists and academics argue that the fight for partnership recognition, either as 'civil' or as 'marriage' is the fundamentally wrong direction for political activism. For example, activist Peter Tatchell argues that: 'marriage was devised to ensure the sexual control of women by men and to regulate the conception and rearing of children' and that other legal arrangements could be made that would recognise a range of relationship forms and cater for practical matters such as next-of-kin and pensions (Tatchell 2006). Controversy over gay marriage sparks substantial debate within both the UK and US gay and lesbian academic community as to the political desirability of assimilation to this heterosexual institution (see Eskridge 1996; Ettelbrick 1997; Ackelsberg and Plaskow 2004; Josephson 2005). Generally, most agree that practical, financial, health and parenting agreements need to be arranged legally but they take issue with appropriating heterosexual language weighed with history of ownership, sexist gender roles and abuse.

While I have sympathy with this argument, I am not sure 'labelling' is the primary issue of concern. Setting aside the social justice or equality arguments in favour of state recognition, New Labour's economic focus must motivate, at least in part, the move towards a society inclusive of lesbian and gay citizens. As noted, the 'gay wedding' industry makes a considerable contribution to the economy. Moreover, the desire to have maximum employment has consequences for families with dependent children or caring responsibilities, as discussed elsewhere in this volume. In order to account for responsibilities outside the workplace, one needs to have a clear understanding of legitimate demands that may take workers away from employment temporarily. So, registering partnerships with the state is one way for the state to get a full picture of the individual commitments of workers. Likewise, in order to have a clear picture of the lives of those needing financial assistance from the state it is necessary to have a formal procedure to identify all possible avenues for alternative assistance, thus saving public money. This perspective is clarified in the following sections which consider parenting responsibilities. It is worth also noting the larger context as across Europe similar partnership policies were already in place in: Belgium, Denmark, Finland, France, Germany, Netherlands, Norway, Sweden and Spain. Recent comparative studies have argued that states which now offer same-sex partnership recognition are those in which, due to high divorce rates, heterosexual marriage is in decline or no longer as valued (Moran 2002; Badgett 2004). Elsewhere, I challenge these findings as, in most countries, heterosexual marriage rates remain steady, so people still value the idea of marriage (Wilson 2005). Policy shifts in countries such as Spain, appear to coincide with a need to recognise, and co-opt, the welfare provided within lesbian and gay relationships and extended 'families of choice' (for more on the care provided within 'families of choice' see Weston 1991; Weeks et al 2001). For example, under new UK legislation same-sex couples, whether they form a civil partnership or not, are required to make joint claims with regards to Child Tax Credit and WTC and benefit claims. Arguments for economic efficiency may be stronger than those for social justice.

To have and to hold ...

In considering the possibilities for parenting among lesbians and gay men, again New Labour has pushed at previous boundaries. Historically, 'homosexuals' have been a 'suspect class', particularly in relation to children. The fear of what 'homosexuals' might do to children and the fear that knowledge of 'homosexuals/ity' would encourage young people to deviate from heterosexuality, underpinned Section 28. Various research conducted over the last 20 years has challenged these assumptions about 'homosexuals' and about the construction of sexual identity during childhood and adolescence (Miller et al 1981; Golombok et al 1983; Green et al 1986; Gottman 1990; Tasker and Golombok 1995; Golombok 1999). While this has made some impact with regards to social attitudes, these fears still lurk within regulations regarding parenting, and with people lesbian and gay parents encounter daily.

There are various routes for lesbians and gay men to become parents. Historically, given the extent of discrimination, the most common route is via a heterosexual encounter, usually marriage. A number of those with same-sex desires gave into social expectations of heterosexuality only to 'come out' later in life. Until recently, in cases where one parent was known to be gay or lesbian child custody was automatically awarded to the heterosexual parent (Lesbian Custody Group 1986). In a few, lesbians were granted custody only if they agreed to not have lesbian partners near the children. Research with lesbian or gay parents has gone some way to supporting more recent legal challenges to such public articulations of homophobia. Similarly, contemporary social attitudes coupled with advances in reproductive technologies have made more likely the possibility of parenthood *as* a lesbian or gay man. Gay fatherhood remains predominantly a phenomena of those who have previously been married but increasingly gay men may choose to donate sperm and be an active biological father of a child within a larger extended 'family of choice', for example, a lesbian couple and biological gay father and his partner. Also, those with significant financial resources can attempt to have a child using a surrogate mother and egg donor. Lesbians may choose donor insemination, via either private fertility clinics or informal arrangements, and donors may be known or unknown to the biological mother or child. One recent survey found that 14% of lesbians have children (Brown, Church and Smallbone 2004).

The 1990 Human Fertilisation and Embryology Act presented the opportunity for lesbians and gay men to access fertility treatments at private fertility clinics. It specifically did not make possible such access within the NHS thus placing a financial burden on those seeking treatment. All those seeking treatment must gain a reference from their doctor, some of which refused to do so for lesbian patients (Donovan 1993, 2000). In addition, in order to access treatment lesbians must undergo counselling to justify why she/they want to become parents and, in accordance with the legislation protecting the 'welfare of the child' and the child's 'need for a father', they must articulate how they will ensure the child will have appropriate male role models. The 1990 Act also maintained the anonymity of sperm donors. Anonymity of donors was removed in the subsequent regulations in April 2005 and now children born via donor insemination will have access to identifying information upon their 18th birthday. This move affected lesbian mothers using donor insemination in three important ways. First, the removal of anonymity has led to a decrease in sperm donations and with this decreasing supply, prices for this service at private clinics have risen. Second, in the intervening years between 1990 and 2005, children born via donor insemination were considered 'legally fatherless'. Thus there was no threat to the mother(s) of homophobic intervention by the donor. This change emphasises the social significance of biological parenthood and has the potential to further undermine the role of social parents, particularly non-biological lesbian mothers. Third, one argument put forth by Mary Warnock is that the state should allow lesbians access to NHS fertility treatment so the state could better monitor these families and their children because 'the practice remains shrouded in secrecy' (2002, 69; see Wilson 2007).

Another route for gay men and lesbians to become parents is through fostering and adoption. Early in New Labour's first term, fostering guidelines were rewritten stating that the primary concern should be the 'right of the child', that 'no one had the right to parent' and that 'gay rights had no place in fostering' (Department of Health Guidelines 1990). While moves to change the guidance did open up space to discuss lesbian and gay parenthood, the outcome allowed local authority and private fostering services to decide individually if they were willing to place a child with lesbian or gay foster parents. The result of this was that many private fostering agencies, particularly those supported by religious organisations, continued to accept only heterosexual foster parents and that the possibility of becoming a foster parent through local authority placements was available only sporadically in geographic locations with a more 'liberal' approach to governance. In placing this initiative by New Labour within a broader context, it is worth noting that, at the time, in EU countries which recognised same-sex partnerships, gay men and lesbians often were excluded from fostering and adoption legislation, for example in the Netherlands and Sweden. So, New Labour could be constructed as leading the way on the grounds of social justice. However, again, the question is 'Why?' Arguably, shifting more children out of the foster system would facilitate the economic goal of decreasing the number of people dependent on the state. This analysis rings true in the justification for recent changes in adoption legislation. The 2002 Adoption and Children Act, implemented in December 2005, enabled same-sex couples to adopt jointly. A small number of lesbians and gay men had adopted previously, as individual parents. Until this legislation was implemented, lesbians and gay men wanting to adopt (or foster) did so as individuals and any partner, although assessed, was not considered as a legal guardian. While the changes do reinforce the two-parent model, they are nevertheless welcomed in that they acknowledge the role of both parents. The government made it clear, however, that the objective of the change was to 'increase the number' of children adopted. Presumably, then, this shift toward 'social justice' was motivated somewhat by the need to reduce numbers of those dependent on the state.

The significance of recognising the social parenting role should not be dismissed. Particularly as in every other regulation, the role of the biological parent is given priority. For example, lesbians who give birth to a child conceived through donor insemination are considered to be the legal parent of that child. Unlike heterosexual married couples where the male partner, who may not be the sperm donor, is listed as the legal father, the female partner of a lesbian biological mother is not given legal status, even if the couple have a civil partnership at the time of conception. Non-biological lesbian parents must apply to the court to be granted parental responsibility. This is yet another financial burden and one which traditionally was used in cases where extended family, for example, grandparents, would be raising the child. It is an option for those legally considered to be more distant from the child than a 'parent'. Without such status, however, the non-biological lesbian parent cannot make decisions for the child with regards to health, education and so on. Even if the non-biological parent chooses to not spend money on the legal fees to gain this right, and even if the couple have not formed a civil partnership, the non-biological parent/partner is held financially accountable for the child with regards to tax credits and benefit claims.

The status of non-biological parents may reflect the historical constructions of 'homosexuals' as potentially harmful to children either with regards to direct abuse of children or, more likely, the potential of moral harm if society is seen to sanction same-sex couples and/or 'families of choice'. Certainly, this fear fuelled Section 28 where the primary concern was protecting children from the knowledge about homosexuality and recognising 'pretend' families. While no charges were brought regarding 'breeches' of Section 28, its existence deterred most local authorities from actively supporting services for lesbian and gay citizens outside the field of health care. As the initial 'moral panic' leading to Section 28 surrounded the possibility of children reading a book portraying gay parents, the absence of support in the field of education was the most noticeable. New Labour attempted a step change in the 2000 Learning and Skills Act and 2000 Sex and Relationship Education (SRE) Guidance. The latter states that 'there are strong and mutually supportive relationships outside marriage ... care needs to be taken to ensure that there is no stigmatisation of children based on their home circumstance' (DfEE 2000, intro., para. 4). Schools are required to acknowledge the value of relationships outside the heterosexual nuclear family and to not discriminate based on the sexual orientation of their parents. Continuing, the Guidance directs teachers to 'deal honestly and sensitively with sexual orientation and answer appropriate questions and offer support' (DfEE 2000, section 1, para.

30).This is significant as Section 28 had served to silence teachers who were asked about issues of sexual orientation and prevent them from offering support – even giving out the phone number of a support line might have cost their job. Moreover, the Guidance tackles homophobic bullying: 'the unacceptability of and emotional distress and harm caused by bullying in whatever form – be it racial, as a result of a pupils' appearance, related to sexual orientation or for any other reason' (DfEE 2000, section 1, para. 30).Taken together these directly require schools to challenge homophobic bullying and discrimination. Given that the exact content of SRE is set by school governors and that parents are able to refuse permission for their children to attend SRE classes, the Guidance can only indirectly encourage significant curriculum changes. So, while they should, I doubt most primary schools have books on the shelf about lesbian and gay families. Nevertheless, the culture is changing. For example, the National Union of Teachers has published guidelines: *Tackling Homophobic Bullying, Supporting LGBT Students* (2004b) and *Negotiating Equality for LGBT Teachers* (2004a). In addition, gay and lesbian activists and voluntary organisations have managed to raise the profile of these policies within the public sector. The DfEE has declared February as 'Lesbian, Gay, Bisexual, Trans History Month' and produced, in conjunction with SchoolsOut!, information and guidance for use in classes. Working together, SchoolsOut! and Stonewall's campaign 'Education for All' is making considerable progress towards the inclusion, acceptance and safety of LGBT young people and teachers in the education system.

New Labour's initiative within education began in 2000 but it was 2003, during its second term, before Section 28 was finally repealed. Undoubtedly, this reflects how worries about harm persist. Such worries were voiced by a minority of MPs during debates about the repeal. It may also highlight some 'path dependency' as it had been an indirect threat rather than a tool directly used against individuals or local education authorities. However, this was a flagship promise during the 1997 New Labour campaign and it did pursue success. Given the difficulties it initially encountered, it is laudable that it issued the SRE Guidance which clearly targeted the heart of homophobic intent in Section 28. This is unsurprising given 'Education, Education, Education' was a New Labour priority. If the state wants to provide an excellently educated workforce in the next generation, it cannot continue to perpetuate social distinctions that might leave some feeling excluded from society.

Love, honour and obey

The introduction of this collection highlights the importance of representation of women in New Labour and particularly as policy elites. Certainly the 'positive images' of 'out' MPs within the Cabinet and as leading members within the Party reflected a willingness to give 'equal respect' to lesbian and gay citizens (Wilson 1993). Of course, gay men and lesbians within New Labour did not have to do all the work themselves. For example, Cherie Booth/Blair represented lesbian and gay clients in high-profile cases challenging discrimination in both UK courts and in the European Court of Human Rights (*Grant v. Southwest Trains*).[2] In addition, members of the Labour Party hold prominent positions in a range of campaign groups that represent issues of concern to lesbian and gay citizens. Campaign groups, regardless of political affiliation, do much of the preliminary work to get issues on the political agenda, raising awareness, educating the public and media, and drafting mock legislation, participating in the consultation process and mobilising lesbian and gay citizens. While there are talented lesbians and gay men working in a variety of organisations in the UK who have effected the changes brought about by New Labour, one lesbian 'representative' has consistently mingled with the New Labour policy elite for 20 years.

The appointment of Angela Mason in 1992 as the first director of Stonewall was controversial to say the least. Michael Cashman, Sir Ian McKellan and other founding members of Stonewall had established the campaign group in response to Section 28 which had caught the lesbian and gay community 'off guard'. Until that time, lesbian and gay political action had been positioned distinctly outside the mainstream. Stonewall was to be a professional lobbying organisation, properly funded, with a clear remit to effect policy and bring about change. Formerly known as Angie Weir, she was described in the *Guardian* as 'a notorious anarchist and member of the Angry Brigade, who had been put on trial in the 1970s for planting bombs on the doorsteps of Conservative Ministers' (Bright 2002). The appointment of Mason may have seemed somewhat radical for a group trying to gain the respect of the establishment. Since her acquittal of the bombing charges in 1972, she had 'come out', trained as a lawyer and worked in Camden's legal department. She had also set up house with her partner, Professor Elizabeth Wilson, and gave birth to a daughter conceived via donor insemination. Her 10 years at Stonewall witnessed unimaginable shifts in public attitudes and policy, much of which she can take credit for – and she has, receiving an OBE in 1999. She confidently guided Stonewall through public debates on lowering the age of consent, gays in the military, discrimination in employment and fostering and adoption. In 2002, her appointment as director of the WEU 'outed' her as New Labour's policy elite. Since leaving Stonewall, she has been criticised for not holding the government to account for failing to repeal Section 28 sooner; for not successfully lobbying for a single equality bill; and for cuddling up too close with the Labour Party during the London mayoral elections. In addition, I was dismayed at the prioritising of issues which were largely supported by male constituents such as the age of consent and gays in the military rather than a single equality bill, civil partnerships or policies affecting lesbian and gay parents. Undoubtedly, the financial support for Stonewall comes largely from gay men with high disposable incomes. So, again, policy advancement may reflect economic realities – 'you dance with them what brung you'. In line with this analysis, we can assess policy changes since her placement within the WEU and see her work within a different, and more powerful, platform to ensure these changes.

Conclusion

Undoubtedly, the WEU has supported legal and policy changes that would incorporate, socially include, and politically enfranchise lesbians and gay men. The shift to the CEHR has been welcomed by Stonewall as it will be the first time challenging sexual orientation discrimination falls under the remit of a state sanctioned equality 'watchdog'. This is important as social attitudes were mixed regarding civil partnership recognition and legislation around non-discrimination in employment (see for example, WEU 2003). Similar antagonistic opinions have been recorded in response to the consultation *Getting Equal: Proposals to Outlaw Discrimination in the Provision of Good and Services* (WEU 2006) where the Christian Right continued to express concern about the recognition of sexual orientation within the school curriculum, the possibility of lesbian and gay groups using public services and the state sanctioned immorality of equality for lesbian and gay citizens. While the government is committed, given EU human rights legislative expectations as well as equality rhetoric, to outlawing discrimination based on sexual orientation, all of the implications of this have yet to filter into public consciousness. For example, no longer would the NHS be able to deny lesbians access to fertility treatment and some question whether the fertility guidelines can continue to insist on the 'need for a father' (BBC 2006).

In summary, the policy changes thus far can be easily mapped onto a larger economic policy trajectory and an EU regulatory framework.

Equal opportunities for workers, recognition of same-sex partnerships, caring roles and 'families' may appear issues of social justice but conveniently will save the state some money. Equalising the age of consent and non-discrimination for those in military service were pushed significantly by the EU equality agenda. However, as Warnock clearly argues, socio-political inclusion may be the cost the state has to pay in order to have regulatory access to lives of lesbian and gay men. Given the positive changes, cynicism may not be the appropriate response, but simply accepting change for the better as a victory for justice and equality without keeping open a critical eye may be the most dangerous response. For example, people have a tendency to forget recent history: only in 2003 were lesbians and gay men able to 'come out' without risk of unemployment or discrimination; only in 2003 could same-sex couples kiss in the street without risk of arrest; only in 2005 were same-sex relationships recognised by the state; only after the passage of the aforementioned Goods and Services Bill will gay men and lesbians be able to sit in a restaurant, book a holiday, have full access to NHS and welfare services without the risk of legal discrimination based on sexual orientation. New Labour has been the most 'lesbian- and gay-friendly' government in history. They have 'acted for' lesbians and gay men; 'taken concerns into policy' and 'made a difference' to their lives; the outcomes of which have effected the political debate significantly in favour of equality, or at least non-discrimination. However, rather than creating a revolution, New Labour initiatives reflected a changing economic and social climate, one that could, presumably, change again.

Notes

[1] *Norris v. Ireland* [1988] 142 Eur. Ct. H.R.

[2] *Grant v. Southwest Trains Ltd* [1998 ICR 449 (ECJ Case C-249/96).

References

Ackelsberg, M. and Plaskow, J. (2004) 'Why we're not getting married', Common Dreams News Center, 1 June, www.commondreams.org (accessed 22 May 2006).

Badgett, L. (2004) 'Variations on an Equitable Theme: Explaining Same Sex Partner Recognition Laws', paper presented to American Political Science Association conference, Chicago.

BBC (2006) 'IVF "need for father"rule may go', 13 July, www.bbc. co.uk (accessed 24 July).

Bright, M. (2002) 'In the pink', *The Observer*, Profile, 24 November.

Brown, K., Church, A. and Smallbone, K (2004) *Do it with Pride*, Brighton: University of Brighton.

DfEE (Department for Education and Employment) (2000) *Sex and Relationship Guidance*, London: DfEE.

Donovan, C. (1993) 'Keeping in in the family: an analysis of doctors' decision-making about access in the provision of donor insemination', unpublished thesis, Edinburgh: University of Edinburgh.

Donovan, C. (2000) 'Who needs a father? Negotiating biological fatherhood in British lesbian families using self-insemination', *Sexualities* 3(2), 149-64.

DTI (Department of Trade and Industry) (2005) *Full Regulatory Impact Assessment for Sexual Orientation*, London: DTI.

Eskridge, W. (1996) *The Case for Same-Sex Marriage: From Sexual Liberty to Civilized Commitment*, New York, NY: Free Press.

Ettelbrick, P. (1997) 'Since when is marriage a path to liberation?', in M. Blasius and S. Phelan (eds) *We are Everywhere: A Historical Source-book of Gay and Lesbian Politics*, New York, NY: Routledge.

General Register Office (2006) www.gro.gov.uk/gro/content/news/Civil_Partnership_numbers.asp (accessed 24 July).

Golombok, S. (1999) 'Lesbian mother families', in A. Bainham, S.D. Sclater, M. Richards, Cambridge Socio-Legal Group *What is a Parent?: A Socio-Legal Analysis*, Oxford: Hart Publishing

Golombok, S., Spencer, A. and Rutter, M. (1983) 'Children in lesbian and single parent households: psychosexual and psychiatric appraisal', *Journal of Child Psychology Psychiatry* 24, 551-72.

Gottman, J. (1990) 'Children of gay and lesbian parents', in F. Hotvedt and M. Sussman (eds) *Homosexuality and Family Relations*, New York, NY: Harrington Park.

Green, R., Mandel, J.B., Hotvedt, M.E., Gray, J. and Smith, L. (1986) 'Lesbian mothers and their children: a comparison with solo parent heterosexual mothers and their children', *Archives of Sexual Behavior* 15, 167-84.

Herman, D. (1993) 'The politics of law reform: lesbian and gay rights struggles into the 1990s', in J. Bristow and A. Wilson (eds) *Activating Theory*, London: Lawrence and Wishart.

Hyde, H.M. (1970) *The Love that Dared not Speak its Name*, Boston, MA: Little Brown.

Jeffery-Poulter, A. (1991) *Peers, Queers and Commons*, London: Routledge.

Josephson, J. (2005) 'Citizenship, same-sex marriage, and feminist critiques of marriage', *Perspectives on Politics* 3(2), 269-84.

Lesbian Custody Group (1986) *Lesbian Mothers' Legal Handbook*, London: The Women's Press.

Matheson, C. (2006) *Wedding Industry in the Pink,* http://news.bbc.co.uk/1/hi/business/4690720.stm (accessed 29 December 2006).

Miller, J., Jacobson, R. and Bigner, J. (1981) 'The child's home environment for lesbians vs. heterosexual mothers: a neglected area of research', *Journal of Homosexuality* 7, 49-56.

Moran, N. (2002) 'The legal recognition of same-sex relationships: a comparative study of the Netherlands, United Kingdom and Ireland within the policy framework of the European Union', unpublished doctoral thesis available from the University of Manchester.

National Union of Teachers (2004a) 'Negotiating equality for LGBT teachers', www.teachers.org.uk (accessed 24 July).

National Union of Teachers (2004b) 'Tackling homophobic bullying, supporting LGBT students', www.teachers.org.uk (accessed 24 July).

Out Now Consulting (2005) Diva and Gay Times Readers' Surveys, London: Out Now Consulting.

Pateman, C. (1988) *The Sexual Contract*, Cambridge: Polity.

Soames, N. (1996) www.rank-outsiders.org.uk.info/history3.shtml (accessed 24 July).

Stormbreak (2000/01) The Gay Life and Style New Millennium Survey, London: Stormbreak Consultancy.

Tasker, F. and Golombok, S. (1995) 'Adults raised as children in lesbian families', *American Journal of Orthopsychiatry* 65, 203-15.

Tatchell, P. (2006) www.petertatchell.net (accessed 7 July 2006).

Warnock, M. (2002) *Making Babies: Is There a Right to Have Children?*, Oxford: Oxford University Press.

Weeks, J. (1981) 'Discourse, desire and sexual deviance: some problems in a history of homosexuality', in K. Plummer (ed) *The Making of the Modern Homosexual*, London: Hutchinson.

Weeks, J. (1990) *Coming Out* (2nd edn), London: Quartet.

Weeks, J., Heaphy, B. and Donovan, C. (2001) *Same-sex Intimacies: Families of Choice and Other Life Experiments*, London: Routledge.

Weston, K. (1991) *Families we Choose: Lesbians, Gays and Kinship*, New York, NY: Columbia University Press.

Wilkinson, S. and Kitzinger, C. (2005) 'Same sex marriage and equality', *The Psychologist* 18 May, 292-93.

Wilson, A. (1993) 'Which equality? Toleration, diversity or respect', in J. Bristow and A. Wilson (eds) *Activating Theory*, London: Lawrence and Wishart.

Wilson, A. (2005) 'The deconstruction of family values', paper given at the American Political Science Association conference, Washington DC (available from apsanet.org).

Wilson, A. (2007) 'With friends like these: the liberalization of queer family policy', *Critical Social Policy* 27(1), 50–76, February.

WEU (Women and Equality Unit) (2003) *Responses to Civil Partnership: A Framework for the Legal Recognition of Same-sex Couples*, London: DTI.

WEU (2006) *Getting Equal: Proposals to Outlaw Discrimination in the Provision of Good and Services*, London: DTI.

ELEVEN

The gender dimensions of New Labour's international development policy

Juanita Elias and Lucy Ferguson

Introduction

In this chapter, we seek to examine the gender dimensions of New Labour's international development work as well as to focus on some of the internal and external limitations of these policies. We note that these limitations stem from a number of different factors. First, institutional factors within the Department for International Development (DfID) have placed constraints on the extent to which policies of 'gender mainstreaming' have really taken hold within the department. Second, a growing emphasis on partnership strategies in international development assistance often result in the sidelining of gender issues in the complex bargaining relationships between donor agencies. Third, we note a tendency for gender issues to be regarded as side-issues; as secondary to the 'big issues' such as fair trade and debt relief (key tenets of the Make Poverty History campaign that was endorsed by the government during 2004 and 2005). Thus while the issue of global poverty became a central policy theme for the New Labour government during 2004/05 (as seen in the launching of the Commission for Africa and Britain's hosting of the G8 summit), a recognition of the gendered nature of poverty has become increasingly lost in this agenda.

We identify two key strands of policy thought on gender and development within New Labour – what we term the 'efficiency' and 'rights' approaches. On the one hand, there is a strong tendency to conceptualise gender issues within a (neo-liberal) economic efficiency paradigm – whereby gender inequality is said to contribute to the overall inability of markets in developing states to function effectively. On the other hand, an important position has emerged that emphasises the need for women in the developing world to secure equal 'rights' and voice to men. This second paradigm has been especially concerned with issues of violence against women and sexual and reproductive rights. However, we also note, particularly in the discussion of the Commission for Africa in the final section of this chapter, that the language of 'women's rights' is often employed in a quite different manner; in terms of the role that civil and political rights and property rights can play a role in enhancing women's economic empowerment and contributing to capitalist development overall.

What both of these paradigms have in common is that they do not view the neo-liberal development policies that have been pursued by international development agencies since the 1980s as all that problematic. Thus the economic efficiency paradigm endorses neo-liberal market solutions – viewing gender inequality as something that is both a hindrance to the market and something that will decline with increased marketisation. While the 'rights' perspective tends to focus on specific women's issues (in particular issues such as violence against women) without considering the way in which gendered patterns of inequality are embedded in the policies of neo-liberalism and how such inequalities impact upon access to rights as well as rights-based activism (Tsikata 2004). By adopting a more critical perspective rooted in an understanding of the centrality of gender inequality to the functioning of the global market economy known as 'gendered political economy' (Waylen 1997), our analysis of New Labour's development policy is rooted in a critique of neo-liberal development policies through 'gendered lenses'.

Our analysis proceeds as follows: first, we look at the context for reform – the background to the policies of gender equality and gender mainstreaming in the area of international development. Second, we examine how this reform agenda was set out within DfID through an examination of the 2000 Target Strategy Paper *Poverty Elimination and the Empowerment of Women: Strategies for Achieving the International Development Targets* (DfID 2000b). Third, we focus on how these policies have been severely constrained by both internal and external factors. Finally, we turn to assess the success of these policies – through an evaluation of how the New Labour government's recent increased emphasis on international development issues suffers from many of the same shortcomings and problems as DfID policies; namely by endorsing an approach to gender and development that fails to consider how commitments to gender equality can be undermined by wider commitments to neo-liberal development and trade policies that can have very negative impacts on gender equality.

Contextualising the policy issue: the Department for International Development

Key to understanding the relationship between gender and international development policy in the Labour government was the establishment of DfID in 1997. The new department, which was separated from the control of the Foreign and Commonwealth Office, was headed by Clare Short. As well as being regarded as a highly experienced politician and very popular with the party's activist base (Young 2000), it is also important to note in the context of this chapter that Short was widely regarded as a feminist (for example, through her involvement in campaigns and a private members bill to ban *The Sun* newspaper's Page 3 (Short 1991; see also Chapter Four)). Two key issues underpinned this decision to establish a new department. The first was the desire to divorce foreign aid policies from wider UK foreign policy objectives (the aim being to prevent foreign aid from being used as a diplomatic bargaining tool). The second was to develop an approach to international development that was less centred on the delivery of aid to needy countries and more focused on delivering assistance to countries in order for them to become self-sustaining and thereby breaking a dependence on aid.

Despite the emphasis on creating a more autonomous development agency, UK international development policy has increasingly come to reflect the policy priorities of the key international financial institutions: the International Monetary Fund (IMF) and the World Bank. DfID emerged at a time when the international financial institutions were coming under increased and sustained criticism from a wide range of civil society groups. Criticisms highlighted the failure of the 'Washington consensus' – the promotion of a set of neo-liberal 'structural' economic reforms imposed on countries in the developing world. These economic reform packages (or structural adjustment policies as they are commonly known) were shown to be especially painful for the poorest and most vulnerable groups of people – including large numbers of women and girls (Desai 2002). As a response, the World Bank in particular sought to come up with new ideas and initiatives that could help stave off such criticisms (Porteous 2005). In 1999, the World Bank launched its Comprehensive Development Framework – an approach that tied together traditional neo-liberal development policies (notably the promotion of a 'vibrant private sector' (Cammack 2003) to wider policies of 'good governance' and commitments to health, education and population policies (among other issues). A key policy instrument within this shifting development agenda was the Poverty Reduction

Strategy Paper — an approach to poverty reduction that placed the emphasis on countries 'owning' their development strategy.

Understanding this shifting development agenda (sometimes referred to as the 'post-Washington consensus') is absolutely critical to discussions of DfID's role in international development policy and politics today. This is because the Poverty Reduction Strategy Paper has assumed a central position in the international politics of aid – with almost the entire official aid community coalescing around this policy tool. Thus DfID's role in the 21st century is starting to look less and less like that of a UK-government bilateral aid agency and more as an institution that operates within an increasingly global and multilateral framework for international development policy and aid. And yet, this international policy environment suited the newly formed DfID well – allowing a policy space for the generation of an essentially 'third way' approach to international development policy (Dixon and Williams 2001; Cumming 2004). Labelled 'tough on debt, tough on the causes of debt' (Dixon and Williams 2001), these policies were characterised by an emphasis on poverty eradication to be achieved through adherence to neo-liberal principles (Short 2004, 80) — an approach broadly identical to those being pursued by the international financial institutions. As we will argue later in this chapter, New Labour's perspective on gender issues in international development has been profoundly influenced by the politics of the post-Washington consensus.

The emerging post-Washington consensus was not the only international policy shift that had a profound influence on New Labour's policies relating to gender and development. As Lovecy in Chapter Four and Durose and Gains in Chapter Five show, the growing international recognition of the importance of 'gender mainstreaming' to policy-making has had a marked influence on New Labour thinking across a range of policy arenas. An emphasis on gender mainstreaming within DfID points towards the significance attached to the Platform for Action (adopted at the UN's Fourth World Conference on Women, in Beijing, 1995) in both national and international policy circles. The Platform for Action became the most influential and the most widely cited international agreement relating to gender issues in the early work on gender and development at DfID. However, DfID was in no way taking the lead in adopting policies recommended in the Platform. The emphasis on gender mainstreaming in development policy had been taken up much earlier by the World Bank and various UN agencies – in particular the United Nations Development Programme) (Hafner-Burton and Pollack 2002; Bergeron 2003; Razavi and Miller 1995). Indeed, it could be suggested that the major driver behind the focus on gender issues at DfID was the increased prominence of gender issues and a gender mainstreaming agenda internationally.

Of course, certain internal factors might also have helped contribute to the adoption of gender-centred policies at DfID, in particular, the policy space afforded to DfID in its early years. Porteous (2005), for example, has pointed to Short's argument in her political memoirs that DfID was granted considerable freedom on policy issues in the early years of DfID's existence (largely because Alastair Campbell was not especially concerned with the work of the department – telling Short that she could be as 'radical' as she liked (Short 2004, 77)). However, in what follows we argue that there is something fundamentally un-radical about the way in which gender has been mainstreamed into UK international development policy.

What New Labour did: the 2000 Target Strategy Paper

An emphasis on gender issues in the work of DfID is reflected in the department's key strategy documents; the International Development White Papers of 1997 and 2000 (DfID 1997; DfID 2000a) and its nine target strategy papers.[1] One of these was the 2000 report *Poverty Elimination and the Empowerment of Women: Strategies for Achieving the International Development Targets* (2000b). This document neatly encapsulated both the efficiency and rights-based approaches to understanding gender issues present within DfID outlined earlier in this chapter. On the one hand the report suggested that 'Gender discrimination is not unjust, it is also inefficient and limits the prospects for development' (DfID 2000b, 10), while elsewhere the report discussed women's rights issues – namely sexual and reproductive rights and violence against women. This dual strategy is nicely summarised by Short in her introductory statement:

> the goal of gender equality needs to be pursued across all
> of the internationally agreed development targets, and in
> the wider process of governance and the pursuit of human
> rights. It sets out why this is an essential precondition for
> development and indicates the steps DfID proposes to take
> in making its contribution to the achievement of this goal.
> (Short 2000, 6)

The report opened with an analysis of why women have remained so marginal to economic development, arguing that women's empowerment (defined as 'individuals acquiring the power to think and act freely, exercise choice, and to fulfil their potential as full and equal members of society' (DfID 2000b)) is a key mechanism through which globalisation can be made to work for women. In this sense, improvements in the status of women within the developing world are viewed as compatible with the achievement of economic development through a neo-liberal model of market-led development. Most notably the report views gender issues in terms of a 'human capital' approach – that training and education are fundamental to improving women's economic status, social status, health and cutting rates of infant and maternal mortality. The Target Strategy Paper employed the language of gender mainstreaming stating that DfID's strategy is 'to ensure that women's empowerment and gender equality are actively pursued in the mainstream of all development activities' (DfID 2000b, 28). These consisted of 10 key objectives outlined in Table 11.1. While Table 11.1 provides examples of actions that fit under each objective, the paper went on to outline key channels through which these objectives could be met. This included providing support to governments, civil society and the private sector, closer cooperation with key donors – the EU, the World Bank, the UN System and other international financial institutions, for example the Inter American Development Bank or the Asian Development Bank, and enhancing DfID's internal commitment to gender mainstreaming through training, knowledge development and sharing.

As we will go on to argue in this chapter, it is this emphasis on working in partnership with other development agencies that has proven to be one of the major limitations to DfID's gender and development agenda. The emphasis on poverty alleviation (or 'pro-poor growth') within the post-Washington consensus complemented and informed DfID's own emphasis on gender equality issues. However, this attempt to combine a gender-friendly approach to poverty reduction while maintaining a commitment to neo-liberal structural adjustment is ultimately limiting because it views gender inequality as a straightforward barrier to economic development – without recognising the ways in which gender inequality can be an integral feature of the market-led growth approach to development sanctioned by the international financial institutions (UNRISD 2005). The problem with this new-found interest in poverty-reduction is that it is characterised by a lack of any discussion concerning the link between economic growth, development and macro-economic policy changes

Table 11.1 Department for International Development objectives and examples of actions

Objective	Examples of actions
Objective 1 To promote equal rights for women and men through international and national policy reform	• Development and implementation of equal opportunity policies • Gender aware approaches to international agreements and regulations • Development of new tools for analysis and international and national policy-making, including better statistics
Objective 2 To secure greater livelihood, security, access to productive assets, and economic opportunities for women as well as men	• Improved access to financial services for women • Improved access for women to affordable energy, water and sanitation and transport services • Reforms to land and inheritance laws • Improved information flows, particularly for women farmers and entrepreneurs • Adherence to core labour standards • Development of 'family-friendly' employment practices
Objective 3 To further close gender gaps in human development particularly education and health	• Development of policies and programmes to remove gender barriers to education • Development of policies and programmes to support achievement of international development targets for maternal mortality and access to reproductive health services • Improvements to national statistical services to provide sex-disaggregate data across all key social indicators
Objective 4 To promote the more equal participation of women in decision-making and leadership roles at all levels	• Capacity-building and other support to women's organisations • Electoral and other reforms to remove barriers to women's participation in public life • Public awareness campaigns to challenge gender stereotypes
Objective 5 To increase women's personal security and reduce gender based violence	• Reform and strengthening of criminal and civil law • Awareness-raising of women's rights among police and judiciary • Public information campaigns • Support to women's organisations • Improved knowledge and statistics

continued .../

Table 11.1 *continued*

Objective	
Objective 6 To strengthen institutional mechanisms and national machineries for the advancement of women in governments and civil society	• Civil service and public spending reforms to establish and support appropriate government structures • Strengthening of role of civil society organisations in advancing gender equality • Public awareness campaigns
Objective 7 To promote equality for women under the law and non-discrimination in access to justice	• Reform and strengthening of criminal and civil law • Support to legal literacy programmes • Training and capacity building for police, judiciary and organisations in civil society • Public information campaigns
Objective 8 To reduce gender stereotyping, and bring about changes in social attitudes in favour of women	• Support to media projects and campaigns, including gender training for journalists and programme makers • Support to women's organisations • Awareness-raising among policy-makers and political leaders
Objective 9 To help develop gender aware approaches to the management of the environment and the safeguarding of natural resources	• Gender aware planning and women's participation in the development of National Strategies for Sustainable Development • Strengthen tenure and common property rights in line with gender equity • Ensure that local planning and access to natural resources is gender aware • Improved data and research
Objective 10 To ensure that progress is made in upholding the rights of both girls and boys within the framework of the Convention on the Rights of the Child	• Implementation of the Convention on the Rights of the Child • Improved data research and statistics • Support to programmes to eliminate the worst forms of child labour

Source: DfID 2000b, 27-30

and the generation of (often highly gendered forms of) inequality and poverty (Bergeron 2003; Thomas 2005).

What happened: evaluating the success of gender mainstreaming within the Department for International Development

The 2000 Target Strategy Paper *Poverty Elimination and the Empowerment of Women* argued that progress towards the objectives outlined in Table 11.1 should be closely monitored (DfID 2000b). In the proceeding discussion, therefore, we look not so much at the extent to which each and every one of these policy objectives has been met. Rather, we draw upon a range of reports that have largely been conducted as part of this monitoring process. We came across nine such reports (MacDonald 2003; Watkins 2004; Edbrooke and Peters 2005; Johnson 2005; Macdonagh 2005; Murison 2005; Pinder 2005; Rose and Subrahmanian 2005; Waterhouse and Neville 2005). Two of these, drawn upon extensively in the following discussion, were written by external consultants and provided general analyses of the successes and failures of the gender mainstreaming process at DfID (MacDonald 2003; Watkins 2004). These two studies in particular point to serious shortcomings in DfID's gender work.

A significant criticism raised in the reports is that the internal policy environment at DfID precludes a substantive focus on gender issues. For example, MacDonald (2003) suggests that there is a lack of institutionalisation of the process of gender mainstreaming into the day-to-day workings of the department. Responsibility for gender mainstreaming lies with Social Development Advisers (SDAs) — the only people who have 'gender competence' written into their job descriptions. However, as Watkins notes, 'Evidence of the success of SDAs in gender mainstreaming in DfID is mixed; there are numerous examples where individual SDAs have been able to successfully promote gender equality objectives, but there is little evidence on how consistently these approaches have been used across the organisation' (Watkins 2004, 14).

In this sense we can see that gender issues tend to be pursued only by committed individuals rather than being placed at the centre of all programmes (Painter 2004, 23). In fact, the internal policy environment at DfID, argues MacDonald, is one in which there is a declining commitment to gender issues especially at senior managerial level. The internal organisational structure of DfID is viewed as being partially to blame for this – the lack of dissemination of internally produced research on gender issues; the lack of gender disaggregated data that provides a practical barrier to any in-depth analysis of DfID's work on gender; a general lack of training and coordination around gender issues; a decline in spending on gender equality; and the lack of a central gender unit. While DfID is praised for having reasonably high levels of female employment at senior managerial level compared to other government departments, a lack of staff with expertise in gender issues is noted (MacDonald 2003).

The perception of a declining commitment to gender issues is also viewed as reflective of a changing international policy environment in which the Platform for Action has been overshadowed as the key internationally agreed set of standards relating to gender equity by the Millennium Development Goals – a set of eight goals (and various associated targets) sanctioned by the UN and aimed at halving extreme poverty by 2015.[2] It is important to note that the target associated with the third goal (promote gender equality and empower women) is to 'eliminate gender disparity in primary and secondary education preferably by 2005 and in all levels of education no later than 2015'. The Millennium Development Goals therefore, effectively sanction an approach in which: (a) gender issues are reduced to easily quantifiable measures of economic efficiency (or 'human capital' development), and (b) 'gender mainstreaming' has been effectively replaced by a development agenda that views gender issues in a much more limited sense. This, as Watkins (2004, 5) notes 'has narrowed the focus of gender equality policy to social sectors, such as girls' education and maternal health, with relatively little attention being given to gender in areas such as economic opportunities and decision-making'. It appears, then, that an outcome of DfID's gender mainstreaming policies is that they have, in fact, resulted in a much closer focus on women and girls rather than gender per se. Thus although DfID has significantly increased its focus on issues such as maternal health (DfID 2004; Macdonagh 2005, 34); the wider goal of mainstreaming gender throughout all of DfID's programmes and activities has stalled. Indeed, it is suggested that an interest in gender issues effectively peaked with the publication of the gender Target Strategy Paper in 2000 (Watkins 2004, 7).

The continuing marginalisation of gender issues in DfID's work (and, as we shall go on to argue, New Labour development thinking more generally) also stems from the shift away from discrete bilateral aid and assistance projects towards an increased emphasis on working with a range of partner agencies in the formulation of country assistance strategies and Poverty Reduction Strategy Papers (as approach clearly endorsed in the eighth Millennium Development Goal 'Develop a global partnership for development'). In this context, gender issues are either sidelined (as evidenced in the gradual process of 'gender evaporation' as DfID's country assistance strategies become increasingly less likely to emphasise gender issues (Macdonagh 2005: 34)) or confined to the 'women's issues' of health, education and welfare. To give an example, as part of the commitment to country ownership of economic reform, Poverty Reduction Strategy Papers are designed to emerge out of a process of 'consultation' between countries, donor agencies and civil society groups. Waterhouse and Neville (2005) in their report to DfID on *Voice and Accountability* note that while certain papers have incorporated a strong gender dimension this is not always the case. Furthermore, the authors note that 'even when women make their voices heard in the process, this may not translate into gender sensitive policy or spending allocations' (Waterhouse and Neville 2005, 20). What such studies point to is how the emphasis on gender equality and women's empowerment that was a hallmark of DfID's earlier policy work seems to have petered out in the face new priorities within the international development community (MacDonagh 2005, 34).

The consequences of this failure to prioritise gender equality issues within DfID has had wider implications for UK international development policies — as we argue in the evaluation of the *Commission for Africa Report* presented in the final section of this chapter (2005).

An assessment of outcomes: mainstreaming the development agenda 2004/05 – any room for gender?

While in the early years of DfID's existence international development issues were somewhat marginal to the New Labour project, by the mid-2000s this had changed considerably. Short has argued that the emerging prioritisation of international development (in particular around issues of debt relief/cancellation and fair trade) is a reflection of the success with which (an independent) DfID was able to present development issues as a legitimate and important area of government policy (and indeed spending) (Short 2004, 91). In 2001, Blair told the Labour Party Annual Conference that Africa was a 'scar on the conscience of the world'. This effectively placed international (in particular African) development issues in a much more central position within the government's agenda than ever before and led to the publication of the *Commission for Africa Report*, in 2005. As such, development policy took centre stage in policy-making in 2005, when Britain's hosting of the G8 summit and its presidency of the EU were used as an opportunity to force the issue of international poverty higher up the international policy-making agenda. At the same time, increased UK government support for international development issues was echoed across a wide range of civil society movements as the Live 8 concerts and the Make Poverty History campaign brought the development debate to a wider British audience than ever before. Thus, in evaluating Labour's record on gender in international development thinking in this final section of the chapter, we move beyond the specific focus on DfID to look at how gender features more broadly in UK development thinking.

Established in 2004 by the Blair government, the tasks of the Africa Commission were 'to define the challenges facing Africa, and to provide clear recommendations on how to support the changes needed to reduce poverty' (Commission for Africa 2005, 3). Williams notes that the Commission was comprised of a multinational membership of African and Western political/business leaders and has largely been regarded as an exercise in UK foreign and development policy that is broadly compatible with the post-Washington consensus (Williams 2005, 531-2). Critics of the Blair/Brown/DfID 'vision' for Africa argue that it reflects a wholly neo-liberal understanding of development, and not necessarily a vision that will contribute to the alleviation of poverty in the continent (Monbiot 2005; Graham 2005).

We found that gender issues are addressed in the report in a manner that reflects New Labour thinking on gender and development more generally – in terms of attempts to combine economic efficiency and rights-based approaches to gender. The highly instrumentalist 'efficiency' approach can be seen in the following two examples. First, in the area of women's political participation it is suggested that the presence of more women MPs would somehow reduce corruption, and that 'many Africans believe women MPs are more likely to listen and attend to basic community needs' (Commission for Africa 2005, 144). Second, in the area of education, gender equality is argued to be 'an investment with very high returns' as the education of girls is likely to decrease the incidence of HIV/Aids and reduce child mortality in a country (Commission for Africa 2005, 184). As such, 'gender equality' in education is understood as a tool for achieving other development goals, rather than as an aim in itself – it is argued that 'educating girls is also an indirect investment in the education of the following generation' (Commission for Africa 2005, 187). The discussion of gender issues in relation to notions of human rights is presented as complementary to the emphasis on building competitiveness and economic efficiency. And yet, some of the most important issues in relation to women's human rights – namely violence against women and sexual and reproductive rights – are largely absent from the report. This is not to suggest that issues of violence against women and sexual and reproductive health are not dealt with in the Commission for Africa report – but that these issues are not viewed in terms of rights (a curious omission given the emphasis on these issues in discussions of women's human rights across academic and policy debates). Rather the emphasis is on how certain types of (gender neutral) human rights can play a role in building efficient and competitive economies and systems of good governance. In this sense, gender issues are evident in these discussions of rights – but only to the extent that women (and children) are most likely to benefit from this renewed emphasis on human rights given that they constitute the majority of Africa's most 'vulnerable' (Commission for Africa 2005, 45). For example, strong liberal African states would be more likely meaningfully to implement the UN's Convention on the Elimination of All Forms of Discrimination against Women (CEDAW) (Commission for Africa 2005, 134).

What we see in the Commission for Africa report is that when attempts are made to mainstream gender into a fundamentally neo-liberal development paradigm, gender issues can only ever be understood in terms of the 'business case'. While DfID's specific work on women and gender has been able to focus on ostensibly 'non-economic' issues surrounding things like gender violence, the policy space within which the Commission for Africa operates is fundamentally constrained by a concern with the 'market fundamentals'.

Gender features strongly in the Commission for Africa Report, albeit in an instrumentalist and primarily neo-liberal manner. However, when international development issues come to the foreground of high-level political negotiations, as happened at the G8 summit in 2005, gender issues were seemingly sidelined. Policy documents preceding the summit include some mention of the goal of gender equality, primarily in relation to achieving universal primary education (G8 2005, 26-7). Previous agreements had committed G8 leaders to supporting gender equality commitments in both the UN's 'Beijing Plus 10' programme and the African Union's 'Solemn Declaration on Gender Equality', arguing for such goals as more women in formal institutions in order to improve African governance (G8 2005, 12). The discourse on gender in G8 policy documents therefore closely reflects that of the mainstream development community, including DfID and the Commission for Africa Report as analysed earlier in this chapter. Gender equality is framed in straightforward 'business case' terms. For example, in the G8 policy documents, 'gender-balanced property rights' are regarded as a prerequisite for the successful market reform of the African agricultural sector (G8 2005, 31). While we would not wish to deny the importance of securing equal property rights for women, our concern is that it is only those rights that are viewed as complementary to a neo-liberal economic development model that are endorsed by the G8.

Furthermore, despite the formal support for gender equality programmes, gender issues featured very little in the key policy debates of the G8 summit. The two priority policy areas that were to be discussed at the G8, as set by the UK government, were Africa and climate change, with counter-terrorism and Middle East policy included as 'other issues'. As such, gender equality in international development became subsumed as an 'issue' within the discussion on Africa (relegated once more to the instrumental level). This is not to say that gender issues are not addressed in UK development policy but that when development comes to the centre stage of policy-making, gender is overshadowed by the 'big issues'. Of course, the UK government was not the only actor to overlook gender issues at the G8 – at the same time, the Make Poverty History campaign's call for 'fair trade, drop the debt and more and better aid' left gender equality issues out of the mainstream civil society debate (WIDE 2005, 3-6).

Conclusion

As seen in the analysis of both the Commission for Africa Report and the G8's Action plan for Africa, 'gender equality' is perceived as critical to achieving economic development. However, an interrogation of the meaning of such development reveals a strongly neo-liberal paradigm, in which development is understood as the extension of free-market capitalism across all areas of social, political and economic life (Cammack 2004).

We would argue that the failure of commitments to gender mainstreaming to alter radically New Labour's approach to development policy assistance stems not only from the internal and external policy environment, but also from the way in which gender inequality is constructed within international development discourse – as a problem that impedes economic development. Viewing gender inequality purely in terms of economic efficiency considerations (the 'business case' for gender equality) is an approach to gender and development that has become integral to the World Bank's attempt at gender mainstreaming (Bergeron 2003). Although during her time at DfID, Clare Short presented the department as having considerable policy autonomy, we would argue that, in fact, DfID's role in international development policy was broadly similar (if not fundamentally shaped by) the post-Washington consensus and the World Bank in particular.

Many of the consultant reports overviewing and critiquing DfID's work on gender are highly critical of this 'business case' approach. MacDonald suggests, for example, that there is little recognition of the ways in which the market economy (and processes of economic 'globalisation' more generally) is itself thoroughly gendered; '[d]ocuments such as the White paper on globalisation ... do not show a clear recognition of the contradiction between cooperation policies that promote gender equality and trade policies which may perpetuate or increase existing inequalities' (MacDonald 2003, 14).

A significant limitation of the emphasis on economic efficiency is that issues such as violence against women are increasingly overlooked in DfID programmes (Edbrooke and Peters 2005, 30). While this oversight is clearly of concern, we would point out that simply reasserting the importance of women's human rights in international development policy is not enough. It is a failure to recognise the role of neo-liberal economic policies in creating and sustaining gender inequality in the first place that is the major flaw in DfID's gender mainstreaming project and New Labour thinking in the area of gender and development more generally. Not addressing gender inequality in a more radical way, and therefore leaving the structures of gender inequality inherent in neo-liberalism intact, limits the scope for any real chance of greater gender equality in international development.

Notes

[1] The nine target strategy papers were as follows: Economic well-being (1999); Better health for poor people (1999); Education for all: The challenge of universal primary education (2000); Poverty eradication and the empowerment of women (2000); Human Rights and poor people (2000); Addressing the water crisis (2000); Environmental sustainability and eliminating poverty (2000); Making government work for poor people (2000); Urbanisation (2000).

[2] The Millennium Development Goals are as follows: (1) eradicate extreme hunger and poverty; (2) achieve universal primary education; (3) promote gender equality and empower women; (4) reduce child mortality; (5) improve maternal health; (6) combat HIV/Aids, malaria and other diseases; (7) ensure environmental sustainability; (8) develop a global partnership for development (see United Nations 2005).

References

Bergeron, S. (2003) 'The post-Washington consensus and economic representations of women in development at the World Bank', *International Feminist Journal of Politics* 5(3), 397-419.

Cammack, P. (2003) 'The governance of global capitalism: a new materialist perspective', *Historical Materialism* 11(2), 37-59.

Cammack, P. (2004) 'What the World Bank means by poverty reduction and why it matters', *New Political Economy* 9(2), 189-212.

Commission for Africa (2005) *Our Common Interest: Report of the Commission for Africa*, London: Commission for Africa.

Cumming, G.D. (2004) 'UK African policy in the Post-Cold War era: from Realpolitik to Moralpolitik?', *Commonwealth and Comparative Politics* 42(1), 106-29.

Desai, M. (2002) 'Transnational solidarity: women's agency, structural adjustment and globalisation', in Naples, N.A. and Desai, M. (eds) *Women's Activism and Globalisation: Linking local struggles and transnational politics*, London: Routledge, 34-44.

DfID (Department for International Development) (1997) *Eliminating World Poverty: A challenge for the 21st century*, London: DfID.

DfID (2000a) *Eliminating World Poverty: Making Globalisation Work for the Poor*, White Paper on International Development, London: DfID.

DfID (2000b) *Poverty Elimination and the Empowerment of Women: Strategies for Achieving the International Development Targets*, London: DfID.

DfID (2004) *Reducing Maternal Death: Evidence and action – a strategy for DfID*, London: DfID.

Dixon, R. and Williams, P. (2001) 'Tough on debt, tough on the causes of debt? New Labour's Third Way foreign policy', *British Journal of Politics and International Relations* 3(2), 150-72.

Edbrooke, J. and Peters, C. (2005) *Evaluation of DfID Development Assistance: Gender equality and women's empowerment – Phase II thematic evaluation: Gender violence*, Working Paper 9, London: DfID.

G8 (2005) *Progress Report by the G8 Africa Personal Representatives on Implementation of the Africa Action Plan*, available at www.fco.gov.uk/Files/kfile/PostG8_Gleneagles_AfricaProgressReport,0.pdf, (accessed 10 May 2006).

Graham, Y. (2005) 'Africa's second "last chance"', *Red Pepper* 132 (July), www.redpepper.org.uk (accessed 4 February 2006).

Hafner-Burton, E. and Pollack, M.A. (2002) 'Mainstreaming gender in global governance', *European Journal of International Relations* 8(3), 339-73.

Johnson, N. (2005) *Evaluation of DfID Development Assistance: Gender Equality and Women's Empowerment − Phase II Thematic Evaluation: Conflict and Post Conflict Reconstruction*, Working Paper 12, London: DfID.

Macdonagh, S. (2005) *Evaluation of DfID Development Assistance: Gender Equality and Women's Empowerment − Phase II Thematic Evaluation: Maternal Mortality*, Working Paper 8, London: DfID.

MacDonald, M. (2003) *Gender Equality and Mainstreaming in the Policy and Practice of the UK Department for International Development*, London: The GAD Network.

Monbiot, G. (2005) 'Africa's new best friends', *Guardian*, 5 July.

Murison, S. (2005) *Evaluation of DFID Development Assistance: Gender Equality and Women's Empowerment − Phase II Thematic Evaluation: Migration and Development*, Working Paper 13, London: DfID.

Painter, G. (2004) *Gender Mainstreaming in Development and Trade Policy and Practice*, Brussels: WIDE.

Pinder, C. (2005) *Evaluation of DfID Development Assistance: Gender Equality and Women's Empowerment − Phase II Thematic Evaluation: Enabling Environment for Growth and Investment*, London: DfID.

Porteous, T. (2005) 'British government policy in sub-Saharan Africa under New Labour', *International Affairs* 81(2), 281-97.

Razavi, S. and Miller, C. (1995) *Gender Mainstreaming: A Study of Efforts by the UNDP, the World Bank and the ILO to Institutionalise Gender Issues*, Geneva: UNRISD.

Rose, P. and Subrahmanian, R. (2005) *Evaluation of DFID Development Assistance: Gender Equality and Women's Empowerment − Phase II Thematic Evaluation: Education*, Working Paper 11, London: DfID.

Short, C. (1991) 'Introduction', in C. Short, K. Tunks and D. Hutchinson (eds) *Dear Clare … this is what women feel about Page 3*, London: Radius.

Short, C. (2000) 'Forward by the Secretary of State', in DfID, *Poverty Elimination and the Empowerment of Women: Strategies for Achieving the International Development Targets*, London: DFID, 6-8.

Short, C. (2004) *An Honourable Deception? New Labour, Iraq and the Misuse of Power*, London: The Free Press.

Thomas, C. (2005) 'Globalization and development in the South', in J. Ravenhill (ed) *Global Political Economy*, Oxford: Oxford University Press, 317-43.

Tsikata, D. (2004) 'The rights-based approach to development: potential for change or more of the same?', *IDS Bulletin* 35(4), 130-3.

United Nations (2005) www.un.org/millenniumgoals (accessed 1 April 2006).

UNRISD (United Nations Research Institute for Social Development) (2005) *Gender Equality: Striving for Justice in an Unequal World*, Geneva: UNRISD.

Waterhouse, R. and Neville, S. (2005) *Evaluation of DfID Development Assistance: Gender Equality and Women's Empowerment. Phase II Thematic Evaluation: Voice and Accountability*, London: DfID.

Watkins, F. (2004) *Evaluation of DfID Development Assistance: Gender Equality and Women's Empowerment – DfID's Experience of Gender Mainstreaming: 1995 to 2004. Report for the Evaluation Department*, London: DfID.

Waylen, G. (1997) 'Gender, feminism and political economy', *New Political Economy* 2(2), 205–20.

WIDE (Women in Development Europe) (2005) *Report: WIDE Annual Conference 2005*, available at www.gadnetwork.org.uk/pdfs/WIDE%20CONF%20REPORT%2005%20(2).pdf (accessed 10 May 2006).

Williams, P. (2005) 'Blair's commission for Africa: Problems and prospects of UK policy', *The Political Quarterly* 76(4), 529–39.

Young, R.A. (2000) 'New Labour and international development', in Coates, D. and Lawler, P. (eds) *New Labour in Power*, Manchester: Manchester University Press.

Part Four
Conclusions

TWELVE

New Labour: towards an engendered politics and policy?

Kirstein Rummery, Francesca Gains and Claire Annesley

New Labour: acting for women, taking on women's concerns, making a difference to women's lives?

In commissioning the chapters for this book, we set out to investigate the extent to which New Labour has feminised politics, that is, whether it has acted for women, taken on women's concerns and made a difference to women's lives (Lovenduski 2005). By drawing together the evidence presented here, we have sought to understand why and when the party was able to act for women, what opportunities and constraints they faced, and examine what effects their actions have had on various groups of women. Finally, our aim was to draw some conclusions about how feminists can mobilise governments to achieve feminist aims and how to engender politics and policy.

The evidence presented so far has demonstrated that New Labour has acted for women in some areas, most clearly through policies and initiatives which have improved the representation of women in the formal political sphere. As Lovecy's Chapter Four shows, the party in opposition and in government has taken crucial steps, initiated by feminists and grass-roots initiatives, to improve the representation of women in the party, Parliament and government. As Durose and Gains point out in Chapter Five, the election of New Labour brought with it opportunities for women through the establishment of the Women's Minister and WEU, by way of the project of devolution and, to a lesser but increasingly important extent, the policy instruments designed to encourage gender mainstreaming.

As the case study chapters in this volume illustrate, New Labour, with its increased representation of women and awareness of women's issues, has also taken on women's concerns into public policy in a range of fields from equal pay, to childcare, to development policy. These are significant not only in the context of New Labour's political and policy achievements, but they have also fundamentally altered the perspective of British political parties. This can be seen explicitly in the way the Conservative Party in opposition has taken on family policy and other issues under the broad 'work–life balance' heading into the party's policy priorities (Branigan 2006) and has recognised the importance of recruiting more women into politics and attracting women voters (Riddell 2006). As a consequence of New Labour's attempt to take on women's concerns into policy, more issues of central concern to women have for the first time become firmly embedded in British politics, in a similar way to the Nordic states since the 1970s. However, as Buchanan and Annesley's chapter on Norway and Sweden shows, governments' commitment to gender issues does not by any means lead to automatic or permanent improvements to women's lives.

Whether New Labour has made a significant difference to women's lives in the UK and internationally is contestable. The bulk of this conclusion is concerned with explaining why the difference made to women's lives has in fact been so limited and what the constraints to progress might have been. We identify the problematic issue of women versus gender, the party's failure to recognise the differential impact of policies on groups of women and the broader institutional and public policy constraints that present themselves.

From feminising to engendering politics

First and foremost, a critical limitation to New Labour's efforts to make a difference to women's lives is that New Labour clearly seeks to make a difference to *women's* lives rather than tackling gender inequalities. The party's narrower stance, which prioritises women and, as Elias and Ferguson point out in Chapter Eleven, girls, overlooks the fact that in order to achieve gender equality, changes have to be made to men's lives as well. For example, gender equality in paid employment is more likely to be achieved if gender equality in informal caring work is forthcoming. As Clarke points out in Chapter Eight, New Labour has taken some limited measures which challenge traditional roles within families (for example, the right to paternity leave), and Rummery highlights in Chapter Nine policy initiatives which offer rewards specifically to carers (for example, the recent pension reforms). However, the bulk of its policies work with the grain of traditional gender roles and do not address the position or role of men.

In other words, rather than seeking to make a difference just to women's lives, a project to feminise politics and policy needs to have its focus firmly on gender – actually on *engendering* politics and policy.

New Labour's focus on women appears to be an advancement in terms of gender equality but, in fact, by addressing women's issues rather than gender issues it slips into reproducing and further engraining old gendered patterns. New Labour's ambition to be 'the most feminist government in our history' is thus restricted by the fact that its feminist approach looks at just women rather than gender solutions, truly 'transforming' gender mainstreaming is little in evidence.

In government, New Labour suffers from the gendered path dependency of existing policy approaches; it is hard to break out of the gendered assumptions of policies that have prevailed for years. A critical juncture is required to challenge the traditional conception of gender roles in society and the economic sphere. A key step in this critical juncture – to break from the gendered socio-economic norm associated with work and care and to develop innovative and responsive policy solutions – would be, as Rummery points out in Chapter Nine, to recognise the complexity of women's lives as workers and carers and as the receivers of care. A simultaneous step would be to draw more men into the role as carers. Or as Wilson put it in Chapter Two, 'the preference would be for a politics that negotiates the complexities of gender seriously confidently'.

Engendering policy: Differential outcomes

New Labour has failed to truly feminise, or engender, politics because it has failed to take adequate account of the complexity of women's lives. In examining how far New Labour has progressed in addressing gender inequalities in policy outcomes, the case studies presented in this book have clearly shown that this failure also extends to policy: 'feminising' policy has been too simplistic a goal. When we examine both how 'women's issues' have been addressed in the policy process, and the outcomes of that process, it is clear that different groups of women have benefited in different ways. It is misleading to look simply at how women have fared in comparison to men, as the evidence suggests that different categories of women have experienced differential outcomes – not just in comparison to men, but also in comparison to other women.

In this section we will therefore address some of the areas within gender where different groups of women have experienced differential outcomes under New Labour, and examine why that has been the case. Using the case studies presented in this book we are going to look at the outcomes for working women, mothers, non-working women and women living in (or at risk of) poverty in turn. It is important to bear in mind that these categories have significant overlaps both longitudinally (over women's life courses) and vertically (across different groups of women at any given point in time).

Working women

Overall, working women (in the context of this section, we mean women engaging in paid work) appear to be some of the biggest winners under New Labour's policies. There has been a clear commitment to the work ideal at several levels, but particularly as a route out of poverty and social exclusion. The failure to raise lone parent benefit, and instead to focus on the provision of childcare, working family and child tax credits sent a clear message that New Labour was committed to making work pay, rather than supporting lone parents (usually mothers) to care for their children. There has also been an explicit acknowledgement in New Labour's policies for working women that *de jure* equality between men and women in the workplace following pre-1997 legislation has not translated into *de facto* equality, with full-time working women earning around 73% of full-time working men's pay when New Labour came to power. It is here that Tessa Jowell's claim that New Labour is 'the most feminist' party may perhaps be justified, if by 'most feminist' one means 'most committed to removing the direct and indirect barriers to equality faced by women in the workplace' (we shall return later to whether this interpretation of 'the most feminist' is justified or correct). However, New Labour's policies have had a differential impact on various groups of women engaging in paid work.

For *women engaged in full-time work*, some of New Labour's policies have had a significant impact. The high priority given by New Labour to making a national system of childcare funding an integral part of economic policy, increased security of job tenure through enhanced maternity leave provision, working family and child tax credits, targeted tax relief being paid to the main carer (usually the mother) and the New Deal for Lone Parents have all made working full time, and returning to work, easier for mothers. Pay reviews in the public sector and the introduction of the NMW (although initially set too low to have a significant impact) have also had a beneficial effect on the pay of full-time working low-paid women.

For women generally (as opposed to just mothers) working full time, the picture does not look so rosy. Although the pay gap between full-time working women and men has closed to 83% since New Labour came to power in 1997, the UK still lags significantly behind other European countries with regards to equal pay. Moreover, despite the policy platform being feminised through the creation of the WEU, many policy changes that could have a significant impact on the lives of working women, including many recommended by the WEU itself, have not been implemented. New Labour has preferred a voluntary approach to addressing the gendered nature of skills differentiation and pay reviews, and has focused on individualised action (such as helping women find childcare) rather than larger-scale collective social and economic action (such as making significant challenges to working hours, the gendered division of labour both in the workforce and in the home, and non-voluntary reviews of pay in the public and private sector).

Moreover, making full-time work pay has had a differential effect on different groups of women, with some full-time working women, particularly those in higher status, higher paid jobs, more likely to return to work, and more likely to benefit from increases in childcare provision, than lower paid women. Increasing the availability of childcare has not made it more affordable: even with increased tax benefits costs remain prohibitively high, particularly for low-paid working parents. Choices may well have increased for middle-class, high-earning women, who have benefited by being able to choose to work full time more easily, but they appear to have been restricted for lone parents and other women, for whom choosing *not* to engage in full-time paid work is becoming increasingly impossible. As Clarke in Chapter Eight asserts, this is in part to do with the overarching policy aim of tackling child poverty through the means of encouraging lone parents into work, rather than tackling women's poverty per se (see also Levitas et al 2006).

However, *women working part time* have had a different experience under New Labour. Women may chose to work part time for a variety of reasons, but for most of them it will be because they are combining paid work with unpaid work, either parenting or caring. For these women, the pay gap that New Labour inherited on gaining power in 1997 has closed slightly, from 58% to 62% of men's hourly earnings. Coates and Oettinger in Chapter Six and Grimshaw in Chapter Seven point out that addressing some of the structural problems associated with part-time working women's poor pay (gender skills differentiation, low levels of minimum wage, failure to engage comprehensively with trade unions over pay, and the expanding use of the private sector in providing services) has either not been a policy priority, or has come into conflict with other, higher priority policy aims and objectives.

Arguably, New Labour is willing to support women as workers as part of its overarching economic policy, but not if that support will conflict with other elements of policy. For example, the increasing involvement of the private sector in the provision of services, a sustained part of New Labour's modernisation and 'Third Way' agenda, has meant that growing sectors of part-time employees who are overwhelmingly women (and who, for example, might otherwise have benefited from pay reviews in the NHS and local authorities) have seen pay and conditions worsen rather than improve. Improving pay and conditions for low-paid women working part time would therefore not appear to be a key New Labour objective if it conflicts with other, more pressing policy commitments.

Mothers

Of course, being engaged in paid work is only a small part of the work that women undertake: many women of working age are mothers, and in fulfilling that role have also attracted New Labour's attention in various ways. However, even looking at a category of 'mothers' within the category of 'women' is oversimplifying differences between groups of women. It is clear that different groups of mothers have experienced different policy outcomes under New Labour.

In some respects, New Labour appears to have been reticent to support *non-working women* simply as mothers. While some initiatives in the Every Child Matters policies, such as the foundation of the NFPI, were specifically to support parents in looking after their children, most of New Labour's policies aimed at mothers have been sought to facilitate their engagement in paid work. As Clarke notes in Chapter Eight, increasing childcare provision, tax credits, Sure Start schemes and New Deal for Lone Parents are all aimed at enabling parents, particularly mothers, to work, rather than parent. There have been no substantial increases in tax credits designed to enable a parent to stay at home and care for their children: there appears to be no policy space for any sustainable alternatives to the two-parent, two-worker (or lone working parent) model of families. The failure to increase lone parent benefit, along with the other policy initiatives aimed at enabling mothers to work has meant that the adult worker model has become dominant (Lewis and Guiliari 2005), and there appears to be very little enthusiasm from New Labour in recognising and valuing the work that women undertake as mothers.

On the other hand, New Labour has been very keen to develop policies that enable *working mothers* to engage in paid work, with a raft of tax credits (some of which extend fairly high up the income ladder) designed to support working families and specifically paid, where possible, to the main carer (usually the mother). The New Deal for

Lone Parents aims to increase lone-mother employment to 70% by 2010, and this is in part designed to help New Labour meet its pledges on reducing child poverty. Increases in maternity leave have also been designed to encourage working mothers to return to work.

However, as Coates and Oettinger stress in Chapter Six, these policies appeared to be designed to encourage mothers to work for economic reasons: to widen the tax base, and to alleviate poverty. There does not appear to be a particularly powerful social justice rationale behind such policies: they are aimed at supporting women as workers, or as people living in poverty, rather than addressing issues of gender inequality per se. Aside from the provision of two weeks' paid paternity leave, very little effort has gone in to addressing the gendered nature of work organisation, and policies appear to have had very little impact on the distribution of paid and unpaid work between mothers and fathers. In other words, gender disparities in both the public and private worlds have remained relatively untouched under New Labour, calling into question just how 'feminist' a party it really is. Extensions in the provision of childcare have also not substantially reduced the cost of childcare, with the result that middle-class, high-earning working mothers have benefited disproportionately from New Labour's policies, while poorer working mothers, particularly those working part time, have experienced greater access to childcare, but are still paying a fairly high proportion of their income for it. Tax credits have also benefited full-time workers proportionately more than part-time, lower-income workers.

In contrast, Wilson in Chapter Ten shows clearly how lesbian mothers under New Labour have gained benefits that do not appear to be driven by economic imperatives, but seem to owe more to a social justice model of gender relations. In other words, New Labour's policies enabling lesbian women to engage in civil partnerships and have the same reproductive rights as heterosexual women appear to be motivated by a desire to remove distinctions between groups of women that are held to be unfair on a gendered basis per se, rather than down to an inequitable distribution of wealth. Neither does extending such benefits to lesbian women appear to be designed with income (tax) generation in mind, although it does bring lesbian mothers into the fold of New Labour's preferred 'two-parent, two-income' model of families. There has been a lack of competing, overarching policy objectives, and this, along with committed activists who found allies willing to engage in pushing forward cost-neutral (at least in economic terms) policy changes have meant that lesbian mothers have secured important civil rights under New Labour. Perhaps crucially, this has not put them on par with heterosexual women (civil partnerships have less legal protection than full marriages – although given marriage's somewhat dubious feminist credentials there may be positive aspects to this for lesbian women), and, equally crucially, it has had negligible economic costs (and some economic benefits) for the state.

Although there have been no specific changes to tax or benefits systems that have enabled *disabled mothers* to combine receiving care and support and giving care and support to their children, there have been changes to health and social care systems under New Labour which have benefited this group of women. In Chapter Nine, Rummery points out that the extension of direct payments/personal budgets has enabled disabled mothers to exercise much greater control over their services and support than was previously the case. Health and social care services are often unsuitable for disabled mothers because they are either focused on meeting the personal care needs of the disabled person, or on protecting children at risk: there are very few services designed to support disabled people as parents. Using direct payments and personal budgets to pay for their own services enables disabled mothers to purchase tailor-made support that can help them care for their children.

However, this policy development was not designed to support disabled mothers in this way: it is an unintended consequence of a policy aimed at reducing the high costs of providing social care services for disabled people, and at making services more responsive to users' needs as part of New Labour's modernisation agenda. It is explicitly not a feminist policy: in fact, its success relies on disabled people being able to employ personal assistants at very low rates of pay, which suggests that a group of marginalised, casualised and underpaid care workers (who are likely to be women) may well be exploited. A benefit for one group of marginalised women (disabled mothers) may be a detriment for another (low-paid workers).

Women outside the public world of work

New Labour's focus on helping 'working' women, particularly working mothers, has perhaps obscured the fact that other groups of women engaged in work are doing so outside the paid, public world. Women who are primarily engaged in caring (or, as discussed above, mothering), or women who are removed from the world of paid work (either through choice, or through structural barriers such as retirement or the inaccessibility of the labour market for disabled women) have not fared so well.

Disabled women are at significant risk of poverty and social exclusion, and there have been no substantial changes in the benefits system to compensate them adequately for the high cost of living with impairments. Policies such as the establishment of the Disability Rights Commission, New Deal for Disabled People and employment protection legislation have focused on encouraging disabled people into work. These policies appear to be driven by economic imperatives: the need to reduce the cost of incapacity and other disability-related benefits, and the need to increase the taxation base to fund public sector improvements. There has been no explicitly feminist or gendered dimension to these policy developments: no recognition of the 'dual burden' of paid and unpaid work experienced by disabled mothers and carers. Although many disabled activists would argue that removing the barriers to paid work is an important goal in its own right, recognising, supporting and compensating disabled women adequately for their unpaid work is also an important goal. However, perhaps crucially, this goal is not one taken up by either disability activists, or by mainstream feminists on disabled women's behalf. Consequently, there has been no window of opportunity or committed policy activist, either inside or outside the machinery of government, to develop policies specifically to support disabled women.

Similarly, there have been very few policy developments designed to support *carers*, despite unpaid, informal care remaining the bedrock around which formal statutory social care services revolve. Benefit rates for carers unable to work have not significantly improved, nor has employment protection for low-paid, part time workers who combine paid work with unpaid care. As with parenting, New Labour has explicitly favoured a worker model of citizenship, with some minor exceptions. New pension rules which enable people to base pension entitlements on their best 20 years' earnings, rather than the average of a lifetime's earnings, will benefit those people (overwhelmingly, but not exclusively women) who have had breaks from paid work to undertake caring responsibilities. However, this still fails to recognise the value of and adequately compensate people for the cost of caring: as Rummery in Chapter Nine and Coates and Oettinger in Chapter Six point out, New Labour has not been overwhelmingly concerned to compensate women for the true cost of caring, with ramifications for women living in, or at risk of, poverty, particularly older women.

Like disabled women, *older women* are removed from the labour market (in this case through the structural imposition of retirement) and so have not benefited from New Labour's focus on 'making work pay' and providing work opportunities for 'those who can'. Measures to help the poorest pensioners (such as increases in the basic state pension) will benefit women disproportionately, as they form the majority of pensioners living in poverty. However, policy developments designed to improve pension provision for older women have been focused on increasing women's access to private and occupational pensions through work, which may well benefit future generations of older women (particularly those benefiting now from measures to improve the pay gap and facilitate combining working with mothering); but will do very little to address the poverty experienced presently by older women, whose income remains, on average, around 53% of that of older men.

Older women will benefit from the increased investment in older people's health and social care services, and from measures (such as direct payments) designed to give them increased control over the kind of social care support they receive. Much as younger disabled women have used direct payments to enable them to fulfil their mothering roles, older disabled women have also used direct payments to enable them to fulfil their caring roles (caring for spouses, parents and disabled children) in ways that were very difficult using state provided or commissioned social care services. However, as with younger disabled women, policy innovations in this area which have benefited older women have been the largely unintended result of developments intended to modernise services, enable easier partnerships with the private sector and increase the cost-effectiveness of services rather than through any gender aware commitment to social justice.

Women living in poverty

While New Labour's status as a feminist party may be in dispute, its commitment to tackling poverty and social exclusion has been well documented. In some respects it does appear to have recognised, and attempted to tackle, the gendered elements of poverty, particularly in looking at some of the structural issues (such as childcare) around work which have had an impact on working mothers. However, in other areas of poverty and social exclusion with a gendered dimension there have been fewer successes. It is clear that New Labour's preferred route for tackling poverty and social exclusion for *British women* is through the world of work. Chapters Six and Seven showed how, despite a raft of policy initiatives designed to make work pay, the lack of commitment to tackling some of the social, economic and structural issues that have led to gender differentials in work and the risk of poverty (such as the gendered balance between paid and unpaid work, part-time working and gendered skills) reflects a lack of commitment to gender mainstreaming in policy generally.

Moreover, the focus on making work pay has deliberately excluded women at risk of poverty in Britain who would either choose not to engage in paid work because of parenting and/or caring commitments, or who have been excluded from paid work because it is inaccessible to them, or they are retired. Coates and Oettinger in Chapter Six and Rummery in Chapter Nine assert that New Labour has been remarkably silent on the issue of poverty experienced by disabled and older women, and non-working mothers and carers: indeed, as Clarke points out in Chapter Eight, when given the opportunity to increase benefits for lone parents it explicitly refused to do so, focusing instead on work as a route out of poverty, as discussed above. New Labour appears to be very unwilling to tackle British women's poverty through income redistribution mechanisms that cannot be tied into an overarching economically-driven work-based policy.

Elias and Ferguson in Chapter Eleven discuss how some progress has been made in getting the gendered dimension of poverty experienced by *women in the developing world* onto the policy agenda (through the mechanism of the DfID). This appears to be happening through two distinct means. First, where there is sustained pressure from outside organisations to improve civil and political rights for women then New Labour appears happy (as it did in the case of lesbian women) to support such aims, so long as they do not conflict with other, overarching policy objectives. Second, where the argument for tackling gender related poverty can be made in economic terms (and particularly where such terms tie in with the aims of such bodies as the World Bank and IMF) – that tackling women's poverty is crucial in tackling poverty generally – then New Labour will also find the resources to support those aims. However, New Labour is less willing to support tackling women's poverty in the developing world as a social justice issue, and crucially, very quick to abandon a commitment to gender-related poverty issues when other, higher priority policy objectives (such as the commitment to working in partnership with outside bodies) come into conflict with that commitment. In this, as in many other areas, there has been no sustained policy commitment to gender mainstreaming or tackling women's issues per se.

The constraints to engendering policy

The analysis above suggests that despite the activism of members and parliamentarians, and policy intentions of New Labour in government, there have been constraints in making a difference to women's lives. In Chapter One of this volume, Annesley and Gains discussed the common constraints on state (particularly government) action which are highlighted when looking at the public policy literature in general and at assessments of New Labour's period in office in particular. Here we reprise this analytical checklist in the light of our case study chapters in Part Three of the book to see if the public policy literature can shed light on why, in government, New Labour faced constraints in formulating and delivering its policy agenda for women. Some constraints were general and applied to all policy activity; some were particular and related to the nature of policies directed at making a difference to women's lives.

First, *electorally*, New Labour in power has been constantly striving to satisfy the finely balanced coalition which elected the party and this creates a tension between the logics of redistribution and fiscal rectitude. New Labour seeks to support the market while ameliorating its worst effects. As Coates and Oettinger in Chapter Six discuss, this compromise initially found practical expression through the maintenance of the previous Conservative government's spending plans in the first two years. Latterly, as Grimshaw highlights in Chapter Seven, this compromise meant although New Labour fulfilled its promise to the unions to introduce a minimum wage, it set the rate low enough to avoid antagonising the business community which had consequences for the numbers of low-paid women workers who were helped by the policy.

Economically in the UK, as elsewhere, the experience of gender mainstreaming is undermined by the institutionalisation of a rational economic framework (True 2003). The government accepts the imperatives of globalisation and signs up to an economic model which does not challenge dominant liberal hegemony (Ludlam and Smith 2001). As Elias and Ferguson show in Chapter Eleven, even where Clare Short was given licence to be as 'radical' as she liked by the Prime Minister's press secretary, Alastair Campbell (Short 2004, 77), the ensuing policies and impressive budget rise of the DfID followed a path set by the agendas and policy frames of the key four international financial institutions. It is clear that New Labour's gender equality policy goals are framed in terms of the economic case and economic goals and its economic model operates within the neo-liberal economic paradigm, failing to recognise that this itself creates and sustains gender inequality. The failure to make progress in feminising politics and policy is because in numerous policy areas – from getting women into work to the gender pay gap to international development policy

– the government works 'with the grain of the market' (Grimshaw, Chapter Seven) and tends to prioritise the 'business case' for gender equality (Elias and Ferguson, Chapter Eleven) over the equality case. The economic approach that oversees and underpins New Labour's attempts to feminise politics and policy thus hinders the extent to which progress can be made.

For example, despite the overt commitment to gender equality that this book identifies, New Labour is still as committed, if not more so, to promoting privatisation and outsourcing of public sector employment which has a significant impact on women's pay and working conditions. As Coates and Oettinger assert in Chapter Six, the 'workerist' emphasis of New Labour's economic policy coupled with the enduring low investment approach to UK political economy detrimentally affects women. Thus achievements on gender equality are hindered by the fact that New Labour is not questioning the 'long hours, low investment' macro-economic model that underpins its version of the adult worker model. A further prime example of this is provided by Grimshaw's analysis of New Labour's attempts to tackle to gender pay gap in Chapter Seven. While it has acted directly in the public sector to improve pay in, for example, the NHS, it has trodden a more cautious path with the NMW and initiatives to tackle the gender pay gap, preferring review after review to direct legislation so as not to upset business interests.

Institutionally, New Labour also had to operate in a contemporary governance arena where the extent to which European government can act independently is tempered by both membership of the EU and the jurisdiction of the European Court of Human Rights (Rhodes 1995). However as Lovecy in Chapter Four, Durose and Gains in Chapter Five, Grimshaw in Chapter Seven and Wilson in Chapter Ten all argue, the impact of European legislation, although a constraint on government autonomy, also presented an opportunity for New Labour to introduce both gender mainstreaming policies and legislation to give legal recognition to same-sex partnerships.

Finally, government action by New Labour is directed at a society with deeply embedded *patriarchal cultural practices* in families and workplaces, schools and public services. Although governments can offer legislative and financial incentives to change behaviour, the way in which citizens respond to governmental policy strictures is inexact and widely varying (Halpern et al 2004). Indeed, the Nordic experience (Chapter Three) demonstrates how long the process of engendering politics and policy can take.

So, although the election of the first Labour government for 17 years with a huge electoral majority and high levels of popular support provided a window of opportunity in Kingdon's (1989) terms, the gendered policy problems which came to the fore were primarily about the relative poverty of women, especially lone parents and the need to encourage more women into the labour force. The dominant policy solutions, which are covered in the case studies in Part Three of this book, were those which all sections of the New Labour coalition could sign up to, and centred on the adult worker model within a liberal economic framework and severely curtailing a 'transformative' mainstreaming agenda (Lewis and Guiliari 2005; Squires 2005).

The extent to which policy solutions were taken up and taken forwards depended upon the commitment of policy entrepreneurs in the core executive and their capacity to act (Cortell and Peterson 1998; Gains 1999). Durose and Gains in Chapter Five point to evidence of influential policy advocacy coalitions operating around the formation of budgetary policy in the Treasury and around the WEU networks of professional civil servants encouraging policy learning on mainstreaming approaches across Whitehall. There clearly were key individuals in government who were driving forward a feminist agenda and who, as Lovecy discusses in Chapter Five, were part of a feminist policy advocacy coalition within the Labour Party through the 1980s and early 1990s. Harriet Harman, Tessa Jowell and Patricia Hewitt in Cabinet consistently sought to highlight and address disparities in policy outcomes for men and women. The evidence from the policy chapters in Part Three shows the importance of departmental Ministers in driving change, for example, in adopting gender mainstreaming targets as discussed by Durose and Gains in Chapter Five and the adoption of gay- and lesbian-friendly policies discussed by Wilson in Chapter Ten. Conversely, in discussing family policy and caring in Chapters Eight and Nine, Clarke and Rummery show that where policy problems straddled a number of ministries and there was no one lead actor, there was little policy coherence and initiatives were subject to a high degree of policy influence by the Treasury.

Of course, New Labour appointed a Minister for Women specifically to act in a coordinating role and adopted gender mainstreaming approaches overseen by the WU. But, as Durose and Gains point out in Chapter Five, most assessments of this role point to an initial weakness with Harriet Harman, who had the role alongside huge responsibilities at the DSS and without strong infrastructural back up from the WU (later the WEU). It was not until first Patricia Hewitt and then Tessa Jowell at the DTI were able to combine portfolio, commitment and the policy infrastructure of gender mainstreaming (primarily through the policy instruments of gender equality PSA targets overseen by the WEU acting as effective watchdog across Whitehall) that real changes began to be felt in other departments (Durose and Gains, Chapter Five). To achieve policy change these actors needed to work effectively with others to forge coalitions and win support for policy proposals. And, as Coates and Oettinger show in Chapter Six, it was critical to get Treasury backing for policy proposals. However this de facto meant adopting policies which fitted the Treasury agenda on labour market flexibility and welfare to work. According to Rummery in Chapter Nine, women carers whose role was unpaid or women unable to work appear to have had less 'joined up' policy attention.

Grimshaw in Chapter Seven argues that even where governments are committed to action, it can be hard to get agreement in the policy networks of actors outside government to agree on how the policy should be implemented (Marsh and Rhodes 1992). He describes the stalemate over agreeing and adopting policies to tackle the gender pay gap despite this being one of the five priorities of the WEU. Three separate reviews have failed to lead to policy proposals on which the government, employers and unions could agree. Grimshaw's chapter also discusses how the potentially ameliorating effect of the minimum wage has been diluted because there is no agreement between social partners on the level required to lift low-paid workers (for which read women) out of poverty.

Finally, the case studies on equal pay and parental leave illustrate the problem of path dependency in tackling traditional gender assumptions after policy implementation (Pierson 2000); despite government support for and incentivisation for a change in behaviour. In Chapter Seven, Grimshaw describes how the Prosser report on women and work made recommendations on achieving cultural change in the workplace aimed at reducing the level of sex segregation and pointing out the difficulty with achieving a change in employer strategies to this end. Clarke too, in Chapter Eight finds deeply rooted implicit normative values and assumptions about the family, gender roles and the relative responsibilities of the state and family in relation to family policy. So, for example, more fathers have taken the opportunity to take paid paternity leave, but very few have used the opportunity of requesting flexible working arrangements.

Overall, the case studies here show that there are significant difficulties to achieving legislative and policy change. Insights from the public policy literature suggest that to understand how feminist actors can achieve change in the UK system close attention should be paid to the work of policy advocacy coalitions in framing policy problems and possible policy solutions and the role of feminists in the core executive, working with networks of policy specialists and the Treasury in pushing forward policy solutions.

Conclusion

So, is New Labour – as Tessa Jowell claimed – the most feminist of all UK governments? In one, limited, sense it is since no other British government to date has sought in the way New Labour has to act for women, take on women's concerns and – although with mixed results – make a difference to women's lives (Lovenduski 2005). There have been key changes that affect women in the areas of childcare, pensions, parental leave and same-sex relationships. Moreover, such incremental changes, often pushed by feminists within the party have made a lasting impact on the political and policy frameworks of the UK political elite, as the adoption of work–life balance issues into Conservative Party policy suggests.

At the same time, however, depending on what is understood by feminism, New Labour can be criticised by not being very feminist at all. New Labour has a narrow conception of feminism that is – to reuse Wilson's phrase from Chapter Two – 'so last season'. Feminism has moved on. New Labour's focus on women rather than gender, its failure to recognise the differential needs of women and impact of policy on women, the focus on paid work over care, and its insistence that the 'business case' is the only and best rationale for tackling gender inequality exemplify the very narrow framework within which the party is operating. A broader version of feminism which considers gender rather than women, care as well as work, and equality in the private as well as public domain is what would make a difference (Rake 2006). Due to New Labour's narrow frame, the party has not succeeded in feminising politics in the sense of making a difference to the unequal gendered relationships in society, politics and policy. It has not made a difference to all women – mostly just those who are working, particularly full time – it has not in any real sense altered the gendered roles in society and due to the dominance of the adult worker model and the economic imperative that underpins it, and it fails to recognise the importance of caring roles that so many women (and men) undertake. What lessons can, then, be learnt for New Labour's fourth term, or alternatively for the first term for the revamped Conservative Party under David Cameron?

A key lesson from this book is that a project to feminise politics has to acknowledge the need to engender policy – find solutions which readjust the relationship between women and men's roles in society. It must recognise the complexity of women and men's lives in their roles as worker, carers and receivers of care as well as recognising the equality case as well as the business case for gender equality.

A second step is to find a political space for feminists with engendering agendas to translate this into policy. A more systematic use of gender mainstreaming presents one opportunity to achieve this. In public policy terms this involves the building of alliances, capacity and infrastructures, and securing resources. Some lessons might be learnt from the experiences in the devolved assemblies of Scotland and Wales where policies engendering politics have been more forthcoming (for example, the right to free care in care homes, the right to breastfeed in public, the banning of smacking children, and direct action to close gender pay gaps). Future research must certainly be carried out in this field to question the structure of windows of opportunity in the UK system of governance. Future research also needs to look at the political agency of women in their attempts engender policy (Annesley 2006).

What is more, alternatives to the liberal model of UK capitalism need to be sought so that governments are no longer constrained in their ability to engender policy by the very gendered nature of liberal capitalism. A sobering lesson for feminists in power to date appears to be that in order to achieve progress, you must be able to frame your aims and objectives in such a way that they fit in with the overarching economic and liberal framework in place: a key aim therefore must be to challenge that framework while working within it. This could take the form of moving towards a gendered political economy (Cook et al 2000) or by pursuing goals such as happiness over economic growth or utility maximisation (Layard 2005; Burchardt 2006). Interestingly, as the current leader of the Conservative Party in opposition, David Cameron has raised as priorities quality of life issues, work–life balance and the need for goals to maximise general well-being rather than GDP (Branigan 2006). The seeds may well have been sown to challenge the hegemony of the economic business case and liberal capitalism in British politics, and create a space to allow a more diverse framing of policy and objectives to reflect the reality of women's and men's lives: it remains to be seen whether feminist activists and politicians in all three UK political parties can rise to the challenge.

References

Annesley, C. (2006) 'Political agency and welfare reform: engendering the adult worker model welfare state', presented to the *Annual Meeting of the American Political Science Association*, Philadelphia, 30 August to 3 September.

Branigan, T. (2006) 'Tories promise to make happiness a priority', *Guardian*, 23 May, 12.

Burchardt, T. (2006) 'Happiness and social policy: barking up the right tree in the wrong neck of the woods', in L. Bauld, K. Clarke and T. Maltby (eds) *Social Policy Review 18*, Bristol: The Policy Press.

Cook, J., Roberts, J. and Waylen, G. (2000) *Towards a Gendered Political Economy*, Basingstoke: Macmillan.

Cortell, A. and Peterson, S. (1999) 'Altered states: explaining domestic institutional change', *British Journal of Political Science* 29(11), 177-203.

Gains, F. (1999) 'Implementing privatization policies in Next Steps agencies', *Public Administration* 77(4), 713-30.

Halpern, D., Bates, C., Mulgan, G., Aldridge, S., with Beales, G. and Heathfield, A. (2004) *Personal Responsibility and Changing Behaviour: The State of Knowledge and its Implications for Public Policy*, London: Prime Minister's Strategy Unit, Cabinet Office.

Kingdon, J. (1984) *Agendas, Alternatives and Public Policies*, Boston, MA: Little Brown.

Layard, R. (2005) *Happiness: Lessons from a New Science*, London: Allen Lane.

Levitas, R., Head, E. and Finch, N. (2006) 'Lone mothers, poverty and social exclusion', in C. Pantazis, D. Gordon and R. Levitas (eds) *Poverty and Social Exclusion in Britain*, Bristol: The Policy Press.

Lewis, J. and Guiliari, S. (2005) 'The adult worker model family, gender equality and care: the search for new policy principles and the possibilities and problems of a capabilities approach', *Economy and Society* 34(1), 76-104.

Lovenduski, J. (2005) *Feminizing Politics*, Cambridge: Polity Press.

Ludlam, S. and Smith, M. (eds) (2001) *New Labour in Government*, Basingstoke: Macmillan.

Marsh, D. and Rhodes, R.A.W. (eds) (1992) *Policy Networks in British Government*, Oxford: Clarendon Press.

Pierson, P. (2000) 'Increasing returns, path dependence, and the study of politics', *American Political Science Review* 94(12), 251-67.

Rake, K. (2006) 'Let's reclaim the f-word', *Guardian*, 8 August, www.guardian.co.uk/gender/story/0,,1839483,00.html#article_continue (accessed 9 August 2006).

Rhodes, R.A.W. (1995) *Understanding Governance*, London: Macmillian.

Riddell, M. (2006) 'Dave's winning ways with women voters', *The Observer*, 28 May, 27.

Short, C. (2004) *An Honourable Deception? New Labour, Iraq and the Misuse of Power*, London: The Free Press.

Squires, J. (2005) 'Evaluating gender mainstreaming in the context of EU diversity strategies', paper given at the Political Studies Association Conference, 5 April, University of Leeds.

True, J. (2003) 'Mainstreaming Gender in Global Public Policy', *International Feminist Journal of Politics* 5(3), 368-96.

Index